101
FUN-TO-CROCHET
•Projects•

Edited by Laura Scott

HOUSE of
WHITE
BIRCHES

PUBLISHERS
SINCE 1947

Editorial Director: Vivian Rothe
Editor: Laura Scott
Editorial Assistant: Marla Freeman
Pattern Editors: Karen Bennett, Colleen McCague
Stitchers: Carmie Anderson, Margaret Dick, Roberta Reinhard
Copy Editor: Cathy Reef
Photography: Sandy Bauman, Tammy Christian, Nora Elsesser
Photography Assistant: Linda Quinlan

Production Manager: Vicki Macy
Creative Coordinator: Shaun Venish
Book Design/Production: Dan Kraner
Production Coordinator: Sandra Beres
Production Assistants: Cheryl Lynch, Jessica Rothe

Publishers: Carl H. Muselman, Arthur K. Muselman
Chief Executive Officer: John Robinson
Marketing Director: Scott Moss

Printed in the United States of America
First Printing: 1996
Library of Congress Number: 96-75146
ISBN: 1-882138-17-1

Every effort has been made to ensure the accuracy and completeness of the
instructions in this book. However, we cannot be responsible for human
error or for the results when using materials other than those specified in
the instructions, or for variations in individual work.

Special thanks to Spinrite Yarns and Dyers, Ltd., for providing the
materials used for completing many of the projects featured in this book.
Also, to Vicki Macy for the watercolor illustrations used throughout.

Cover projects clockwise from top left: Birdhouse Tissue Box, Pineapple Star Doily,
Sweet Dreams, Valentine Plant Poke, Easter Plant Pokes and Victorian Ornaments.
Center projects: Open Swirls Afghans, Teddy Bear Pocket Pal.
Back cover projects clockwise from top left: Blueberry Delight,
Rudolph's Christmas Cheer and Piglets-for-Sale Doorstop.

What a delight it has been to put this book together for you! Between juggling our spouses, children, careers, friends and the endless list of "to-dos," there is often precious little time to devote to our favorite hobby—crochet. This book brings you more than 101 (we managed to squeeze in a few extras for you!) crochet patterns that really are fun to crochet.

It's important to experience the feeling of completion and accomplishment that comes from finishing an entire project. With this book, you'll find more than 100 projects that will give you this kind of satisfaction after just a few evenings of stitching.

If you are a beginning crocheter, or if you have a friend or family member who wants to learn to crochet, this book will prove invaluable. The majority of these projects can be crocheted by beginners. On Page 174 we've given you general instructions followed by a fully illustrated Stitch Guide. You'll also find numerous tips and hints mixed in with the patterns to help sharpen your crocheting skills.

And, of course, the biggest delight of this book is the patterns. From toys and baby outfits to Christmas decorations and kitchen accessories with much more in between, you'll find wonderful yarn and thread projects to make for any and every occasion.

All of us who worked together to bring you this book wish you many relaxing and rewarding hours of fun crochet.

Laura Scott, Editor

Laura Scott

101 Fun-to-Crochet Projects

Contents

Baby Love

Toys, Toys, Toys!

Christmas Magic

Bazaar Fun

Little Pretties

Kitchen Fixin's

Home Sweet Home

Baby Love

Nothing evokes the image of love and tenderness like delicate baby items carefully crocheted with loving hands. The designs presented here—including crib blankets, bottle cozies, sweater sets, and nursery accent pieces—offer a variety of items to delight both mother and baby.

Pretty Baby Sets

*What darling little girl wouldn't love to be wrapped in our pink **Sugar 'n' Spice Baby Set**? She'll simply cooo with delight! Or, if it's a quick gift you need, simple stitches and techniques make our aqua-colored **Quick & Easy Baby Set** the answer to your dilemma.*

Sugar 'n' Spice

Sweater

Back & Fronts

Row 1: Beg at bottom with light pink, ch 104, sc in 7th ch from hook, [ch 3, sk 2 chs, sc in next ch] rep across, ch 3, turn. (33 ch-3 sps)

Row 2 (RS): 2 dc in first ch sp, 3 dc in each rem ch sp across, ch 4, turn.

Let's Begin!

Experience Level: Intermediate

Size: 6–9 months

Materials

☐ Bernat® Coordinates® Basic® sport weight yarn: 4 oz light pink #2001, 1 oz white #2000

☐ Size F/5 crochet hook

☐ Size 0 steel crochet hook

☐ 1½ yds ¼"-wide white satin ribbon

☐ Yarn needle

Gauge: 5 dc and 3 patt rows = 1"

To save time, take time to check gauge.

Pattern Notes: Beg ch-3 counts as first dc unless otherwise indicated.

Join rnds with a sl st unless otherwise stated

Row 3: Sk 3 dc, sc in next sp between dc sts, [ch 3, sk 3 dc, sc in next sp between dc sts] rep across to within last 3 dc, ch 3, sc in 3rd ch of beg ch-3, ch 3, turn.

Rows 4–21: Rep Rows 2 and 3. At end of Row 21, do not ch 4, fasten off.

Turn work, place markers in each 8th sp from edge for fronts, leaving 17 sps for back.

Back yoke

Row 22: Attach light pink yarn in first ch-3 sp, ch 3, 3 dc in next sp, 3 dc in each sp across back to within last sp, 1 dc in last sp, ch 3, turn. (47 dc sts across row)

Rows 23–30: Dc in each dc across, ch 3, turn, fasten off at end of Row 30.

Right front yoke

Row 22: Attach light pink yarn in first st at edge, ch 3, 2 dc in first ch sp, 3 dc in each rem sp across, with 1 dc in sp of marker, ch 3, turn. (22 dc)

Rows 23–27: Dc in each dc across, ch 3, turn, do not ch 3, turn at end of Row 27.

Row 28: Sl st in each of next 6 sts, ch 3, dc in each rem st across, ch 3, turn. (16)

Rows 29 & 30: Dc in each dc across, ch 3, turn,

fasten off at end of Row 30.

Left front yoke
Row 22: Attach light pink yarn in same sp as marker, ch 3 (only st worked in this sp), 3 dc in each rem sp across, ch 3, turn. (22 dc)

Rows 23–27: Dc in each st across, ch 3, turn.

Row 28: Dc in each of next 15 sts, ch 3, turn. (16)

Rows 29 & 30: Dc in each dc across, ch 3, turn, fasten off at end of Row 30.

With WS facing, sew shoulder seams. Turn RS out.

Right Sleeve
Row 1: Attach light pink in sp next to marker, ch 3, work 37 dc evenly sp around armhole opening, ch 3, turn. (38 dc)

Rows 2 & 3: Dec 1 dc over next 2 dc, dc in each rem dc across, ch 3, turn. (37)(36)

Rows 4–15: Dc in each dc across, ch 3, turn, fasten off at end of Row 15.

Left Sleeve
Rows 1–15: Rep Rows 1–15 of right sleeve.

Sew sleeve seams closed.

Trim
Sleeve trim *(Make 2)*
Row 1: Attach white at sleeve joining, ch 1, [sc in each of next 2 sts, sk 1 st] rep around, ch 1, turn.

Rows 2 & 3: Sc in each sc across, ch 1, turn, fasten off at end of Row 3.

White ruffle trim
Rnd 1: Attach white at right bottom of sweater, ch 1, sc in same st, working along right edge, work 3 sc in each dc row, around neck edge, *dc in each of next 5 sts, 2 dc in each of next 3 rows *, dc in each st of neck, rep from * to * for other side of neck, working along left edge, work 3 dc in each dc row, at bottom work 2 extra sc in corner, work 3 sc in each sp across bottom of sweater, ending with 2 extra sc in corner sp, join in beg sc.

Rnd 2: [Ch 3, sl st in next st] rep around, join in 3rd ch of beg ch-3, ch 3, turn.

Rnd 3: Sl st in next ch-3 sp, [ch 3, sl st in next ch-3 sp] rep around, join in 3rd ch of beg ch-3, fasten off.

Bonnet
Note: Do not join rnds; use yarn marker to mark rnds.

Back
Rnd 1: With light pink, ch 4, join to form a ring, work 6 sc in ring.

Rnd 2: Work 2 sc in each sc around. (12)

Rnds 3–12: Sc around, inc 6 sc evenly sp around. (72 sc at end of Rnd 12)

Rnds 13–15: Sc in each sc around, ch 4 and turn at end of Rnd 15.

Sides & Top
Row 1: Sk 2 sts, sc in next st, [ch 3, sk 2 sts, sc in next st] rep until there are 19 ch-3 sps, ch 3, turn.

Rows 2–10: Rep Rows 2 and 3 of sweater back and fronts. At end of Row 10, ch 1, turn.

Row 11: Working in front lps only, sl st loosely in each st across, do not turn, at right side of bonnet, [ch 3, sc in next row] 5 times, [ch 3, sk 2 sts, sc in next st] 5 times across bottom of neck, [ch 3, sc in next row] 5 times, ch 3, turn.

Rows 12 & 13: Rep Rows 2 and 3 of sweater back and fronts, fasten off at end of Row 13.

Ruffle Trim
Row 1: Attach white, holding back of bonnet facing, in first rem free lp of Row 12 of face opening, [ch 3, sl st in next lp] rep across, ch 3, turn.

Row 2: [Ch 3, sl st in next ch lp] rep across, fasten off.

Bonnet Tie
Cut a 24" length white satin ribbon. Tie ends into knots to keep from fraying. Weave tie through ch-3 sps on last row of bonnet at neckline edge.

Booties *(Make 2)*
Instep
Row 1: With white, ch 9, sc in 2nd ch from hook, sc in each rem ch across, ch 1, turn. (8)

Rows 2–9: Sc in each sc across, ch 1, turn. At end of Row 9, ch 22 (leg opening), sl st in first sc of Row 9, fasten off.

Foot
Rnd 1: Attach light pink in 11th ch of leg opening, sc in each ch, each st around instep and each ch on other side of instep, do not join, mark each rnd. (46)

Rnd 2: Sc around, in 2 sc evenly sp around. (48)

Rnds 3–5: Sc in each st around.

Sole
Rnd 6: Ch 3, working in back lps only, dc in each st around, join in 3rd ch of beg ch-3.

Rnd 7: Ch 3, dc in each st around, join in 3rd ch of beg ch-3.

Rnd 8: Ch 1, dec 1 sc every 4th st around, join.

Row 9: With WS facing, fold in half lengthwise, working through both thicknesses, sl st across edge, fasten off.

Sole trim
Attach light pink in any rem lp of Rnd 5, ch 1, sc in each lp around, join in beg sc, fasten off.

Leg
Rnd 1: Attach light pink in a ch at back of leg opening, ch 1, sc in same ch, ch 3, sk 2 chs, [sc in next ch, ch 3, sk 2 chs] rep around, join.

Rnd 2: Sl st in ch-3 sp, ch 3, 2 dc in same sp, 3 dc in each rem ch-3 sp around, join in 3rd ch of beg ch-3.

Rnd 3: [Ch 3, sk 3 dc, sc in sp between dc] rep around, join in 3rd ch of beg ch-3.

Rnds 4 & 5: Rep Rnds 2 and 3.

Rnd 6: Rep Rnd 2.

Rnd 7: Working in back lps only, sl st in each st around, join, fasten off.

Ruffle
Attach white in rem free lp of Rnd 6, [ch 3, sl st in next lp] rep around, join in 3rd ch of beg ch-3, fasten off.

Bootie Ties
Cut two 15" ties white satin ribbon. Tie ends into knots to keep from fraying. Weave through eyelet row at top of bootie foot. Tie ends in a bow.

—*Designed by Aline Suplinskas*

Quick & Easy Baby Set
Sweater
Row 1: Ch 126, dc in 6th ch from hook, dc in next ch, ch 1, sk 1 ch, [dc in each of next 2 chs, ch 1, sk 1 ch] rep across, ending with dc in last ch, ch 3, turn.

Row 2: Sk first ch-1 sp, 2 dc, ch 1, 2 dc in next ch-1 sp, [sk 1 ch-1 sp, 2 dc, ch 1, 2 dc in next ch-

Let's Begin!

Experience Level: Beginner

Size: Newborn–4 months

Materials
- Bernat® Coordinates® 2-ply baby yarn: 5 oz. aqua basic #1003
- Size E/4 crochet hook
- Stitch markers
- Yarn needle
- 24" ⅜"-wide white satin ribbon
- 36" ¼"-wide white satin ribbon
- 4 (⅜") white buttons

Gauge: 5 sc and 5 sc rows = 1"
To save time, take time to check gauge.

Pattern Notes: Turning ch-3 counts as first dc of next row throughout unless otherwise indicated.

Join rnds with a sl st unless otherwise stated.

1 sp] rep across, ending with dc in last st, ch 3, turn. (20 shells)

Rows 3–13: [2 dc, ch 1, 2 dc in ch-1 sp of shell] 20 times, dc in last dc, ch 3, turn, at end of Row 13, ch 1, turn.

Row 14: Sc in each dc and each ch-1 sp across, fasten off, turn. (102 sc)

Divide for armholes, place markers in 26th st from each edge for fronts, leaving 50 sc for back.

Back Sleeves & Yoke
Row 1: Ch 29 (sleeve), sc in 2nd ch from hook, sc in each rem ch across, sc in each of next 50 sc across back, ch 29 (2nd sleeve), turn.

Row 2: Sc in 2nd ch from hook, sc in each rem ch, sc in each sc across back and sleeve, turn. (106 sc)

Rows 3–20: Sc in each sc across, ch 1, turn, fasten off at end of Row 20.

Left Front & Sleeve Front
Row 1: Attach yarn at side edge, ch 1, sc in each of next 26 sc, ch 29 (sleeve), turn.

Row 2: Sc in 2nd ch from hook, sc in rem chs, sc in each of next 26 sc, ch 1, turn. (54 sts)

Continued on Page 14

Precious Pink Bunny

This soft and cuddly bunny makes a sweet accent piece for a little girl's nursery.

Body

Rnd 1: Beg at front of body with baby pink, ch 2, 6 sc in 2nd ch from hook. (6)

Rnd 2: 2 sc in each st around. (12)

Rnd 3: [Sc in next sc, 2 sc in next sc] rep around. (18)

Rnd 4: [Sc in each of next 2 sc, 2 sc in next sc] rep around. (24)

Rnds 5–10: Sc in each sc around.

Rnd 11: Sc in each of next 8 sc, [sc in next sc, 2 sc in next sc] 4 times, sc in each of next 8 sc. (28)

Rnd 12: Rep Rnd 5.

Rnd 13: Sc in each of next 8 sc, [sc in each of next 2 sc, 2 sc in next sc] 4 times, sc in each of next 8 sc. (32)

Rnd 14: [Sc in each of next 7 sc, 2 sc in next sc] rep around. (36)

Rnds 15–20: Rep Rnd 5.

Stuff body at end of Rnd 20.

Rnd 21: [Sc in each of next 4 sc, dec 1 sc over next 2 sc] rep around. (30)

Rnd 22: [Sc in each of next 3 sc, dec 1 sc over next 2 sc] rep around. (24)

Rnd 23: [Sc in each of next 2 sc, dec 1 sc over next 2 sc] rep around. (18)

Rnd 24: [Sc in next sc, dec 1 sc over next 2 sc] rep around. (12)

Stuff body.

Rnd 25: [Dec 1 sc over next 2 sc] rep around, fasten off. (6)

Sew opening closed.

Let's Begin!

Experience Level: Beginner

Size: 4½" tall, plus ears

Materials

☐ Bernat® Berella "4"® worsted weight yarn: 1¾ oz baby pink #8943, small amount white #8942 and scrap of black #8894

☐ Size G/6 crochet hook or size needed to obtain gauge

☐ Yarn needle

☐ 1¾" white pompon

☐ 2 (1") white pompons

☐ ½" light pink pompon

☐ 2 white 12" chenille stems

☐ Fiberfill

☐ 18" ¼"-wide white satin ribbon

☐ Sewing needle and thread

Gauge: 4 sc and 4 sc rnds = 1"

To save time, take time to check gauge.

Pattern Notes: This item is not recommended as a toy for children under 3 years of age.

Do not join rnds; mark beg of rnds with scrap of CC yarn.

Head

Rnds 1–4: Beg at top of head with baby pink, rep Rnds 1–4 of Body. (24)

Rnd 5: Sc in each sc around.

Rnd 6: [Sc in each of next 3 sc, 2 sc in next sc] rep around. (30)

Rnd 7: [Sc in each of next 9 sc, 2 sc in next sc] rep around. (33)

Rnd 8: [Sc in each of next 10 sc, 2 sc in next sc] rep around. (36)

Rnds 9–13: Rep Rnd 5.

Rnd 14: [Sc in next sc, dec 1 sc over next 2 sc] rep around. (24)

Rnd 15: [Sc in each of next 2 sc, dec 1 sc over next 2 sc] rep around. (18)

Stuff head.

Rnd 16: [Sc in next sc, dec 1 sc over next 2 sc] rep around. (12)

Rnd 17: Sc in each sc around, fasten off, leaving a length of yarn. Sew head to body.

Front Legs
First leg

Rnds 1 & 2: Beg at foot with baby pink, rep Rnds 1 and 2 of Body. (12)

Rnds 3–8: Sc in each sc around. At the end of Rnd 8, ch 1, turn.

Row 9: 2 sc in first st, sc in next st, hdc in each of next 2 sts, 2 hdc in next st, 3 hdc in next st, ch 1, turn.

Row 10: Hdc in each of next 6 sts, sc in each of next 4 sts, ch 1, turn.

Row 11: Sc in each of next 4 sc, hdc in each of next 6 sts, fasten off, leaving a length of yarn.

Stuff leg. Sew to body with Row 11 of leg at Rnd 9 or 10 of body. Stuff haunch section as you close. *Note: Hdc section of haunch will be at top.*

Second leg

Rnds 1–8: Rep Rnds 1–8 of first leg. (12)

Row 9: 3 hdc in next st, 2 hdc in next st, hdc in each of next 2 sts, sc in next st, 2 sc in next st, ch 1, turn.

Row 10: Sc in each of next 4 sts, hdc in each of next 6 sts, ch 1, turn.

Row 11: Hdc in each of next 6 sts, sc in each of next 4 sts, fasten off, leaving a length of yarn.

Stuff leg. Sew to other side of body in same manner as first leg.

Back Legs
First leg

Rnds 1–8: Rep Rnds 1–8 of first front leg.

Row 9: 2 sc in next st, sc in next st, hdc in next st, 2 hdc in next st, 3 hdc in each of next 2 sts, ch 1, turn.

Row 10: Hdc in each of next 7 sts, sc in each of next 5 sts, ch 1, turn.

Row 11: Sc in each of next 5 sts, hdc in each of next 7 sts, ch 1, turn.

Row 12: Hdc in each of next 7 sts, sc in each of next 5 sts, fasten off, leaving a length of yarn.

Stuff leg. Sew Row 12 of leg at Rnd 19 of body, stuffing haunch section as you progress.

Second leg

Rnds 1–8: Rep Rnds 1–8 of first front leg.

Row 9: 3 hdc in each of next 2 sts, 2 hdc in next st, hdc in next st, sc in next st, 2 sc in next st, ch 1, turn.

Row 10: Sc in each of next 5 sts, hdc in each of next 7 sts, ch 1, turn.

Row 11: Hdc in each of next 7 sts, sc in each of next 5 sts, ch 1, turn.

Row 12: Sc in each of next 5 sts, hdc in each of next 7 sts, fasten off.

Stuff leg. Sew to other side of body in same manner as first leg.

Ears

Inner ears (*Make 2*)

Row 1: With white, ch 14, beg in 2nd ch from hook and continuing across, [sc in each of next 3 chs, hdc in each of next 3 chs, dc in next ch, hdc in each of next 3 chs, sc in each of next 3 chs], working on opposite side of foundation chain, rep between [] once, do not join, fasten off.

Row 2: With RS facing, join baby pink with a hdc, hdc in each of next 11 sts, 3 dc in each of next 2 sts, hdc in each of next 12 sts, fasten off.

Outer ears (*Make 2*)

Row 1: With baby pink, rep Row 1 of inner ear, do not fasten off, ch 1, turn.

Row 2: Hdc in each of next 12 sts, 3 dc in each of next 2 sts, hdc in each of next 12 sts, ch 1, turn.

Row 3: Lay inner ear on top of outer ear with WS tog, working through both thicknesses, sl st in each of next 15 sts, 3 sc in next st, sl st in each of next 14 sts, fasten off.

Pinch bottom of ear tog; sew to top of head, leaving ½" sp between ears.

Finishing

Sew 1" white pompons side by side on lower part of face for cheeks.

Sew ½" light pink pompon above cheeks for nose.

With black yarn and yarn ndl, embroider satin stitch eyes, leaving 1" between eyes.

Cut chenille stems into 4" lengths; thread 4 lengths through face under nose and above cheeks.

Bind in center and twist in shape. Trim to desired length.

Sew large white pompon in place for tail.

Tie ribbon in a bow around neck.

—*Designed by Sheila Leslie*

Quick & Easy Baby Set

Continued from Page 11

Rows 3–16: Sc in each sc across, ch 1, turn.

Row 17: Sc in each sc across, ending 3 sc from neck edge, ch 1, turn. (51 sts)

Row 18: Rep Row 3.

Rows 19 & 20: Rep Rows 17 and 18, fasten off at end of Row 20. (48 sts)

Right Front & Sleeve Front

Row 1: Ch 29, sc in 2nd ch from hook, sc in each rem ch across, beg at underarm, sc across 26 sc of right front, ch 1, turn. (54 sts)

Row 2: Sc in each sc across, ch 1, turn.

Rows 3–20: Rep Rows 3–20 of left front and sleeve front.

Sew underarm sleeve seams. Sew top of sleeves and shoulder seams.

Sleeve Trim

Rnd 1: Attach yarn at underarm seam, ch 1, sc evenly sp around in every other row end, join in beg ch-1.

Rnd 2: Ch 1, sc in each sc around, join in beg ch-1, fasten off.

Rep for 2nd sleeve.

Sweater Trim

Rnd 1: Attach yarn at bottom left corner, ch 2, sc in same st for corner, [ch 2, sk 2 sts, sc in next st] rep around outer edge of sweater with ch 2, sc in same st for corner in each outer corner around, join in 2nd ch of beg ch-2, fasten off.

Sew 4 buttons down top front edge of sweater. Button in ch-2 sps of opposite side.

Cap

Note: *Do not join rnds; mark beg of rnd with scrap of CC yarn.*

Rnd 1: Ch 4, join to form a ring, 6 sc in ring. (6 sts)

Continued on Page 19

Bootie Bonanza

Create these fanciful booties for your special little one. Shown from the top down are: **Baby & Me Booties**, **Miniature Booties**, **Baby's Sunday Sandals** *and* **Swan Booties**.

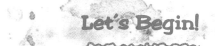

Baby & Me Booties

Let's Begin!

Experience Level: Intermediate

Size: Newborn–6 months(adopted kids doll) Instructions are given for 0–6 months size with doll size in parentheses. When only 1 number is given, it applies to both sizes. (See Pattern Note below.)

Materials
☐ Bernat® Softee® 2-ply baby yarn: ½ oz white #1706 (MC), small amount lilac #1634 (CC)

☐ Size D/3(G/6) crochet hook or size needed to obtain gauge

☐ 36" ¼"-wide white satin ribbon

Gauge: 5 dc = 1"; 2 dc rnds = ¾" with size D hook; 4 dc and 2 dc rnds = 1" with size G hook

To save time, take time to check gauge.

Pattern Notes: Infant booties are worked with size D hook; doll booties are worked with size G hook.

Join rnds with a sl st unless otherwise stated.

Pattern Stitch
Dc cluster: Holding back last lp of each indicated dc on hook, dc in each of next 2 sts, yo and draw through all lps on hook.

Bootie (Make 2)
Sole
Rnd 1: Beg at center of sole with MC, ch 14(8), 2 dc in 4th ch from hook, dc in each of next 9(3) chs, 6 dc in last ch, working on opposite side of foundation ch, dc in each of next 9(3) chs, 3 dc in same ch as beg, join in 14th ch of beg ch-14. (30, 18)

Rnd 2: Ch 3, dc in same st, 2 dc in next st, dc in each of next 10(4) sts, 2 dc in each of next 6 sts, dc in each of next 9(3) sts, 2 dc in each of next 3 sts, join in 3rd ch of beg ch-3. (41, 29)

Bootie Sides
Rnd 3: Working in back lps only for this rnd, ch 3, dc in each st around, join in 3rd ch of beg ch-3. (41, 29)

Rnd 4: Ch 3, dc in each of next 11(8) sts, dc cluster, dc in each of next 12(8) dc, dc cluster, dc in each of next 13(8) dc, join in 3rd ch of beg ch-3.

Vamp
Draw up a lp of MC, remove hook. The toe of the bootie is worked over the 12(8) sts between the dc-cluster sts of Rnd 4.

Row 5: With toe of bootie facing you, attach CC in first st after dc cluster of Rnd 4 to your right, ch 2, keeping the last lp of each st on hook, dc in each of next 11(7) sts, yo and draw through all lps on hook, ch 1 to lock, fasten off, leaving a slight length.

Secure length of yarn and weave into toe.

Instep
Rnd 6: Pick up dropped lp of MC from Rnd 4, ch 2, hdc in each of next 10(7) sts, dc cluster, dc cluster in each of next 2 sts as follows: in next st (it will be the same st as first st of vamp in Rnd 4) and in side edge of vamp, work 3 hdc across vamp, dc cluster in each of next 2 sts as follows: in side edge of vamp and in next st that is the same st as last st of vamp in Rnd 4, dc cluster over each of next 2 sts, hdc in each of next 12(7) sts, join in 2nd ch of beg ch-2, fasten off.

Bootie Top
Rnd 7: Attach CC yarn in same st as fastened-off st, working in back lps only for this rnd, ch 3, dc in each of next 29(21) sts, join in 3rd ch of beg ch-3. (30, 22)

Rnd 8: Ch 3, [fpdc around the post of next dc, bpdc around the post of next dc] rep around, join in 3rd ch of beg ch-3. (30, 22)

Rnds 9 & 10: Ch 3, [fpdc around fpdc, bpdc around bpdc] rep around, join in 3rd ch of beg ch-3, fasten off at the end of Rnd 10.

Note: Bootie top can be worked for more rnds by rep Rnd 9 to desired length.

Edging
Rnd 11: Attach MC in any st at back of bootie, ch 1, sl st, [ch 1, sl st in next st] rep around, join in beg ch-1, fasten off.

Work loose end into piece.

Finishing
Weave 18" length of ribbon through Row 7, beg and anding at center front. Tie ends in bow.

—*Designed by Barbara Batson*

Baby's Sunday Sandals

Let's Begin!

Experience Level: Intermediate

Size: Newborn–6 months

Finished Measurement:
Approximately 4" long

Materials
- ☐ 4-ply worsted weight yarn: 50 yds yellow and small amount white
- ☐ Size G/6 crochet hook
- ☐ 2 (¾") yellow buttons

Gauge: 4 sc = 1"

To save time, take time to check gauge.

Pattern Notes: Join rnds with a sl st unless otherwise stated.

Toe end is wider than heel end.

Bootie (Make 2)

Sole

Rnd 1: With yellow, ch 12, sc in 2nd ch from hook, sc in each of next 7 chs, hdc in next ch, 2 hdc in next ch, 5 hdc in last ch (toe end), working on opposite side of ch, 2 hdc in next ch, hdc in next ch, sc in each of next 7 chs, 2 sc in next ch, join in beg sc.

Rnd 2: 2 sc in first sc of last rnd, sc in each of next 10 sts, [2 sc in next sc, sc in next sc] 3 times, sc in each of next 9 sts, 2 sc in next sc, sc in last sc, join in beg sc.

Rnd 3: 2 sc in next sc, sc in each of next 11 sc, [2 sc in next sc, sc in next sc] twice, [sc in next sc, 2 sc in next sc] twice, sc in each of next 11 sc, 2 sc in next sc, sc in next sc, join in beg sc, ch 1, turn.

Rnd 4: Working in back lps only for this rnd, sc in each st around (this forms a ridge around sole), join in beg sc, fasten off. (39 sts)

Top

Row 1: Beg in Rnd 3 of sole, join white with a sl st in 9th st from heel end, [ch 3, sk next st, sl st in next st] 4 times, ch 3, turn.

Rows 2–11: Sl st in first ch-3 sp, [ch 3, sl st in next ch-3 sp] 4 times, ch 3, turn.

Row 12: Sl st in first ch-3 sp, [ch 3, sl in next ch-3 sp] 4 times, fasten off.

Row 13: Beg at heel end of Rnd 3, counting along unworked side, sk first 8 sts, attach white with a sl st in next st, ch 1, sl st in first ch-3 sp of top, [ch 1, sk next st on Rnd 3, sl st, ch 1, sl st in next ch-3 sp of top] 3 times, ch 1, sk next st on Rnd 3, sl st in next st, fasten off.

Tightly wrap a 12" piece of yellow yarn 5 times around center of bootie toe. Tie on WS to hide ends; trim.

Heel & Strap for Left Bootie

Row 1: With heel end of sole closest and top of bootie facing away from you, join white in same st as last sl st worked, [ch 3, sk next sc, sl st in next st] rep around, sl st in first 2 ch-3 sps of toe (do not ch), turn.

Row 2: Sl st in first ch-3 sp of heel, [ch 3, sl st in next ch-3 sp] rep around, sl st in first 2 ch-3 sps of toe (do not ch), turn.

Rows 3–4: Sl st in first ch-3 sp, [ch 3, sl st in next ch-3 sp] rep across, sl st in same ch-3 sp as on Row 2, do not ch, do not fasten off.

Strap

Ch 12, sl st in 6th ch from hook, [ch 2, sk next 2 chs, sl st in next ch] twice, ch 1, join in 12th ch of beg ch-12, fasten off.

Sew on buttons.

Heel & Strap for Right Bootie

Rows 1–3: Rep Rows 1–3 of left heel.

Strap

Ch 12, sl st in 6th ch from hook, [ch 2, sk next 2 chs, sl st in next ch] twice, ch 1, join in 12th ch of beg ch-12.

Continue heel

Rows 4: Sl st in first ch-3 sp of heel, [ch 3, sl st in next ch-3 sp] rep across, sl st in same ch-3 sp as on Row 2 of heel, fasten off.

—*Designed by Leann Walters*

Swan Booties

Let's Begin!

Experience Level: Advanced

Size: Newborn–3 months

Materials
- ☐ 3-ply baby yarn: 50 yds white and small amount black
- ☐ Size F/5 crochet hook
- ☐ Yarn needle
- ☐ Small amount 6-strand black embroidery floss

Gauge: 6 sc and 6 rows = 1"

To save time, take time to check gauge.

Pattern Note: Join rnds with a sl st unless otherwise stated.

Bootie (Make 2)

Body & Head

Row 1: With white, ch 26, sc in 2nd ch from hook and in each ch across, ch 1, turn.

Rows 2–23: Sc in each sc across, ch 1, turn. (25 sc)

Row 24: Sc in each sc across, join in beg sc to form a ring, ch 1, do not turn.

Rnd 25: Sc in each sc around, join in beg sc, ch 1.

Rnd 26: Sc in first sc, [sk next sc, sc in next sc] rep around.

Rnd 27: [Sc in next sc, sk next sc] rep around, join in beg sc, ch 1. (6 sc)

Rnds 28–38: Sc in each sc around, join in beg sc, ch 1.

Rnd 39: 2 sc in each sc around, join in beg sc, ch 1. (12 sc)

Rnd 40: [Sc in next sc, 2 sc in next sc] rep around, join in beg sc.

Rnd 41: [Sc in each of next 2 sc, 2 sc in next sc] rep around, join in beg sc.

Rnds 42–45: Sc in each sc around, join in beg sc.

Rnd 46: [Sc in each of next 2 sc, sk next sc] rep around, join in beg sc.

Rnd 47: Sc in each sc around, join in beg sc.

Rnd 48: [Sc in next sc, sk next sc] rep around, join in beg sc.

Stuff head.

Rnd 49: Sc in each sc around, join in beg sc, fasten off, leaving 8" end, weave through sts and pull tight.

Sew top of bootie by sewing ends of 8 rows tog at toe end.

Sew heel of bootie.

Ruffled Cuff

Row 1: Join white with sc at back of bootie, 21 sc around top of bootie. (22 sc)

Row 2: Ch 4, [sk next sc, dc in next sc, ch 1] rep around, join in 3rd ch of beg ch-4, ch 1.

Row 3: [Sc, ch 5, sc, ch 5, sc, ch 5] in first ch-1 sp and in each ch-1 sp around, join in beg sc, fasten off.

First Wing

Row 1: Ch 7, sc in 2nd ch from hook, dc in next ch, 3 tr in each of next 2 chs, dc in next ch, sc in last ch, ch 1, turn.

Rows 2–4: Sc across, ch 1, turn.

Row 5: Sc in first sc, hdc in next sc, dc in next sc, 3 tr in each of next 4 sc, dc in next sc, hdc in next sc, sc in last sc, ch 1, turn.

Row 6: [Sc in front lp of next st, sk next st, sc in front lp of next st] rep across, sc in last st.

Row 7: Ch 5, sc in 2nd ch from hook and in each of next 3 chs, sl st in same st as beg ch-5, turn.

Row 8: Sl st in each of next 5 sts, ch 3, turn, sk first ch, sc in each of next 2 chs and in each of next 5 sl sts, sl st in next unworked st of Row 6, turn.

Row 9: Sk sl st, sl st in each of next 7 sc, ch 3, turn, sk next ch, sc in each of next 2 chs and in each of next 7 sl sts, sl st in next unworked sc of Row 6, turn.

Row 10: Sk sl st, sl st in each of next 9 sc, ch 3, turn, sc in 2nd ch and in each of next 9 sl sts, sl st in next unworked ch of Row 6, turn.

Rep Row 10, adding 2 sc at end of each feather, until 9 feathers have been made, fasten off, leaving 24" end. Sew wing to bootie.

Second Wing

Rows 1–6: Rep Rows 1–6 of first wing.

Row 7: Ch 22, sc in 2nd ch from hook, sc across, sl st in same sc as beg ch-22, turn.

Row 8: Sl st in each of next 19 sc, ch 1, turn, sc in each sl st across, sl st in next unworked sc from Row 6, turn.

Rep Row 8, dec 2 sts at end of each feather, until 9 feathers have been made, fasten off, leaving 24" end. Sew wing to bootie.

Fold head forward onto top of neck and st into place. Sew head in place on bootie.

Beak

Rnd 1: With black embroidery floss, ch 2, 5 sc in 2nd ch from hook, join in beg sc, ch 1.

Rnds 2 & 3: Sc in each sc around, join in beg sc, ch 1.

Row 4: Sc in each of next 2 sc, ch 1, turn.

Row 5: Sc next 2 sc tog, fasten off, leaving 6" end.

Row 6: Attach black yarn with sc on other side of beak, sc in next sc, ch 1, turn.

Row 7: Sc next 2 sc tog, fasten off.

Sew beak onto head.

Tie

With white, ch 75. Beg at back of bootie, weave through Row 2 of top of bootie. Tie in bow at back.

—Designed by Leann Walters

Miniature Booties

Sole

Rnd 1: Ch 10, dc in 4th ch from hook, dc in each of next 5 chs, 5 dc in last ch, working on opposite side of foundation ch, dc in each of next 5 chs, 4 dc in last ch, join in 3rd ch of beg ch-10. (21 sts)

Rnd 2: Ch 3, working in back lps only, dc in each st around, join in 3rd ch of beg ch-3. (21 sts)

Instep

Row 3: Ch 3, turn, working in front lps only, dc in same st as ch-3, dc in each of next 3 sts, sl st in 3rd st on side of bootie (left side of instep attached). (5 sts)

Row 4: Ch 1, turn, sc in each of next 5 dc, sl st to 3rd st on right side of bootie (corner of instep). (18 sts)

Beading

Rnd 5: Ch 3 (counts as first hdc), [sk 1 sc, hdc in next sc, ch 1] rep 7 times, join in 2nd ch of beg ch-3. (9 hdc)

Experience Level: Beginner

Size: 14"–16" doll

Actual Measurements: 2½" sole

Materials

☐ 2-ply baby yarn: 21 yds white

☐ Size G/6 crochet hook

☐ 24" ¼"-wide pink satin ribbon

Gauge: 4 sts = 1"

To save time, take time to check gauge.

Pattern Notes: Join rnds with a sl st unless otherwise stated.

To make doll booties that won't easily slip off the doll, thread elastic through beading rnd instead of ribbon.

Rnd 6: Ch 1, sc in each hdc and each ch-2 sp around, join in beg sc. (18 sts)

Cuff

Rnd 7: Ch 1, sc in next sc, [ch 1, dc in next sc, ch 1, sc in each of next 2 sc] rep around, join in beg sc, fasten off. (6 scallops around)

Finishing

Weave 12" length of ribbon through beading rnd and tie in a bow.

—Designed by Kathleen Schmitz

Quick & Easy Baby Set

Continued from Page 14

Rnd 2: 2 sc in each sc around. (12 sts)

Rnds 3–12: Sc around, inc 6 sc evenly sp around. (72 sc at end of Rnd 12)

Rnds 13 & 14: Sc in each sc around, ch 1, turn at end of Rnd 14.

Row 15: Sc in each of next 60 sc, ch 1, turn.

Rep Row 15 until piece meas 2½" from beg of Row 15, ch 3, turn after last rep.

Continued on Page 22

Pretty Baby

Make this delicate sweater with matching bonnet and booties for dress-up occasions.

Sweater

Row 1: Beg at lower edge, ch 83, sc in 2nd ch from hook and in each ch across, ch 1, turn. (82 sts)

Rows 2 & 3: Sc in each st across, ch 1, turn.

Row 4: Sc in each st across, ch 3, turn.

Row 5: Dc in next st and in each st across, ch 2, turn. (82 sts)

Row 6: Hdc in next st and in each st across, ch 3, turn.

Row 7: Working in back lps only, dc in next st and in each st across, ch 2, turn.

Rows 8–15: [Rep Rows 6 and 7] 4 times.

Row 16: Rep Row 6.

Right Front

Row 17: Working in back lps only, dc in each of next 18 sts, ch 2, turn. (19 sts)

Rows 18–21: [Rep Rows 6 and 7] twice.

Carriage Robe
instructions begin on Page 27

Let's Begin!

Experience Level: Beginner

Size: 2–5 months

Materials
- Bernat® Coordinates® Basic® sport weight yarn: 8 oz. lemon basic #2002
- Size F/5 crochet hook or size needed to obtain gauge
- 3 yds ⅜"-wide coordinating satin ribbon
- Yarn needle

Gauge: 4 sts and 2 patt rows = 1"

To save time, take time to check gauge.

Pattern Notes: To change size to fit newborn, use baby yarn and size E/4 crochet hook. Gauge with E hook is 5 sts and 3 patt rows = 1".

Join rnds with a sl st unless otherwise stated.

Row 22: Hdc in each of next 11 sts, ch 3, turn.

Row 23: Working in back lps only, dc dec over next 2 sts, dc in each of next 9 sts, ch 2, turn.

Row 24: Hdc in each of next 7 sts, dec over next 2 sts, hdc in last st, fasten off.

Back
With RS facing, attach yarn in 3rd st over from right front, ch 3.

Row 1: Working in back lps only, dc in each of next 39 sts, ch 2, turn. (40 sts)

Row 2: Hdc in each of next 39 sts, ch 3, turn.

Rows 3–8: [Rep Rows 1 and 2] 3 times, fasten off.

Left Front
With RS facing, attach yarn in 3rd st over from back, ch 3.

Row 1: Working in back lps only, dc in each of next 18 sts, ch 2, turn. (19 sts)

Row 2: Hdc in each of next 18 sts, ch 3, turn.

Rows 3 & 4: Rep Rows 1 and 2.

Row 5: Rep Row 1, fasten off, turn.

With WS facing, attach yarn in 8th st from edge, ch 2.

Row 6: Hdc in each of next 11 sts, ch 3, turn.

Row 7: Working in back lps only, dc in each of next 8 sts, dec over next 2 sts, dc in last st, ch 2, turn.

Row 8: Hdc dec over next 2 sts, hdc in each of next 8 sts, fasten off.

Sew shoulder seams.

Sleeve (Make 2)
Row 1: With RS facing, attach yarn at underarm in first sk st, ch 3, dc in next st, dc around armhole, working 2 dc in end of dc rows and 1 dc in end of hdc rows, ch 2, turn. (26 sts)

Row 2: Hdc in each of next 25 sts, ch 3, turn.

Row 3: Working in back lps only, dc in each of next 25 sts, ch 2, turn.

Rows 4–11: [Rep Rows 2 and 3] 4 times.

Row 12: Rep Row 2, ch 1, turn.

Rows 13–16: Sc in each st across, ch 1, turn, fasten off at end of Row 16.

Sew seams.

Trim
Row 1: With RS facing, attach yarn in lower right-hand corner, ch 1, sc evenly sp across right front to upper right-hand corner, 2 sc in corner, ch 4, [dc, ch 1] 20 times evenly sp across neck, ch 4, 2 sc in corner, sc evenly sp across left front, ch 2, turn.

Row 2: Hdc in each st and ch-1 sp around, fasten off.

Finishing
Cut a 30" length of ribbon. Weave through sps in neck.

Bonnet
Back
Row 1: Beg at back neck edge, ch 18, dc in 4th ch from hook and in each ch across, ch 2, turn. (16 sts)

Row 2: Hdc in each of next 15 sts, ch 3, turn.

Row 3: Working in back lps only, dc in each of next 15 sts, ch 2, turn.

Rows 4–7: [Rep Rows 2 and 3] twice.

Row 8: Hdc in each of next 15 sts, fasten off.

Front
Row 1: With RS facing, attach yarn at right neck edge, ch 3, work 15 dc evenly sp along row ends, working in back lps only, dc in each of next 16 sts, work 16 dc along other end of rows, ch 2, turn. (48 sts)

Row 2: Hdc in each of next 47 sts, ch 3, turn.

Row 3: Working in back lps only, dc in each of next 47 sts, ch 2, turn.

Rows 4 & 5: Rep Rows 2 and 3.

Row 6: Hdc in each of next 47 sts, ch 1, turn.

Row 7: Working in back lps only, sc in each st across, ch 1, turn.

Rows 8–11: Sc in each st across, ch 1, turn, at end of Row 11, do not fasten off.

Ribbon Casing

Working along bottom of bonnet, sc in end of Row 10, ch 4, [dc, ch 1] 20 times across back neck edge, ch 4, sl st in corner, ch 2, turn.

Cut a 30" length of ribbon. Weave through ribbon casing.

Edging

3 hdc in ch-4 sp, hdc in each dc and ch-1 sp across to corner, 4 hdc in ch-4 sp in corner, fasten off.

Booties *(Make 2)*

Rnd 1: Beg at toe, ch 3, join to form a ring, ch 3, 9 dc in ring, join in 3rd ch of beg ch-3.

Rnd 2: Ch 3, dc in same st, 2 dc in each st around, join in 3rd ch of beg ch-3. (20 sts)

Rnds 3–5: Ch 3, dc in each of next 19 sts, join in 3rd ch of beg ch-3.

Foot

Row 1: Ch 3, dc in each of next 19 sts, ch 3, turn.

Rows 2–4: Dc in each of next 19 sts, ch 3, turn.

Row 5: Dc in each of next 19 sts, ch 1, turn, fold bootie in half, working in both sides at the same time, sl st across 10 sts, fasten off.

Leg

Row 1: Attach yarn in heel seam at top edge, ch 4, [dc, ch 1] 10 times around ankle edge, join in 3rd ch of beg ch-4, ch 2, turn.

Row 2: Hdc in each ch-1 sp and dc around, join in beg hdc, ch 3, turn. (21 sts)

Row 3: Working in back lps only, dc in each of next 20 sts, join in beg dc, ch 2, turn.

Row 4: Hdc in each of next 20 sts, join in beg hdc, ch 2, turn.

Row 5: Rep Row 3.

Row 6: Rep Row 4, fasten off.

Finishing

Cut ribbon into 2 (15") lengths. Weave a length through each bootie in Row 1 of leg.

—Designed by Rosalyn F. Manesse

Quick & Easy Baby Set

Continued from Page 19

Shell Edging

Row 1: Sk 1 st, 2 dc, ch 1, 2 dc in next st, [sk 3 sts, 2 dc, ch 1, 2 dc in next st] 14 times, dc in last st, ch 3, turn. (15 shells)

Row 2: [2 dc, ch 1, 2 dc in ch-1 sp of shell] 15 times, dc in last dc, ch 3, do not turn.

Neckline Trim

Sc in same st, ch 2, sc in next row, [ch 2, sk 2 sts, sc in next sp] rep around to within last 2 shell rows, ch 2, sc in next row, ch 2, sc in last row, fasten off.

Finishing

Cut ribbon into 2 (12") lengths. Tack 1 length to each front bottom corner of cap for ties.

Booties *(Make 2)*

Instep

Row 1: Ch 9, sc in 2nd ch from hook, sc in each rem ch across, turn. (8 sts)

Rows 2–8: Ch 1, sc in each sc across, turn, at end of Row 8, ch 22, join in beg sc of Row 8, fasten off.

Foot

Rnd 1: Attach yarn in 12th ch, sc in each ch, sc in each st around instep, sc in each rem ch, do not join, mark beg of Rnds 2–9 with CC scrap of yarn.. (46)

Rnds 2–5: Sc in each sc around.

Sole

Rnd 6: Working in back lps only, sc around, dec every 8th st around.

Rnds 7–9: Sc around, dec 1 sc in every 8th st around.

At end of Rnd 9, ch 1, turn WS out, fold flat across, sc through both thicknesses across, fasten off.

Sole trim

Attach yarn in rem front lp of Rnd 7, ch 1, sc in

each rem lp around, join in beg sc, fasten off.

Leg

Rnd 1: Attach yarn at center back of foot, ch 1, sc in same st, ch 1, sk 1 st, [sc in next st, ch 1, sk 1 st] rep around, join in beg sc.

Rnd 2: Ch 1, working in ch-1 sps, [2 sc in each of next 3 ch-1 sps, sc in next ch-1 sp] 4 times, join in beg sc. (28 sc)

Rnds 3–5: Ch 1, sc in each sc around, join in beg sc.

Rnd 6: [Ch 3, dc, ch 1, 2 dc] in same st, sk 3 sts, [2 dc, ch 1, 2 dc in next st, sk 3 sts] rep around, join in 3rd ch of beg ch-3.

Rnd 7: Sl st into ch-1 sp, ch 3, dc, ch 1, 2 dc in same ch-1 sp of shell, [2 dc, ch 1, 2 dc in next ch-1 sp of shell] rep around, join in 3rd ch of beg ch-3, fasten off.

Finishing

Cut remaining satin ribbon into 2 18" lengths. Weave length through ch sps at base of bootie foot. Tie ends into a bow.

—Designed by Aline Suplinskas

Hush, Little Baby

Include the date on which your precious new baby entered the world on this pillow.

Let's Begin!

Experience Level: Beginner

Size: 10" x 12"

Materials

☐ Bernat® Coordinates® Basic® sport weight 3-ply baby yarn: 3½ oz white #2000

☐ Bernat® Softee® Baby Sparkle 2-ply baby yarn: 1 oz each sky #4600, peach #4311 and lemon #4305

☐ Size J/10 afghan crochet hook

☐ Size J/10 crochet hook or size needed to obtain gauge

☐ Fiberfill

☐ Yarn needle

Gauge: 5 sc and 5 sc rnds = 1"

To save time, take time to check gauge.

Pattern Note: Join rnds with a sl st unless otherwise stated.

Pillow Front & Back *(Make 2)*

Row 1: With afghan crochet hook and white, ch 45, retaining all lps on hook, insert hook in 2nd ch, draw up a lp, [insert hook in next ch, draw up a lp] rep across, yo and draw through 1 lp on hook, [yo, draw through 2 lps on hook] rep across until 1 lp rem on hook.

Continued on Page 25

Comfy Romper

This one-piece romper is designed for comfort as well as attractiveness.

Let's Begin!

Experience Level: Advanced beginner

Size: Newborn–3 months

Materials
- ☐ Bernat® Coordinates® Basic® sport weight yarn: 4 oz sky basic #2005 (MC)
- ☐ Bernat® Softee® 2-ply baby yarn: small amount white #4703 (CC)
- ☐ Size C/2 crochet hook
- ☐ Size E/4 crochet hook or size needed to obtain gauge
- ☐ 4 (½") white buttons
- ☐ 2½ yds ¼"-wide white ribbon
- ☐ 2 (2½") strips 1"-wide hook-and-loop tape

Gauge: 5 dc = 1"; 3 rows = 1¼" with size E/4 hook

To save time, take time to check gauge.

Pattern Note: To make larger size (4–6 months) use sport weight yarn and size H/8 and E/4 crochet hooks.

Front

Row 1: Beg at middle of crotch with MC and larger hook, ch 15 loosely, dc in 4th ch from hook and in each ch across, ch 3, turn. (13 sts)

Rows 2–5: Dc in each st across, ch 3, turn.

Row 6: Dc in same st and in each st across, 2 dc in last st, ch 3, turn. (15 sts)

Row 7: Dc in each st across, ch 3, turn.

Rows 8 & 9: Rep Row 6. (19 sts)

Row 10: Dc in same st and in each st across, 2 dc in last st, ch 10, fasten off.

Attach yarn in 3rd ch of turning ch-3 at beg of Row 10, ch 12.

Row 11: Dc in 4th ch from hook, dc in each of next 8 chs, dc in each of next 21 sts, dc in each of next 10 chs, ch 3, turn. (41 sts)

Rows 12–19: Dc in each st across, ch 3, turn.

Ribbon casing

Row 20: With RS facing, working in front lps only, dc in each of next 19 sts, ch 1, sk next st, dc in each of next 20 sts, do not ch, turn, working back across same row, dc in back lps (now in front) of each st across, ch 3, turn.

Row 21: Working in both lps of both front and back dc, dc in each st across Row 20 to form tube for ribbon casing, ch 3, turn.

Right front

Row 22: Dc in each of next 16 sts, working in back lps only, dc in each of next 3 sts, ch 1, sk next st, dc in back lp of each of last 3 sts, ch 3, turn.

Rows 23 & 24: Dc in each st across, ch 3, turn.

Row 25: Dc in each of next 2 sts, ch 1, sk next st, dc in each st across, ch 3, turn.

Rows 26 & 27: Rep Rows 23 and 24.

Row 28: Dc in each of next 19 sts, ch 1, sk next st, dc in each of last 3 sts, ch 3, turn.

Row 29: Dc in each st across, ch 12.

Row 30: Dc in 4th ch from hook and in each st across, ch 3, turn.

Row 31: Rep Row 25.

Rows 32 & 33: Dc in each st across, ch 3, turn.

Shoulder

Row 34: Dc in each of next 19 sts, ch 3, turn.

Row 35: Dec over next st, dc in each st across, ch 3, turn.

Row 36: Dc in each of next 16 sts, dec over last 2 sts, fasten off.

Left front

Note: For boy's romper, work last 7 sts in front lps and work buttonholes.

Row 22: Attach yarn at beginning of Row 21 at left side seam, ch 3, dc in each of next 16 sts, dc in back lp of each of next 7 sts (buttonhole side will overlap), ch 3, turn.

Rows 23–28: Dc in each st across, ch 3, turn.

Row 29: Dc in each st across, ch 12.

Row 30: Dc in 4th ch from hook and in each ch and st across, ch 3, turn.

Rows 31–33: Dc in each st across, ch 3, turn.

Shoulder

Row 34: Dc in each of next 19 sts, ch 3, turn.

Row 35: Dec over next st, dc in each st across, ch 3, turn.

Row 36: Dc in each of next 16 sts, dec over next 2 sts, fasten off.

Back

Rows 1–19: Rep Rows 1–19 of Front.

Ribbon casing

Row 20: With RS facing, working in front lps only, dc in each st across, do not ch, turn, working back across same row, dc in back lps only (now in front) of each st, ch 3, turn.

Row 21: Working in both lps of both front and back dc, dc in each st across Row 20 to form ribbon casing, ch 3, turn.

Rows 22–29: Dc in each st across, ch 3, turn, at end of Row 29, ch 10 (sleeve), fasten off.

Attach yarn at beg of Row 29, ch 12 (sleeve).

Row 30: Dc in 4th ch from hook and in each of next 9 chs, dc in each of next 41 sts, dc in each of next 10 chs, ch 3, turn.

Rows 31–34: Dc in each st across, ch 3, turn.

First shoulder

Row 35: Dc in each of next 19 sts, ch 3, turn.

Row 36: Dec over next st, dc in each st across, fasten off.

Second shoulder

Attach yarn in beg ch-3 of Row 34, ch 3.

Rows 1 & 2: Rep Rows 35 and 36 of Back.

With RS tog, sew shoulder, underarm and side seams.

Neck Trim

With CC and size C hook, attach yarn at right front neckline. Holding a tight tension, ch 2.

Row 1: Hdc evenly sp around neckline, working an extra hdc at row ends, fasten off.

Attach MC at beg of row, ch 2.

Row 2: Sc in same st, *ch 2, sc in next st, rep from * across, fasten off.

Leg Trim

Row 1: Attach CC at seam of crotch, with smaller hook, ch 2, 2 hdc in each row end up side of crotch, hdc in each st along side of leg, 2 hdc in each row end down other side of crotch, fasten off, attach MC at beg of row, ch 1.

Row 2: Rep Row 2 of neck trim. Rep Rows 1 and 2 for other leg.

Sleeve Trim

Rnd 1: Attach CC at end of sleeve, with smaller hook, ch 2, 2 hdc in each row end around, join in 2nd ch of beg ch-2, fasten off, attach MC at beg of row, ch 1.

Rnd 2: Rep Row 2 of neck trim.

Rep Rnds 1 and 2 for other sleeve.

Finishing

Sew hook-and-loop tape at end of each crotch piece, having front overlapping back.

Weave ribbon through hdc rows at neck and around cuffs just above trim. Tie in a bow.

Weave ribbon through casing in Row 20. Tie front.

Sew buttons opposite buttonholes.

—Designed by June Hardy

Hush, Little Baby

Continued from Page 23

Row 2: Retaining all lps on hook, draw up a lp around 2nd vertical post, [draw up a lp around

next vertical post] rep across, yo and draw through 1 lp on hook, [yo and draw through 2 lps on hook] rep across.

Rows 3–30: Rep Row 2.

Row 31: Insert hook around 2nd vertical post, draw up a lp and pull through st on hook, [draw up a lp around next vertical post and pull lp through st on hook] rep across, fasten off.

Note: *Completed piece, Rows 1–31, will meas 8", with a 44-st width of 10".*

Border

Rnd 1 (RS): With crochet hook, attach white in any corner st, ch 1, [work 3 sc in corner st, sc evenly sp across edge to within next corner] rep around, join in beg sc.

Rnd 2: Ch 1, sc in each sc around with 3 sc in each center corner sc around, join in beg sc.

Rnd 3: Rep Rnd 2, fasten off.

Rnd 4: Attach sky, rep Rnd 2, fasten off.

Rnd 5: Attach white, rep Rnd 2, fasten off.

Rnd 6: Attach peach, rep Rnd 2, fasten off.

Rnd 7: Attach white, rep Rnd 2, fasten off.

Cross-Stitch

Following Chart A for color changes, cross-stitch rocking horse on pillow front.

Cross-stitch birth date on right-hand edge of pillow front following Chart B.

Following graph for st placement, cross-stitch "Hush Little Baby" on pillow back.

Finishing

With WS tog and pillow front facing, attach white in any center corner st, ch 1, working through both thicknesses, sc in each st around, with 3 sc in each corner st, stuff with fiberfill before closing 4th edge, join in beg sc, fasten off.

—Designed by Diane Leichner

CHART A

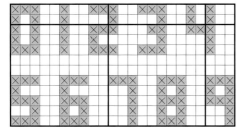

COLOR KEY
x Sky
o Peach
6 Lemon

CHART C

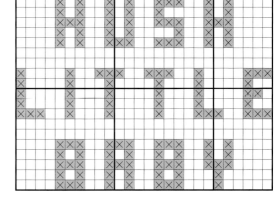

CHART B

Carriage Robe

Smaller than a crib blanket, this carriage robe is just right for strollers and car seats.

Let's Begin!

Experience Level: Beginner

Size: 29" x 33"

Materials
☐ Bernat® Berella "4"® 4-ply worsted weight yarn (3.5 oz per ball): 2 balls white #8942 and 1 ball each baby yellow #8945 and baby green #8948

☐ Size F/5 crochet hook

☐ Yarn needle

Gauge: 5 dc or 5 sc = 1"; 2 dc rows = 1"; 2 sc rows = ½"

To save time, take time to check gauge.

Carriage Robe

Row 1: With white, ch 159, dc in 4th ch from hook, 3 dc in next ch, dc in next ch, [sk 2 chs, dc in next ch, 3 dc in next ch, dc in next ch] rep across, ending with dc in last ch, turn.

Note: *For remainder of carriage robe, work in back lps only.*

Row 2: Ch 3 (counts as first dc), sk next st, dc in next st, 3 dc in next st, dc in next st, [sk 2 sts, dc in next st, 3 dc in next st, dc in next st] rep across, ending with sk 1 st, dc in 3rd ch of beg ch-3, fasten off.

Row 3: Attach baby yellow in 3rd ch of turning ch, ch 1, sc in same st, sk 1 st, sc in next st, 3 sc in next st, sc in next st, [sk 2 sts, sc in next st, 3 sc in next st, sc in next st] rep across, ending with sk 1 st, sc in turning st, ch 1, turn.

Row 4: Continuing with baby yellow, rep Row 3, at end of row do not ch 1, fasten off.

Row 5: Attach white in first st, rep Row 2, do not fasten off, turn.

Row 6: Rep Row 2.

Rows 7 & 8: With baby green, rep Rows 3 and 4.

Rows 9–84: Rep Rows 5–8, alternating baby yellow and baby green sc rows between white dc rows 19 more times.

Rows 85 & 86: Rep Rows 5 and 6, do not fasten off at the end of Row 86, ch 2, turn.

Row 87: Sk 2 sts, sc in next st, [ch 2, sk 2 sts, sc in next st] rep across, fasten off.

Weave in all loose ends.

—Designed by Aline Suplinskas

Baby Bottle Cozies

Babies will love looking at these adorable animals during feeding time.
Each whimsical cozy will help keep Baby's bottle warm too!

Elephant Cozy

Let's Begin!

Experience Level: Beginner

Size: Fits any standard 8-oz baby bottle

Materials

☐ Bernat® Berella "4"® 4-ply worsted weight yarn: 2½ oz. dark oxford heather #8893, small amount each rose #8921 and light denim #8794

☐ Size H/8 crochet hook

☐ Felt: small amount each black, white and red

☐ Glue

☐ Fiberfill

☐ Elastic cord

☐ Yarn needle

Gauge: 4 sc and 4 sc rows = 1"
To save time, take time to check gauge.

Pattern Notes: Do not join rnds unless otherwise indicated.

Bottle should be removed from cozy before giving to an unattended infant.

Body

Rnd 1: With dark oxford heather, ch 2, work 6 sc in 2nd ch from hook. (6)

Rnds 2–5: Sc around, inc 6 sc evenly sp each rnd. (30)

Rnd 6: Working in back lps only, sc in each st around, sl st in next st, ch 1. (30)

Rnds 7–28: Sc in each sc around.

Rnd 29: Working in front lps only, sc in each st around.

Rnd 30: Sc in each sc around, fasten off, leaving a length for sewing.

Whipstitch front lps of Rnd 30 to rem back lps of Rnd 28. Run a length of elastic cord under Rnd 30. Knot elastic to tightly, making sure bottle will slip in and out of cozy easily. Weave in elastic ends.

Bottom ruffle

With top of cozy facing, attach rose with sl st around any sc post of Rnd 6 of body, ch 4, 2 tr around same sc, work 3 tr around each rem sc post around, join with a sl st in 4th ch of beg ch-4, fasten off. Weave in loose end.

Top ruffle

With top of cozy facing, attach light denim with sl st around any sc post of Rnd 7 of body, ch 3, 2 dc around same sc, work 3 dc around each rem sc post around, join with a sl st in 3rd ch of beg ch-3, fasten off.

Weave in loose end. Slip bottle into cozy.

Trunk

Rnd 1: With dark oxford heather, ch 2, in 2nd ch from hook work 1 sc, 2 hdc, 1 sc, 2 hdc, join with a sl st in beg sc, ch 1. (6)

Rnd 2: Working in back lps only, sc in each st around, join with a sl st in beg sc. (6)

Rnds 3 & 4: Sc in each st around, do not join rnds.

Rnd 5: Sc around, inc 3 sc sts evenly sp around. (9)

Rnds 6–9: Sc in each st around.

Rnd 10: Rep Rnd 5. (12)

Rnds 11 & 12: Rep Rnd 6.

Rnds 13 & 14: Sc around, inc 6 sc evenly sp around. (24)

At the end of Rnd 14, fasten off, leaving a length for sewing.

Stuff trunk with fiberfill; sew to center of cozy. Curl trunk upward slightly.

Left Ear
Part A

Row 1: With dark oxford heather, ch 2, in 2nd ch from hook work 2 sc, 2 hdc, ch 1, turn. (4)

Row 2: Work 2 hdc in each hdc and 2 sc in each sc, ch 1, turn. (8)

Row 3: Work 2 sc in each sc and 2 hdc in each hdc, ch 1, turn. (16)

Row 4: [Hdc in next st, 2 hdc in next st] 4 times, [sc in next st, 2 sc in next st] 4 times, ch 1, turn. (24)

Row 5: Sc in each of next 12 sts, [hdc in next st, 2 hdc in next st] 6 times, fasten off. (30)

Part B

Row 1: With dark oxford heather, ch 2, in 2nd ch from hook work 2 hdc, 2 sc, ch 1, turn. (4)

Row 2: Work 2 sc in each sc and 2 hdc in each hdc across, ch 1, turn. (8)

Row 3: Work 2 hdc in each hdc and 2 sc in each sc across, ch 1, turn. (16)

Row 4: [Sc in next st, 2 sc in next st] 4 times, [hdc in next st, 2 hdc in next st] 4 times, ch 1, turn. (24)

Row 5: [Hdc in next st, 2 hdc in next st] 6 times, sc in each of next 12 sts, do not fasten off. (30)

Joining

Place Part A and Part B tog with WS facing, matching sc ends and hdc ends, sc across Row 5 working through both thicknesses, sl st in last st, fasten off, leaving a length for sewing. Sew to cozy with hdc ends at top of head.

Right Ear

Part A (work after part B)

Rep Part A for left ear, except do not fasten off.

Part B (work before part A)

Rep Part B for left ear, except fasten off.

Joining

Join in same manner as for left ear; sew to right side of head.

Lower Lip

With dark oxford heather, ch 5, dc in 3rd ch from hook, dc in each of next 2 chs, fasten off, leaving a length for sewing.

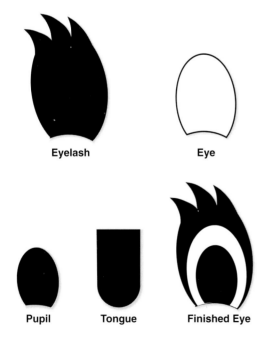

Eyelash   Eye

Pupil   Tongue   Finished Eye

With WS on underside, sew under trunk.

Felt Features

Eyes

Cut 2 black felt eyelash backgrounds. Cut 2 white felt eyes. Cut 2 black felt pupils. Glue to face just above trunk.

Mouth

Cut 1 red felt mouth. Glue to center of lower lip.

Lion Cozy

Let's Begin!

Experience Level: Beginner

Size: Fits any standard 8-oz baby bottle

Materials

☐ Bernat® Berella "4"® 4-ply worsted weight yarn 2½ oz light tapestry gold #8886, small amount each walnut #8916, cinnabar #8810 and black #8994

☐ Size H/8 crochet hook

☐ Felt: small amount each black, white, red and gold

☐ Fiberfill

☐ Glue

☐ Elastic cord

☐ Yarn needle

Gauge: 4 sc and 4 sc rows = 1"
To save time, take time to check gauge.

Pattern Notes: Do not join rnds unless otherwise indicated.

Bottle should be removed from cozy before giving to an unattended infant.

Body

Rnds 1–30: With light tapestry gold, rep Rnds 1–30 of Elephant body.

Ears (Make 2)

Inner ear

Rnd 1: With walnut, ch 2, 6 sc in 2nd ch from hook. (6)

Rnd 2: Work 2 sc in each sc around, join with a sl

Continued on Page 33

Sweet Dreams

Show Baby off proudly on outdoor excursions with this matching coverlet and pillow set sized for the carriage.

Let's Begin!

Experience Level: Beginner

Size:
Carriage Cover: 20" x 28½"
Pillow: 8" x 10"

Materials
- ☐ Bernat® Berella "4"® worsted weight yarn (3.5 oz per ball): 2 balls each white #8942, pink #8943 and baby blue #8944; 1 ball baby ombre #9045
- ☐ Size G/6 crochet hook
- ☐ Fiberfill
- ☐ 3 yds ¼"-wide pink satin ribbon
- ☐ Yarn needle

Gauge: 3 patt sts = 1"; motif= 4½" square
To save time, take time to check gauge.

Pattern Note: Join rnds with a sl st unless otherwise stated.

Carriage Cover

Motif (*Make 24: 8 each of pink, baby blue & white*)
Row 1: Ch 25, insert hook in 2nd ch from hook, draw lp through, insert hook in next ch, draw lp through, yo and draw through all 3 lps on hook, ch 1, *insert hook in next ch, draw lp through, insert hook in next ch, draw lp through, yo and draw through all 3 lps on hook, ch 1, rep from * across, ending with ch 1, turn. (12 patt sts)

Row 2: Insert hook in first st, *draw lp through, insert hook under ch-1, draw lp through (there will be 1 strand of yarn of previous row between the 2 lps of yarn just drawn up on this row), yo and draw through all 3 lps on hook, ch 1, insert hook in next st *, rep from * to * across, ending with ch 1, turn.

Rows 3–18: Rep Row 2, do not ch 1 at end of Row 18, fasten off, leaving a length of yarn for sewing.

Assembly
Sew motifs tog according to photo. With RS tog, taking small sts, sew through both layers (do not overcast). Make sure direction of the st patt remains the same.

Border
Rnd 1: With RS facing, join baby blue with a sl st in top left corner, ch 1, sc in same st, 12 sc along side evenly sp across each square, continue around outside edge, having 3 sc in each corner, join with a sl st in beg sc, fasten off.

Rnd 2: Join pink where baby blue was fastened off, rep Rnd 1.

Rnd 3: Rep Rnd 2 with white yarn.

Ruffled Edging
Join baby ombre in top left corner, sc in same sc, *5 dc in next sc, sc in next sc, rep from * around, sc in last sc, [ch 1, sc in next sc] rep across top edge, join with a sl st in beg sc, fasten off.

Ribbon Trim
Cut 5 (12") pieces of ribbon. Using photo as a guide, thread 1 end of ribbon through yarn ndl; pull up from WS; remove ndl. Thread other end of ribbon into yarn ndl; pull up from WS ¼" from first end. Tie in a tight knot. Tie in a bow; trim ends.

Pillow

Front Motif (*Make 12: 4 each of pink, baby blue & white*)

Row 1: Ch 13, insert hook in 2nd ch from hook, draw lp through, insert hook in next ch, draw lp through, yo and draw through all 3 lps on hook, ch 1, *insert hook in next ch, draw lp through, insert hook in next ch, draw lp through, yo and draw through all 3 lps on hook, ch 1, rep from * across, ending with ch 1, turn.

Rows 2–9: Rep Rows 2–9 of Carriage Cover.

Sew motifs tog according to Fig. 2 in same manner as carriage cover motifs.

Cut an 8" length of ribbon and tie into a bow in one corner.

Back
Row 1: With white, ch 37, work in patt as for motifs.

Rows 2–34: Work in est patt, do not fasten off at end of Row 34.

Assembly
With WS tog, join front and back by working sc through both layers all around, having 7 sc sts across each motif and 3 sc in each corner. Stuff lightly before closing, join with a sl st in beg sc, fasten off.

Edging

Join baby ombre in any corner, ch 3, 4 dc in same st, *sk 1 sc, sc in next sc, sk 1 sc, 5 dc in next sc, rep from * around, join with a sl st in 3rd ch of beg ch-3, fasten off.

—Designed by Colleen Sullivan

Lion Cozy

Continued from Page 30

st in beg sc, fasten off. (12)

Outer ear

Rnd 1: With light tapestry gold, ch 2, 6 sc in 2nd ch from hook. (6)

Rnd 2: Work 2 sc in each sc around, do not fasten off. (12)

Finishing

With wrong sides tog and walnut side facing, sc through both thicknesses around entire outer edge, join with a sl st in beg sc, fasten off, leaving a length for sewing. (12)

Sew ears to side of head 3 rnds below top of cozy.

Mane

Cut several 5-inch strands from light tapestry gold, cinnabar and walnut yarns. Holding 1 strand of each color tog, knot around face for fringe, with 1 row in front of ears and 1 row behind ears. Trim mane shorter around top of head and ears, but longer under chin.

Legs *(Make 2)*

Rnd 1: With light tapestry gold, ch 2, 5 sc in 2nd ch from hook. (5)

Rnds 2 & 3: Work 2 sc in each sc around. (20)

Rnd 4: Sc in each of next 6 sts, [dec 1 sc over next 2 sts] 4 times, sc in each of next 6 sc. (16)

Rnd 5: Sc in each of next 4 sts, [dec 1 sc over next 2 sts] 4 times, sc in each of next 4 sts. (12)

Rnds 6–8: Sc in each st around. (12)

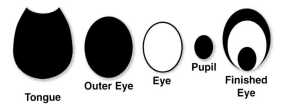

Tongue **Outer Eye** **Eye** **Pupil** **Finished Eye**

At end of Rnd 8, stuff leg with fiberfill.

Rnd 9: [Dec 1 sc over next 2 sts] 6 times. (6)

Rnd 10: Sl st in every other sc around, fasten off, leaving a length for sewing.

Sew to front lower body.

Arms *(Make 2)*

Rnd 1: With light tapestry gold, ch 2, work 6 sc in 2nd ch from hook. (6)

Rnd 2: Work 2 sc in each sc around. (12)

Rnd 3: Sc around, inc 4 sc evenly sp around. (16)

Rnd 4: Sc in each of next 4 sc, [dec 1 sc over next 2 sc] 4 times, sc in each of next 4 sc. (12)

Rnd 5: Sc in each of next 4 sc, [dec 1 sc over next 2 sc] twice, sc in each of next 4 sc. (10)

Rnds 6–8: Sc in each sc around. (10)

At the end of Rnd 8, stuff arm with fiberfill.

Rnd 9: [Dec 1 sc over next 2 sc] 5 times. (5)

Rnd 10: Sl st in every other st around, fasten off, leaving a length for sewing.

Sew to front body below mane.

Cheeks

Rnd 1: With light tapestry gold, ch 3, 7 hdc in 3rd ch from hook, sl st in 3rd ch of beg ch-3, fasten off, leaving a length for sewing. (8)

Sew to face with cheeks touching at center face.

Nose

With black, ch 2, 4 sc in 2nd ch from hook, join with a sl st to form a ring, fasten off, leaving a long length of yarn.

Sew nose above and between cheeks. Embroider a line down between cheeks and make a smiling mouth by sewing a line under each cheek. For spots on cheeks, bring ndl up through cheek; go back down through cheek beside same sp ndl was brought up. Make 4 or 5 spots on each cheek, fasten off. Work in loose end.

Tail

With light tapestry gold, ch 25, working across back of ch, sl st in 2nd back bump on ch, sl st in each rem back bump of ch, fasten off.

Sew tail between Rnds 6 and 7 of back body.

Knot 1 strand each light tapestry gold, walnut and cinnabar in end ch of tail. Trim ends.

Continued on Page 35

Soft Shells Crib Blanket

Tenderly cover your sweetly sleeping infant with this lacy blanket.

Crib Blanket

Row 1 (RS): With lilac and dreamland, ch 116, sc in 2nd ch from hook, sc in each rem ch across, ch 1, turn. (115)

Row 2: Sc in each sc across, ch 1, turn.

Let's Begin!

Experience Level: Beginner

Size: 35" x 43"

Materials

☐ Bernat® Softee® baby yarn (1¾ oz per skein): 7 skeins dreamland #1151, 5 skeins white #1706 and 4 skeins each lemon #1312 and lilac #1634

☐ Size F/5 crochet hook

Gauge: 4 sc = 1"; 2 sc rows = ½"; 3 shell rows = 1½"

To save time, take time to check gauge.

Pattern Notes: Join rnds with a sl st unless otherwise stated.

Work with 2 strands of yarn held tog throughout—1 strand dreamland and 1 of either white, lilac or lemon—unless otherwise stated.

Rows 4 and 5 est patt st rep throughout center and on parts of border.

To add a new yarn color, fasten off last color and attach new color before pulling through last lp of last st at end of row.

Do not fasten off dreamland, except where specified on border rnds.

Row 1 est RS of afghan, working afghan from top to bottom.

Pattern Stitch

Shell: 2 dc, ch 2, 2 dc in indicated st.

Row 3: Sc in first sc, [sk 2 sc, shell in next sc, sk 2 sc, sc in next sc] rep across, ending with sk 2 sc, sc in last sc, ch 3, turn.

Row 4: Dc in same sc, [sc in ch-2 sp of next shell, shell in next sc] rep across, ending with 2 dc in last sc, ch 1, turn.

Row 5: Sc in first dc, [shell in next sc, sc in ch-2 sp of next shell] rep across, ending with sc in 2nd ch of end ch, ch 3, turn.

Rows 6–89: Alternating 3 rows white, 3 rows lemon, 3 rows white and 3 rows lilac, rep Rows 4 and 5 until 29 patt of shell stripes are completed (87 rows of shells plus 2 beg sc rows = 89 rows), ch 3, turn, continue in lilac and dreamland.

Row 90 (WS): [Hdc in next dc, sc in next dc, sc

in next ch-2 sp, sc in next dc, hdc in next dc, dc in next sc] rep across, ch 1, turn.

Row 91 (RS): Sc in each st across, fasten off.

Border

With 2 strands lilac, RS facing, draw up a lp in side of top of dc to the left of corner ch on long edge, 5 sts from corner. (Each dc counts as 2 sts; each sc counts as 1 st.)

Rnd 1 (RS): Work down long side, ch 1, *sc in top of dc, sc in sc (over side edge of) and over base of next dc, rep from * to corner, sc, ch 2, sc in corner st, rep patt on opposite long edge, working over ch-3 and in top of ch, working across bottom and top, sc in each sc (or chs of top) across, at the end of rnd, join in beg sc, ch 1, turn.

Rnd 2 (WS): Sc in next sc and in each sc around, working sc, ch 2 and sc in each corner ch-2 sp around, join in beg sc, ch 1, fasten off.

Rnd 3: Attach 1 strand dreamland and 1 strand white in turning ch, sc in next sc, [sk 2 sc, shell in next sc, sk 2 sc, sc in next sc] rep around outer edge, working [sk 1 sc, sc, sk 1 sc, shell in ch-2 sp] in 5 sts from corner, continue with ch 2, sc and shell patt.

Notes: *On long sides, sk 3 sc (instead of 2) after shell twice to come out even at corners. (22 shells on side, 18 on top and bottom)*

At end of rnd, join last dc of shell to beg sc, turn, sl st into ch-2 sp of shell, ch 1.

Rnd 4: *Sc in ch-2 sp, shell in next sc, rep from * around, working at each corner sc in 2nd dc of corner shell, shell in ch-2 sp, sc in next dc, at end of rnd, join last dc of shell to beg sc, turn, sl st to ch-2 sp of shell, ch 1, fasten off.

Rnd 5: With 2 strands of lemon, draw up a lp, ch 1, sc in next st and in each st around, work sc, ch 2, sc in each ch-2 sp, join with a sl st in beg sc.

Rnd 6: *Ch 3, sl st, ch 3 and sl st in ch-2 sp, ch 3, sl st in center sc between shells, rep from * around, working at each corner ch 3, sl st in st just before ch-2 sp, ch 3, sl st, ch 3, sl st in ch-2 sp, ch 3, sl st in sp just after ch-2 sp, continue with ch-3 sl st in center sc, join in 3rd ch of beg ch-3, fasten off.

Weave in loose ends.

—Designed by Katherine Eng

Lion Cozy

Continued from Page 33

Felt Features

Legs

Cut 2 foot pads and 6 toe pads from gold felt. Glue each in place on legs.

Arms

Cut 2 arm pads and 6 finger pads from gold felt. Glue in place on arms.

Tongue

Cut 1 tongue from red felt. Glue center bottom between cheeks.

Eyes

Cut 2 backgrounds and 2 pupils from black felt. Cut 2 eyes from white felt. Glue eyes to face on each side of nose.

—Designed by Cindy Harris

Finishing Seams

There are 3 methods of joining seams: slip stitch, single crochet or weaving. The secret for all 3 is to work loosely.

• Slip stitch (a ridge is produced when seams are slip stitched): Pin pieces together. If RS are together, the raised ridge will appear on the inside of your garment. If slip stitches are worked with the WS together, the ridge will form on the right side, which is sometimes preferred for decorative purposes. Insert hook into the top loops of both pieces being joined and slip stitch loosely around.

• Single crochet: Use the same technique, except use a hook and single crochet.

• Weaving: Pin pieces RS together. With yarn needle and matching yarn, sew pieces together with an overcast stitch, catching the top loop of each stitch on both pieces.

Toys, Toys, Toys!

Create fanciful playthings with a personal touch for the tots in your life. The patterns included in this chapter offer a variety of toys and games for little boys and girls—from cuddly stuffed animals to a purrrrfect kitty cat game board.

Rosie Bear

This cheerful bear is as sweet as a rose from the tips of her ears to the tips of her toes!

Let's Begin!

Experience Level: Intermediate

Size: 18" tall

Materials

☐ 4-ply worsted weight yarn: 8 oz white, 3 oz each pink and pink ombré, 2 oz green, and scraps of black and blue

☐ Size G/6 crochet hook or size needed to obtain gauge

☐ Size H/8 crochet hook

☐ Scrap of pink felt

☐ Sewing thread: pink and green

☐ 3 yds white cotton yarn

☐ 2 (15mm) black buttons with 4 sewing holes in each button

☐ 19" 2"-wide white lace

☐ 1 yd ¼"-wide blue satin ribbon

☐ Snap fastener

☐ Yarn needle

☐ Sewing needle

☐ Polyester fiberfill

Gauge: 4 sc and 4 sc rnds = 1" with size G hook

To save time, take time to check gauge.

Pattern Note: Do not join rnds unless otherwise indicated. Mark rnds with yarn marker.

Bear

Head

Rnd 1: With smaller hook and white, ch 2, 8 sc in 2nd ch from hook. (8)

Rnd 2: 2 sc in each sc around. (16)

Rnd 3: [Sc in next sc, 2 sc in next sc] rep around. (24)

Rnd 4: [Sc in each of next 2 sc, 2 sc in next sc] rep around. (32)

Rnd 5: [Sc in each of next 3 sc, 2 sc in next sc] rep around. (40)

Rnds 6 & 7: Sc in each sc around.

Rnd 8: [Sc in each of next 4 sc, 2 sc in next sc] rep around. (48)

Rnds 9 & 10: Rep Rnd 6.

Rnd 11: [Sc in each of next 5 sc, 2 sc in next sc] rep around. (56)

Rnds 12–14: Rep Rnd 6.

Rnd 15: 2 sc in each of next 12 sc (side head), sc in each of next 16 sc (mark center of these 16 sts for face), 2 sc in each of next 12 sc (opposite side of head), sc in rem 16 sc. (80)

Rnds 16–22: Rep Rnd 6.

Rnd 23: [Sc in each of next 2 sc, dec 1 sc over next 2 sc] rep around. (60)

Rnds 24–26: Rep Rnd 6.

Rnd 27: Rep Rnd 23. (45)

Rnd 28: [Sc in each of next 3 sc, dec 1 sc over next 2 sc] rep around. (36)

Neck

Rnds 29 & 30: Sc in each sc around, at end of Rnd 30, do not fasten off. Stuff top part of head with fiberfill.

Muzzle

Rnd 1: With smaller hook and white, ch 10, 2 sc in 2nd ch from hook, sc in each of next 7 chs, 4 sc in next ch, working on opposite side of foundation ch, sc in each of next 7 chs, 2 sc in last ch. (22)

Rnd 2: 2 sc in next sc, sc in each of next 10 sc, 2 sc in next sc, sc in each of next 10 sc. (24)

Rnds 3 & 4: Sc in each sc around.

Rnd 5: Sc in each of next 14 sc (mark center of these 14 sc for nose), fasten off, leaving a 20" length of yarn.

Nose

With black and yarn ndl, work satin st for nose (Fig. 1).

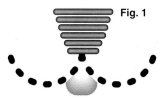

Fig. 1

Mouth

With black and yarn ndl, sew mouth using straight sts (Fig. 1).

Tongue

Cut tongue from pink felt using tongue template

for pattern. With sewing ndl and pink thread, sew tuck in top of tongue as indicated. Sew tongue at center of mouth (Fig. 1).

Tongue Actual Size

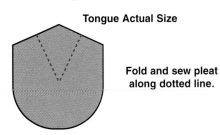

Fold and sew pleat
along dotted line.

Ears *(Make 2)*
Backs

Rnd 1: With size H hook and white, ch 2, 8 sc in 2nd ch from hook. (8)

Rnd 2: 2 sc in each sc around. (16)

Rnd 3: [Sc in next sc, 2 sc in next sc] rep around. (24)

Rnd 4: Sc in each sc around, ch 1, fold ear in half, change to smaller hook.

Rnd 5: Working through both thicknesses, matching sts and pulling sts tight, [dec 1 sc over next 2 sc] 6 times, ch 1, turn.

Row 6: Sc in each of next 6 sts, turn.

Ear ruffle

Row 7: Working in back lps only of Row 6, [ch 4, sc, ch 4, sc, ch 4] in each st across, ending with sl st in last st after final ch-4, fasten off.

Ear centers

Rnd 1: With size G hook and pink, ch 2, 7 sc in 2nd ch from hook. (7)

Rnd 2: 2 sc in each of next 4 sc, fasten off, leaving a length of yarn.

Place pink center in center of ear, having the 3 unworked sc sts of Rnd 1 at base of ear (opposite the ruffle) and the 8 sc of Rnd 2 pointing toward the ruffle of ear.

Eyelids *(Make 2)*
With smaller hook and blue, ch 5, sl st in 2nd ch from hook, sl st in each rem ch across, fasten off, leaving a length of yarn.

Finishing
Sew muzzle to face with nose touching Rnd 14 of head; stuff muzzle before closing.

Follow diagram below to make eye indentations 2" apart on Rnd 12 of head as follows: With yarn ndl and white cotton yarn, insert ndl in on odd numbers and out on even numbers; pull ends slightly to indent.

Eye Indentations

With yarn ndl and white, sew black buttons to face over eye indentations. Fasten off yarn on inside of head; stuff rem of head.

Sew eyelids over button eyes.

Sew ears, shaping by folding side corners toward front and tacking in place. Sew ears to each side of head over Rnds 5–13.

Body
Note: Beg at Rnd 30 of head.

Rnd 31: [Sc in each of next 5 sc, 2 sc in next sc] rep around. (42)

Rnd 32: [Sc in each of next 6 sc, 2 sc in next sc] rep around. (48)

Rnd 33: [Sc in each of next 7 sc, 2 sc in next sc] rep around. (54)

Rnd 34: [Sc in each of next 8 sc, 2 sc in next sc] rep around. (60)

Rnds 35–45: Sc in each sc around.

Note: Marker should now be at center back of body; place another marker at center front.

Rnd 46: Sc in each of next 24 sts, [2 sc in next sc, sc in each of next 2 sts] 4 times (tummy), sc in each of next 24 sc. (64)

Rnd 47: Sc in each of next 26 sc, [2 sc in next sc, sc in each of next 2 sc] 4 times (tummy), sc in each of next 26 sc. (68)

Rnd 48: Sc in each of next 28 sc, [2 sc in next sc, sc in each of next 2 sc] 4 times (tummy), sc in each of next 28 sc. (72)

Rnds 49–51: Sc in each sc around.

Rnd 52: Back body inc: Using marker at center back as guide, sc in each st around, having [2 sc in next sc, sc in each of next 2 sc] 4 times across center back of body. (76)

Rnd 53: Rep Rnd 52. (80)

Rnds 54–56: Sc in each sc around. (80)

Rnd 57: [Sc in each of next 8 sc, dec 1 sc over next 2 sc] rep around. (72)

Rnd 58: [Sc in each of next 7 sc, dec 1 sc over next 2 sc] rep around. (64)

Rnd 59: Sc in each of next 4 sc, [dec 1 sc over next 2 sc, sc in each of next 4 sc] rep around. (54)

Rnd 60: [Sc in next sc, dec 1 sc over next 2 sc] rep around. (36)

Rnds 61–64: Sc in each sc around, fasten off at end of Rnd 64, leaving a length of yarn.

Stuff body with fiberfill. Fold opening across flat with 18 sts front and 18 sts back; sew across opening.

Tail

Rnd 1: With smaller hook and white, ch 2, 8 sc in 2nd ch from hook. (8)

Rnds 2–4: Sc in each sc around, fasten off at end of Rnd 4, leaving a length of yarn.

Stuff tail with fiberfill. Sew edge flat across. Sew to center body back between Rnds 56 and 57.

Paw & Arm *(Make 2)*

Rnd 1: With smaller hook and pink, ch 2, 7 sc in 2nd ch from hook.

Note: *Mark rnds with yarn marker.* (7)

Rnd 2: 2 sc in each sc around. (14)

Rnd 3: [Sc in next sc, 2 sc in next sc] rep around. (21)

Rnd 4: [Sc in each of next 2 sc, 2 sc in next sc] rep around. (28)

Rnd 5: [Sc in each of next 3 sc, 2 sc in next sc] rep around, sl st in next st, fasten off. (35)

Top of paw

Rnds 1–5: With white, rep Rnds 1–5 of paw and arm. At end of Rnd 5, do not fasten off.

Paw joinings

Rnd 6: With WS of paws tog, working through both thicknesses with white side facing and matching sts, sc in each of next 22 sts, do not fasten off, continue with arm.

Arm

Rnd 7: Sc in each rem sc of the front and back of paw, mark with yarn marker. (26)

Rnds 8–15: Sc in each sc around. (26)

Arm back extension

Note: *This will give arms a forward position after*

being sewn to body. Sl st so that you will be working on 13 center back sts.

Row 1: Sl st in first st, sc in each of next 11 sts, sl st in next st, turn.

Row 2: Sk first sl st, sl st in next st, sc in each of next 9 sts, sl st in next st, turn.

Row 3: Sk first sl st, sl st in next st, sc in each of next 7 sc, sl st in next st, turn.

Row 4: Sk first sl st, sl st in next st, sc in each of next 5 sts, sl st in next st, fasten off, leaving a length of yarn.

Paw ruffle

Working in sc sts of paw joining, attach white, [ch 4, sc in next sc] rep around paw joining, fasten off. Work loose end into arm.

Paw & Leg *(Make 2)*

Note: *Mark rnds with yarn marker.*

Rnd 1: With smaller hook and pink, ch 5, sc in 2nd ch from hook, sc in each of next 2 chs, 4 sc in next ch, working on opposite side of foundation ch, sc in each of next 2 chs, 2 sc in last ch. (11)

Rnd 2: 2 sc in first st, sc in each of next 3 sts, 2 sc in each of next 4 sts, sc in each of next 2 sts, 2 sc in last st. (17)

Rnd 3: Sc in first st, [2 sc in next st, sc in each of next 3 sts] rep around. (21)

Rnd 4: Sc in each of next 2 sts, 2 sc in next st, sc in each of next 4 sts, 2 sc in each of next 2 sts, sc in each of next 2 sc, 2 sc in each of next 2 sc, sc in each of next 7 sts, 2 sc in last sc. (27)

Rnd 5: 2 sc in next sc, sc in each of next 7 sc, 2 sc in each of next 2 sts, sc in each of next 5 sts (toe end), 2 sc in each of next 2 sts, sc in each of next 10 sts. (32)

Rnd 6: Sc in each of next 2 sts (heel end), 2 sc in next sc, sc in each of next 9 sc, 2 sc in each of next 2 sc, sc in each of next 5 sts, 2 sc in each of next 2 sts, sc in each of next 9 sts, 2 sc in each of last 2 sts. (39)

Rnd 7: Sc in each sc around, fasten off. (39)

Rnd 8: Working in back lps only for this rnd, attach white, sc in each st around. (39)

Rnd 9: Sc in each sc around.

Rnd 10: Sc in each of next 14 sts, [dec 1 sc over next 2 sc] 5 times, sc in each of next 15 sts. (34)

Rnd 11: Sc in each of next 12 sts, [dec 1 sc over next 2 sc, sc in next sc] 3 times, sc in each of next 13 sts. (31)

Rnd 12: Sc in each of next 13 sc, [dec 1 sc over next 2 sc] twice, sc in each of next 14 sc. (29)

Rnds 13–25: Sc in each sc around.

Back leg extension

Note: This is to position leg when sewn to body.

Row 1: Mark off center 14 sts of back of leg, sl st in next st, sc in each of next 12 sc, sl st in next st, turn.

Row 2: Sk sl st, sl st in next st, sc in each of next 10 sc, sl st in next st, turn.

Row 3: Sk sl st, sl st in next st, sc in each of next 8 sc, sl st in next st, fasten off.

Foot ruffle

Attach white in any rem free lp of Rnd 7 of leg, working with size G hook, [ch 4, sc in next lp] rep around, join, fasten off.

Floral Decorations

Garland Stems & Leaves

With smaller hook and green, ch 78 (measures about 20"), sc in 2nd ch from hook, sc in each of next 5 chs of foundation ch, [ch 4, sl st in 2nd ch from hook, dc in next ch, sc and sl st in next ch, sl st in next ch of foundation ch at base of leaf, sc in each of next 7 chs of foundation ch] rep across ch, fasten off, leaving a 1" length of yarn.

Bracelet Stems & Leaves

With smaller hook and green, ch 25, rep in same manner as for garland stems and leaves.

Roses (*Make 31*)

With smaller hook and pink ombré, ch 5, 4 sc in 2nd ch from hook, 5 sc in each of next 2 chs, 3 sc in next ch, sl st in same last ch, fasten off, leaving a 3" length for sewing.

Individual Leaves (*Make 6*)

With smaller hook and green, ch 4, sl st in 2nd ch from hook, dc in next ch, sc and sl st in next ch, sl st in next ch, fasten off. Weave in loose end.

Double-Leaf Stem

With smaller hook and green, ch 10, sc in 2nd ch from hook, *sc in each of next 3 chs, ch 4, sl st in 2nd ch from hook, dc in next ch, sc and sl st in next ch, sl st in next ch *, sc in each of next 4 chs, rep from * to * once, sc in rem 3 chs, fasten off.

Finishing

Garland

Attach 16 roses to garland. Cross ends of garland around bear's neck; sew snap fastener. Tack ends of garland to tummy.

Bracelet

Attach 6 roses to bracelet. Place around wrist; tie ends tog.

Individual Flowers

Attach 5 roses to 5 leaves. Attach 1 to each ear for earrings, 1 to top of each foot and 1 to top side of tail.

Head Decoration

Lp lace to form a bow; tightly tie satin ribbon around center. Tie rem ends of ribbon in bow in front of lace. Attach to center top of head.

Attach 3 roses across double-leaf stem; attach to bow in front of ribbons.

Attach rem rose to rem leaf; attach to head behind bow.

—Designed by Peggy P. Johnston

Selecting Appropriate Yarns

Choosing the right yarn for your design is not easy—there are many new and interesting textured yarns, tweeds and bold novelty fibers available. But here is a formula that will help:

When designing something simple with minimal detail, let the yarn have the spotlight. For these items try the tweeds, textures and novelty yarns.

When creating elaborate designs, choose a yarn that will complement and enhance rather than dominate and detract from the item.

When in doubt, let your statement be *understatement.*

Fantasyland Unicorn

This playful, imaginative creature will delight children of all ages.

Let's Begin!

Experience Level: Intermediate

Size: 10½" tall

Materials

- ☐ 4-ply yarn: 6 oz white, 2 oz yellow and small amounts green and red
- ☐ Size G/6 crochet hook
- ☐ 6-strand black embroidery floss
- ☐ Yarn needle
- ☐ Fiberfill

Gauge: 3 sc and 3 sc rnds = 1"

To save time, take time to check gauge.

Pattern Notes: Work with 2 strands of yarn unless otherwise indicated.

Do not join rnds unless otherwise indicated. Use a yarn marker to mark rnds.

Legs are made in left- and right-side pairs. Complete 1 side, then make 2nd side.

Bottom of Head
Rnd 1: With 2 strands white, ch 2, 7 sc in 2nd ch from hook. (7)

Rnd 2: 2 sc in each sc around. (14)

Rnd 3: 2 sc in next st, sc in each rem st around. (15)

Rnds 4–8: Rep Rnd 3. At end of Rnd 8, sl st in next st, fasten off. (20)

Set aside.

Legs *(Make 2 pairs)*
Rnd 1: With 2 strands white, ch 5, 3 sc in 2nd ch from hook, [2 sc in next ch] twice, 3 sc in end ch, working on opposite side of foundation ch, [2 sc in next ch] twice. (14 sts)

Rnds 2–13: Sc in each sc around. At end of Rnd 13, sl st in next st, fasten off.

Make 2nd leg in same manner, but do not fasten off at end of Rnd 13, ch 8.

Rnd 14: Sc where sl st was made in first leg, sc in each of next 6 sts of first leg, mark for center back of legs, sc in each of next 7 sts, sc in each ch of ch-8, sc in each of next 7 sts of 2nd leg, mark for center front, sc in each of next 7 sts, sc in opposite side of ch-8, sc to center back. (44)

Rnds 15 & 16: Sc in each st around. At the end of Rnd 16, sl st in next st, fasten off.

Make 2nd pair of legs, but do not fasten off, ch 1.

Body

Rnd 1: Mark ch-1 for center back of body, sc where sl st was made on first pair of legs, sc to front, ch 1, mark for center front of body, sc to back.

Rnd 2: Sc in ch-1, sc to front, sc in ch-1, sc to back, end 1 st away from center.

Rnd 3: Sc next 2 sts tog, sc to front, ending 1 st away from center, sc next 2 sts tog, sc to back, ending 2 sts away from center.

Rnd 4: Sc next 2 sts tog, sc in next st (center back), sc next 2 sts tog, sc to front, ending 1 st away from center, 2 sc in each of next 2 sts, sc to back.

Rnd 5: Sc next 2 sts tog between dec groups of previous rnd, sc to front, 2 sc in st between incs of previous rnd, sc to back, ending 2 sts away from center.

Sew opening between legs closed. Stuff legs firmly.

Rnd 6: Sc next 2 sts tog, sc in next st (back), sc next 2 sts tog, sc to front, ending at inc of previous rnd, 2 sc in each of next 2 sts, sc to back.

Rnd 7: [Sc next 2 sts tog] 3 times, sl st in next st, fasten off, leaving a 20" length of yarn.

Neck & Head

Rnd 1: Attach 2 strands white with sc in 11th st from center front of body, sc in each of next 21 sts. (22 sts)

Rnd 2: Cross over and sc in first st of last rnd, sc in each of next 10 sts, sc where sl st was made in bottom of head, sc around, sc to end of rnd.

Rnd 3: Sc in each of next 10 sts, draw up a lp in next st, sk next st, draw up a lp in next st, yo and draw through all 3 lps on hook, sc in each of next 18 sts, dec as on other side of head, sc to end of rnd.

Stuff; sew back opening.

Rnd 4: Sc in each of next 9 sts, dec, sc in each of next 16 sts, dec, sc to end.

Rnd 5: Sc in each of next 8 sts, dec, sc in each of next 14 sts, dec, sc to end.

Rnd 6: [Sc next 2 sts tog, sc in each of next 13 sts] twice.

Rnd 7: [Sc next 2 sts tog, sc in each of next 12 sts] twice.

Rnd 8: [Sc next 2 sts tog, sc in each of next 11 sts] twice.

Stuff head and neck.

Rnd 9: [Sc next 2 sts tog, sc in each of next 4 sts] 4 times.

Rnd 10: [Sc next 2 sts tog, sc in each of next 3 sts] 4 times.

Rnd 11: [Sc next 2 sts tog, sc in each of next 2 sts] 4 times, fasten off, leaving a 10" length of yarn for sewing.

Finish stuffing head; sew closed.

Ears (*Make 2*)

Row 1: Beg at 5th rnd from top of head, attach 1 strand of white with sc at side of head, 2 sc toward back of head, turn, 3 sc toward front of head, ch 1, turn. (6)

Rows 2 & 3: Sc in each st across, ch 1, turn.

Rows 4–6: Sc first 2 sts tog, sc to within last 2 sts, sc last 2 sts tog, fasten off at end of Row 6.

Horn

Rnd 1: Beg at center of head 1 rnd away from ears, attach 1 strand white with sc, 9 sc in circle. (10)

Rnds 2–5: Sc next 2 sts tog, sc in each rem st around.

Flatten last rnd and pick up a lp in next 2 layers of sts, yo and draw all lps off hook, fasten off.

Mane

Thread yellow yarn onto yarn ndl. Insert ndl under lp of a st on back of neck; pull yarn through, leaving 3" length. Knot close to st; cut, again leaving 3" length.

Work 3 close rows with 3" lengths down back of neck. Work shorter ends between ears and base of neck. Separate plies of yarn; brush out and trim.

Tail

Cut 10 (14"-long) strands of yellow; tie tog in middle with overhand knot. Sew knot to unicorn below 3rd rnd from top in back. Separate plies of yarn; brush out and trim.

Garland

With green for leaves, [ch 5, sc in 2nd ch from hook, dc in next ch, hdc in next ch, sc in last ch] twice (1 leaf set completed), ch 3, rep between [] 6 times, fasten off, leaving 3" length of yarn for tying.

With red for flowers, *ch 4, sc in 4th ch from hook, [ch 3, sc in same ch as last sc] 4 times, fasten

Continued on Page 51

Bunny Rattle

Make a bouncing bunny for your baby! This soft and cuddly toy has a rattle hidden deep inside to keep little ones amused.

Let's Begin!

Experience Level: Beginner

Size: 12" tall including ears

Materials

☐ Coats & Clark® Red Heart® worsted weight yarn: 4 oz white #311, 3 oz pale yellow #322 and small amounts each of light mint #364 and petal pink #373

☐ Size J/10 crochet hook

☐ Yarn needle

☐ Polyester fiberfill

☐ Small plastic bottle with child-safety cap

☐ 20 dried beans

Gauge: 4 sc and 4 sc rnds = 1"

To save time, take time to check gauge.

Pattern Notes: Patt is worked in continuous rnds unless otherwise stated.

Weave in all ends as work progresses.

Head & Body

Rnd 1: With white, ch 3, join with a sl st to form a ring, ch 1, 2 sc in each ch around. (6 sc)

Rnds 2–5: Sc around, inc 6 sc evenly sp. (12 sc)(18 sc)(24 sc)(30 sc)

Rnds 6–14: Sc in each sc around. (30 sc)

Rnd 15: Sc 2 tog around. (15 sc)

Rnd 16: Sc in each sc around, fasten off. (15 sc)

Stuff head firmly. Attach pale yellow.

Rnd 17: 2 sc in each sc around. (30 sc)

Rnd 18: Rep Rnd 2. (36 sc)

Rnds 19–32: Sc in each sc around. (36 sc)

Place dried beans in plastic bottle; place in center of body, stuffing firmly all around.

Rnds 33–37: Sc around, dec 6 sc evenly sp, stuffing as you close. (30 sc)(24 sc)(18 sc)(12 sc)(6 sc)

Rnd 38: [Sl st in every other st] 3 times, fasten off.

Ears (Make 2)

Rnd 1: Ch 3, join with a sl st to form a ring, ch 1, 2 sc in each ch around. (6 sc)

Rnd 2: Sc in each sc around. (6)

Rnd 3: Sc in each sc around, inc 2 sc evenly sp.

Rnds 4–7: Rep Rnds 2 and 3. (8 sc)(10 sc)(10 sc)(12 sc)

Rnds 8–13: Sc in each sc around. (12)

Rnd 14: Sc in each sc around, dec 4 sc evenly sp. (8 sc)

Rnds 15 & 16: Sc in each sc around, fasten off at end of Rnd 16, leaving 12" tail. (8 sc)

Flatten ears; sew to top of head 1" apart.

Arms (Make 2)

Rnd 1: With white, ch 3, join with a sl st to form a ring, ch 1, 2 sc in each ch around. (6 sc)

Rnds 2 & 3: Sc around, inc 6 sc evenly sp. (12 sc)(18 sc)

Rnds 4 & 5: Sc in each sc around. (18 sc)

Rnd 6: Sc 2 tog around. (9 sc)

Rnd 7: Sc in each sc around. (9)

Rnd 8: Sc around, inc 3 sc evenly sp. (12 sc)

Rnds 9–13: Sc in each sc around, fasten off at end of Rnd 13. (12 sc)

Rnd 14: Attach pale yellow in last st made, sc in each sc around, join with a sl st in beg sc, ch 1, turn. (12 sc)

Rnd 15: Working in back lps only, 2 sc in each st around. (24 sc)

Rnds 16–18: Sc in each sc around. (24 sc)

Rnd 19: Rep Rnd 6, join with a sl st in beg sc. (12 sc)

Rnd 20: [Ch 3, sl st in next st] rep around, fasten off.

Stuff arm to Rnd 13 only. With pale yellow, whipstitch across rem lps of Rnd 14 to close top of arm; sew seam of arm to side of body.

Legs (Make 2)

Rnds 1–13: Rep Rnds 1–13 of arms.

Rnds 14–16: Sc in each sc around, fasten off after Rnd 16. (12 sc)

Rnds 17–23: Attach pale yellow in last st made, Rep Rnds 14–20 of arm.

Stuff legs to Rnd 16 only.

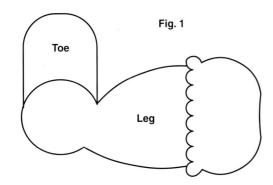

Fig. 1

Toe

Leg

Toes

Rnds 1–3: Rep Rnds 1–3 of arms. (18 sc)

Rnds 4–7: Sc in each sc around, fasten off at end of Rnd 7, leaving 12" tail. (18 sc)

Stuff toe; sew to end of leg (Fig. 1). Sew legs to body in sitting position 2½" apart by sewing through rem lps of Rnds 17.

Tail

Rnd 1: With white, ch 3, join with a sl st to form a ring, ch 1, 2 sc in each ch around. (6 sc)

Rnds 2–4: Sc around, inc 6 sc evenly sp. (12 sc)(18 sc)(24 sc)

Rnds 5 & 6: Sc in each st around. (24 sc)

Rnd 7: Sc 2 tog around. (12 sc)

Rnd 8: Sc around, dec 4 sc evenly sp, fasten off, leaving 12" tail. (8 sc)

Stuff tail; sew to back of body.

Finishing

Mouth

With 1 ply of petal pink and yarn ndl, embroider smiling mouth using reverse st (Fig. 2).

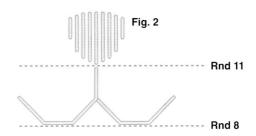

Fig. 2

Rnd 11

Rnd 8

Nose

With 1 ply of petal pink and yarn ndl, satin-st triangular nose ¾" long at top of mouth.

Eyes

With 1 ply of light mint and yarn ndl, satin-st ¾"-long oval eyes on both sides of nose over Rnds 7–9.

—Designed by Cindy Harris

Stuffing Toy Projects

By stuffing crocheted pieces as you work, one is not as likely to stretch the fabric, and can immediately see how things are shaping up.

Adjust the stuffing as needed with the blunt end of the hook through the stitches.

Pocket Pals

Make a puppy, bear, doll and bunny small enough to hide in little pockets.

47

Let's Begin!

Experience Level: Beginner

Size: Approximately 4" tall

Materials

- Bernat® Berella "4"® 4-ply yarn: 2 oz white #8942, 1½ oz each pastel peach #8947 and honey #8795, 1 oz scarlet #8933, ¾ oz pale clay #8806, ½ oz black #8994, and small amounts each baby pink #8943, winter white #8941, walnut #8916, light tapestry gold #8886 and light colonial blue #8862
- Size E/4 crochet hook
- Size G/6 crochet hook or size needed to obtain gauge
- 3 (1"-diameter) white pompons
- ½"-diameter pink pompon
- Sewing needle and white thread
- 13" ½"-wide satin ribbon
- Fiberfill
- Yarn needle

Gauge: 4 sc and 4 sc rnds = 1" with size G hook

To save time, take time to check gauge.

Pattern Notes: Work with larger hook throughout except where indicated.

Do not join rnds unless otherwise indicated; use scrap of CC yarn to mark rnds.

Puppy

Head

Rnd 1: With pastel peach, ch 2, 6 sc in 2nd ch from hook. (6)

Rnd 2: 2 sc in each sc around. (12)

Rnd 3: [2 sc in each of next 3 sc, sc in each of next 3 sc] rep around. (18)

Rnd 4: Sc in each sc around.

Rnd 5: [Sc in each of next 2 sc, 2 sc in next sc] rep around. (24)

Rnd 6: [Sc in each of next 5 sc, 2 sc in next sc] rep around. (28)

Rnds 7–12: Rep Rnd 4.

At the end of Rnd 12, stuff head with fiberfill.

Rnd 13: *[Dec 1 sc over next 2 sc] 3 times, sk next sc, rep from * around. (12)

Body

Rnd 14: [Sc in next sc, 2 sc in next sc] rep around. (18)

Rnd 15: Rep Rnd 4.

Rnd 16: [Sc in each of next 2 sc, 2 sc in next sc] rep around. (24)

Rnds 17–23: Rep Rnd 4.

Rnd 24: Sc in each of next 22 sc, sl st in next sc, ch 1, working in back lps only, hdc in same st as ch-1, hdc in each of next 10 sts, hdc in next st, sl st in same st, fasten off, leaving a length of yarn.

Stuff body with fiberfill. Thread yarn ndl with rem length of yarn, press hdc sts flat to form bottom; sew hdc sts to sc sts opposite.

Legs (*Make 2*)

Rnd 1: With pastel peach, ch 2, 6 sc in 2nd ch from hook. (6)

Rnd 2: 2 sc in each sc around. (12)

Rnds 3–9: Sc in each sc around, at end of Rnd 9, sl st in next st, ch 1, turn.

Row 10: Sk sl st, sc in each of next 6 sts, fasten off.

Stuff legs with fiberfill. Sew legs to body with Row 10 at bottom.

Arms (*Make 2*)

Rnds 1 & 2: Rep Rnds 1 and 2 of legs. (12)

Rnds 3–8: Sc in each sc around, at the end of Rnd 8, sl st in next st, fasten off.

Stuff arms with fiberfill. Sew Rnd 8 flat across; sew arms to each side of body.

Snout

Rnd 1: With pastel peach, ch 2, 4 sc in 2nd ch from hook. (4)

Rnd 2: 2 sc in each sc around. (8)

Rnd 3: [2 sc in each of next 2 sc, sc in each of next 2 sc] rep around. (12)

Rnd 4: [2 hdc in next sc, hdc in each of next 5 sc] rep around, sl st in next st, fasten off, leaving a length of yarn. (14)

Stuff snout with fiberfill; sew to face.

Eye Patch

With walnut, ch 2, in 2nd ch from hook work 3 sc, hdc, 3 dc, hdc and 1 sc, sl st to join, fasten off.

Sew eye patch to right side of face just above and to the left of snout, opposite position at which right eye will be worked later.

Face

With black yarn and yarn ndl, embroider satin-st eyes and nose and straight-st mouth, as shown in photo.

Ears

First ear
Row 1: With walnut, ch 10, sc in 2nd ch from hook, sc in each of next 2 chs, hdc in each of next 4 chs, dc in next ch, 6 dc in last ch, working on opposite side of foundation ch, dc in next ch, hdc in each of next 4 chs, sc in each of next 3 chs, ch 1, turn.

Row 2: Sc in each of next 7 sts, hdc in each of next 2 sts, 2 sc in each of next 4 sts, sl st in each of next 9 sts, fasten off.

Second ear
Row 1: Rep Row 1 of first ear.

Row 2: Sl st in each of next 9 sts, 2 sc in each of next 4 sts, hdc in each of next 2 sts, sc in each of next 7 sts, fasten off.

Sew ears to head with 9-sl-st edge of each ear facing forward.

Tail

Rnd 1: With pastel peach, ch 2, 4 sc in 2nd ch from hook. (4)

Rnd 2: [Sc in next sc, 2 sc in next sc] rep around. (6)

Rnds 3–5: Sc in each sc around.

Rnds 6 & 7: Sc around, inc 1 sc st around. (8) At the end of Rnd 7, sl st in next st, fasten off. Stuff tail lightly with fiberfill; sew to back body.

Tag

With light tapestry gold, ch 2, 5 sc in 2nd ch from hook, sl st to join, fasten off, leaving a length of yarn.

Collar

With scarlet, ch 24, fasten off, leaving a length of yarn.

Lp rem length of yarn from tag over middle of collar; secure at back of tag with a few sts.

Place collar around neckline; sew ends tog at back.

Weave in loose ends.

Bear

Head
Rnds 1–13: With honey, rep Rnds 1–13 of puppy.

Body
Rnds 14–24: With honey, rep Rnds 14–24 of puppy.

Legs
Rnds 1–10: With honey, rep Rnds 1–10 of puppy.

Arms
Rnds 1–8: With honey, rep Rnds 1–8 of puppy.

Snout
Rnd 1: With winter white, ch 2, 6 sc in 2nd ch from hook. (6)

Rnd 2: 2 sc in each sc around. (12)

Rnd 3: [Sc in each of next 5 sc, 2 sc in next sc] rep around. (14)

Rnd 4: Sc in each sc around, sl st in next st, fasten off. Stuff snout with fiberfill; sew to face

Face

With black yarn and yarn ndl, embroider satin-st eyes and nose and straight-st mouth, as shown in photo.

Ears *(Make 2)*

Row 1: With honey, ch 2, 4 sc in 2nd ch from hook, ch 1, turn. (4)

Row 2: Sc in first sc, 2 sc in each of next 2 sc, sl st in next sc, fasten off.

Sew ears to top of head.

Bow Tie

Row 1: With size E hook and light colonial blue, ch 5, sc in 2nd ch from hook, sc in each of next 3 chs, ch 1, turn. (4)

Row 2: Sc in each sc across, ch 1, turn.

Row 3: [Dec 1 sc over next 2 sc] twice, ch 1, turn. (2)

Row 4: Dec 1 sc over next 2 sc, ch 1, turn. (1)

Row 5: Sc in sc, ch 1, turn. (1)

Row 6: 2 sc in sc, ch 1, turn. (2)

Row 7: 2 sc in each sc across, ch 1, turn. (4)

Row 8: Sc in each sc across, ch 1, turn.

Row 9: Sc in each sc across, fasten off.

Tie

With smaller hook and light colonial blue, ch 26, fasten off.

Tack bow tie to middle of tie; place around neckline. Sew ends of tie tog at back.

Weave in loose ends.

Doll

Head

Rnds 1–12: With pale clay, rep Rnds 1–12 of puppy.

Rnd 13: *[Dec 1 sc over next 2 sc] 3 times, sk next sc, rep from * around, sl st in next st, fasten off.

Top of Dress

Rnd 14: Attach scarlet sc in same st in which pale clay was fastened off, 2 sc in next sc, [sc in next sc, 2 sc in next sc] rep around. (18)

Rnd 15: Sc in each sc around.

Rnd 16: [Sc in each of next 2 sc, 2 sc in next sc] rep around. (24)

Rnds 17 & 18: Sc in each sc around.

At end of Rnd 18, sl st in next st, fasten off scarlet.

Lower Body

Rnd 19: Working in back lps only, attach white, sc in each st around. (24)

Rnds 20–24: Rep Rnds 20–24 of puppy.

Skirt

Rnd 1: Attach scarlet in rem free lp of Rnd 18, ch 3, dc around, inc 16 dc evenly sp around, sl st to join in 3rd ch of beg ch-3. (40)

Rnd 2: Ch 2, hdc in each st around, sl st to join in 2nd ch of beg ch-2.

Rnd 3: [Ch 2, dc in same st, sk next st, sl st in next st] rep around, join, fasten off.

Legs (Make 2)

Rnds 1–10: With pale clay, rep Rnds 1–10 of puppy.

Arms (Make 2)

Rnd 1: With pale clay, ch 2, 5 sc in 2nd ch from hook. (5)

Rnd 2: 2 sc in each sc around. (10)

Rnd 3: Sc in each sc around, sl st in next st, fasten off.

Rnd 4: Attach scarlet, sc in each sc around. (10)

Rnds 5–8: Sc in each sc around, at end of Rnd 8, sl st in next st, fasten off.

Stuff arms lightly with fiberfill. Sew arms to body.

Face

For nose, with pale clay, build up several satin sts in center of face, as shown in photo.

Embroider satin-st eyes with black, as shown in photo.

For V-shaped mouth, embroider straight sts with scarlet, as shown in photo.

Hair

With black and yarn ndl, make a series of 7 or 8 lps across Rnd 2 at top of head for bangs.

Cut 40 strands of black 10" long. Place 2 at a time across head. With separate strand of black and yarn ndl, backstitch down a center part line, securing strands to head.

Bring strands to sides of head. Tie a strand of black yarn around strands to make a ponytail at each side of head. Tack hair to side of head. Tie a length of scarlet yarn around each ponytail; tie end in a bow.

Collar

With scarlet, ch 23, dc in 3rd ch from hook, [sk next ch, sl st in next ch, ch 2, dc in same ch] rep across, ending with sl st in same ch as last dc, fasten off.

Sew collar around neckline.

Bunny

Head

Rnds 1–13: With white, rep Rnds 1–13 of puppy.

Body

Rnds 14–24: With white, rep Rnds 14–24 of puppy.

Legs (Make 2)

Rnds 1–10: With white, rep Rnds 1–10 of puppy.

Arms (Make 2)

Rnds 1–8: With white, rep Rnds 1–8 of puppy.

Inner Ear (Make 2)

Row 1: With baby pink, ch 12, sc in 2nd ch from

hook, sc in each of next 2 chs, hdc in each of next 4 chs, dc in each of next 3 chs, 5 dc in last ch, working on opposite side of foundation ch, dc in each of next 3 chs, hdc in each of next 4 chs, sc in each of next 3 chs, fasten off.

Row 2: With RS facing, attach white in first sc of Row 1, ch 1, sc in same sc as beg ch-1, sc in each of next 10 sts, 2 hdc in next st, 3 hdc in next st, 2 hdc in next st, sc in each of next 11 sts, fasten off.

Outer Ear *(Make 2)*

Row 1: With white, rep Row 1 of inner ear, do not fasten off, ch 1, turn.

Row 2: Sc in each of next 11 sts, 2 hdc in next st, 3 hdc in next st, 2 hdc in next st, sc in each of next 11 sts, ch 1, turn.

Row 3: With inner ear facing and outer ear on bottom, working through both thicknesses, sl st in each st around, fasten off.

Sew ears to top of head.

Face

With black yarn and yarn ndl, embroider eyes with satin st over Rnds 8 and 9 of head, as shown in photo.

Sew 2 white pompons side by side below each eye over Rnd 11.

For whiskers, cut 4 lengths of white sewing thread each 6" long. Pull threads through the st just above and between cheeks; tie tightly. Trim ends.

Sew pink pompon above and between cheeks over whiskers for nose.

Finishing

Sew rem white pompon to back body for tail.

Tie satin ribbon around neckline in a bow.

—Designed by Sheila Leslie

Fantasyland Unicorn

Continued from Page 44

off, rep from * 6 times.

Sew flowers to leaf sets with yellow so center of each flower stands out. Dampen and press out garland. Tie around neck of unicorn.

With green, make 1 (3-leaf) set; attach flower with yellow. Sew to top of head between ears.

Eyes

With black embroidery floss, embroider eyes and mouth in satin st, as shown in photo. Sew long sts for nostrils with black embroidery floss.

—Designed by Janet Chavarria

Crocheting With Rag Strips

Crocheting with rag strips has become a popular craft. The large gauge makes rag projects go so quickly they are seldom left abandoned.

The procedure for crocheting garments from rag strips is basically the same as for rugs, but here are some helpful hints that will speed you on your way to an exciting new wardrobe:

• To make your rag strips, select firmly woven or knitted light- to medium-weight fabrics. Fabric strips tend to twist as you work with them, so try to find fabrics that are the same on both sides.

• Be sure the fiber content of your fabrics is compatible with your project. Cotton and cotton blends have more body, while rayons, which work up softer, tend to be more clinging. Polyesters are extremely stiff when crocheted. Make a trial swatch, using hooks sizes J to Q, depending upon your fabrics.

• For a size 12 women's long-sleeved sweater you will need approximately 600 yards of fabric strips. The usual strip width is ¾", so you will need approximately 11 yards of 45"-wide fabric.

• For lighter weight sweaters, cut strips narrower and use a smaller hook, but be sure you have chosen fabrics that don't ravel easily.

• Strips may be cut all at once before you begin crocheting. Commercial cutting tools are available at craft and sewing supply stores.

• Strips may be sewn together as work progresses, or before crocheting begins. Reduce frequent seaming by cutting strips on the bias, stopping just short of the selvedge, and beginning again at the selvedge edge a strip-width from the previous cut.

Wilbur Worm

*The sections of this colorful caterpillar pull apart for
hours of entertainment while toddlers learn about colors and sizes.*

Let's Begin!

Experience Level: Beginner

Size: 25" long

Materials

☐ Bernat® Nice & Soft® worsted weight yarn: 2 oz scarlet #4216, 1½ oz each carrot #4347 and lotus #4634; 1 oz each electric green #4517 and wine #4288; and ½ oz each rose #4211, royal #4641 and bright yellow #4346

☐ Bernat® Berella "4"® 4-ply yarn: 2 oz hunter green #8981, 1 oz light tapestry gold #8886, and small amounts each winter white #8941 and black #8994

☐ Size G/6 crochet hook

☐ Fiberfill

☐ 13½" 1½"-wide hook-and-loop tape

☐ Sewing needle and thread

☐ Tapestry needle

Gauge: 4 sc and 4 sc rows or rnds = 1"

To save time, take time to check gauge.

Pattern Notes: This item is not recommended as a toy for children under 3 years of age.

Body is crocheted in 9 different colored segments, following rnds of head as indicated.

Do not join rnds unless otherwise indicated; mark rnds with a scrap of CC yarn.

Weave in loose ends as work progresses.

Eyes *(Make 2)*

Row 1: With winter white, ch 7, sc in 2nd ch from hook, sc in each rem ch across, ch 1, turn. (6)

Rows 2–5: Sc in each sc across, ch 1, turn,

Row 6: Dec 1 sc over next 2 sc, sc in each of next 2 sc, dec 1 sc over next 2 sc, ch 1, turn. (4)

Row 7: [Dec 1 sc over next 2 sc] twice, ch 1, turn.

Row 8: Dec 1 sc over next 2 sc, do not turn. (1)

Rnd 9: Sc evenly sp around, working 3 sc in each corner, sl st to join in sc of Row 8, fasten off.

Pupils

Row 1: With black, ch 5, sc in 2nd ch from hook, sc in each rem ch across, ch 1, turn. (4)

Rows 2 & 3: Sc in each sc across, ch 1, turn.

Row 4: [Dec 1 sc over next 2 sc] twice, ch 1, turn. (2)

Row 5: Dec 1 sc over next 2 sc, do not turn. (1)

Rnd 6: Sc evenly sp around, working 3 sc in each corner, sl st to join in sc of Row 5, fasten off, leaving a length of yarn.

Finishing

Sew pupil in lower right corner of eye.

Attach black to Rnd 9 of eye on left edge, ch 1, sc in each st around, with 3 sc in each corner st and catching in sts of pupil that lie along edge of eye, sl st to join in beg sc, fasten off, leaving a length of yarn.

Nose

Rnd 1: With carrot, ch 2, 6 sc in 2nd ch from hook. (6)

Rnd 2: 2 sc in each sc around. (12)

Rnd 3: [Sc in next st, 2 sc in next st] rep around. (18)

Rnd 4: [2 sc in next st, sc in each of next 2 sts] rep around. (24)

Rnd 5: [Sc in each of next 2 sts, dec 1 sc over next 2 sts] rep around. (18)

Rnd 6: [Dec 1 sc over next 2 sts, sc in next st] rep around. (12)

Stuff nose with fiberfill.

Rnd 7: [Dec 1 sc over next 2 sc] rep around, sl st in next st, fasten off, leaving a length of yarn. (6)

Weave rem length of yarn through sts of Rnd 7, pull to close opening, knot to secure.

Mouth

With black yarn, ch 20, fasten off, leaving a length of yarn.

[With black, ch 5, fasten off, leaving a length of yarn] twice.

Head

Rnd 1: With scarlet, ch 2, 6 sc in 2nd ch from hook. (6)

Rnd 2: 2 sc in each st around. (12)

Rnd 3: [Sc in next st, 2 sc in next st] rep around. (18)

Rnd 4: [2 sc in next st, sc in each of next 2 sts] rep around. (24)

Rnd 5: [Sc in each of next 3 sts, 2 sc in next st] rep around. (30)

Rnd 6: Sc in next st, 2 sc in next st, [sc in each of

next 4 sts, 2 sc in next st] 5 times, sc in each of next 3 sts. (36)

Rnd 7: [Sc in each of next 5 sts, 2 sc in next st] rep around. (42)

Rnd 8: Sc in each of next 2 sts, 2 sc in next st, [sc in each of next 6 sts, 2 sc in next st] 5 times, sc in each of next 4 sts. (48)

Rnd 9: Sc in each of next 7 sts, 2 sc in next st] rep around. (54)

Rnd 10: Sc in each of next 3 sts, 2 sc in next st, [sc in each of next 8 sts, 2 sc in next st] 5 times, sc in each of next 5 sts. (60)

Rnd 11: [Sc in each of next 9 sts, 2 sc in next st] rep around. (66)

Rnd 12: Sc in each of next 4 sts, 2 sc in next st, [sc in each of next 10 sts, 2 sc in next st] 5 times, sc in each of next 6 sts. (72)

Rnd 13: [Sc in each of next 11 sts, 2 sc in next st] rep around. (78)

Rnd 14: Sc in each of next 5 sts, 2 sc in next st, [sc in each of next 12 sts, 2 sc in next st] 5 times, sc in each of next 7 sts. (84)

Rnd 15: [Sc in each of next 13 sts, 2 sc in next st] rep around. (90)

Rnd 16: Sc in each sc around.

Rnd 17: Rep Rnd 16.

At the end of Rnd 17, draw up a lp, remove hook.

Working with tapestry needle and rem lengths of yarns, sew nose to Rnd 1 of head.

Sew eyes over Rnds 4–15 centered above nose with ¾" sp between.

Sew long mouth chain centered under nose over Rnd 11; sew short chs at each end of mouth at a slight angle, as shown in photo.

Rnd 18: Sc in each of next 6 sts, dec 1 sc over next 2 sts, [sc in each of next 13 sts, dec 1 sc over next 2 sts] 5 times, sc in each of next 7 sts. (84)

Rnd 19: [Sc in each of next 12 sts, dec 1 sc over next 2 sts] rep around. (78)

Rnd 20: Sc in each of next 5 sts, dec 1 sc over next 2 sts, [sc in each of next 11 sts, dec 1 sc over next 2 sts] 5 times, sc in each of next 6 sts. (72)

Rnd 21: [Sc in each of next 10 sts, dec 1 sc over next 2 sts] rep around. (66)

Rnd 22: Sc in each of next 4 sts, dec 1 sc over next 2 sts, [sc in each of next 9 sts, dec 1 sc over next 2 sts] 5 times, sc in each of next 5 sts. (60)

Rnd 23: [Sc in each of next 8 sts, dec 1 sc over next 2 sts] rep around. (54)

Rnd 24: Sc in each of next 3 sts, dec 1 sc over next 2 sts, [sc in each of next 7 sts, dec 1 sc over next 2 sts] 5 times, sc in each of next 4 sts. (48)

Rnd 25: [Sc in each of next 6 sts, dec 1 sc over next 2 sts] rep around. (42)

Rnd 26: Sc in each of next 2 sts, dec 1 sc over next 2 sts, [sc in each of next 5 sts, dec 1 sc over next 2 sts] 5 times, sc in each of next 3 sts. (36)

Rnd 27: [Sc in each of next 4 sts, dec 1 sc over next 2 sts] rep around. (30)

Rnd 28: Sc in next st, dec 1 sc over next 2 sts, [sc in each of next 3 sts, dec 1 sc over next 2 sts] 5 times, sc in each of next 2 sts. (24)

Rnd 29: [Sc in each of next 2 sts, dec 1 sc over next 2 sts] rep around. (18)

Stuff head with fiberfill, slightly flattening. Continue to stuff as work progresses.

Rnd 30: [Sc in next st, dec 1 sc over next 2 sts] rep around. (12)

Rnd 31: [Dec 1 sc over next 2 sts] rep around, sl st in next st, fasten off, leaving a length of yarn.

Weave yarn through rem sts, pull to close opening; knot to secure.

Body
First segment
Rnds 1–14: With hunter green, rep Rnds 1–14 of head. (84)

Rnds 15 & 16: Rep Rnd 16 of head.

Rnds 17–29: Rep Rnds 19–31 of head. (6)

Second segment
Rnds 1–13: With carrot, rep Rnds 1–13 of head. (78)

Rnds 14 & 15: Rep Rnd 16 of head.

Rnds 16–27: Rep Rnds 20–31 of head. (6)

Third segment
Rnds 1–12: With lotus, rep Rnds 1–12 of head. (72)

Rnds 13 & 14: Rep Rnd 16 of head.

Rnds 15–25: Rep Rnds 21–31 of head. (6)

Fourth segment
Rnds 1–11: With electric green, rep Rnds 1–11 of head. (66)

Rnds 12 & 13: Rep Rnd 16 of head.

Rnds 14–23: Rep Rnds 22–31 of head. (6)

Fifth segment

Rnds 1–10: With light tapestry gold, rep Rnds 1–10 of head. (60)

Rnds 11 & 12: Rep Rnd 16 of head.

Rnds 13–21: Rep Rnds 23–31 of head. (6)

Sixth segment

Rnds 1–9: With wine, rep Rnds 1–9 of head. (54)

Rnds 10 & 11: Rep Rnd 16 of head.

Rnds 12–19: Rep Rnds 24–31 of head. (6)

Seventh segment

Rnds 1–8: With rose, rep Rnds 1–8 of head. (48)

Rnds 9 & 10: Rep Rnd 16 of head.

Rnds 11–17: Rep Rnds 25–31 of head. (6)

Eighth segment

Rnds 1–7: With royal, rep Rnds 1–7 of head. (42)

Rnds 8 & 9: Rep Rnd 16 of head.

Rnds 10–15: Rep Rnds 26–31 of head. (6)

Ninth segment

Rnds 1–6: With bright yellow, rep Rnds 1–6 of head. (36)

Rnds 7 & 8: Rep Rnd 16 of head.

Rnds 9–13: Rep Rnds 27–31 of head. (6)

Finishing

With hook-and-loop tape sections tog, cut tape into 9 sections each 1½" in length; round off corners of each section with scissors.

Pull sections apart. Sew first piece to center of back of head; sew 2nd piece of same section to center of Rnd 1 of First segment.

*Pull next section apart. Sew first piece to center back of same segment; sew 2nd piece of same section to center of Rnd 1 of next segment, rep from * until all hook-and-loop tape sections are used, joining segments tog in order of size as work progresses.

—*Designed by Martha Lobmeyer*

The Origins of Crochet

In the early days of crochet, pattern designs and instructions were passed down by word-of-mouth—few patterns were written down. The truth about the origins of crochet are, therefore, very vague.

It is generally thought, though, that crochet began much the same as knitting, coming from the East and traveling to the Mediterranean. The word "crochet" is of French origin, coming from the verb *crocher,* which means "to hook." The French are accredited with developing and spreading the art of crochet.

In the 16th century, crochet was referred to as "nun's work," since nuns made altar cloths, vestments and all sorts of church linens either entirely in crochet or trimmed with crocheted lace.

By the 1780s, the crochet capital of the world was Cork, Ireland, where crocheted lace making became a thriving industry. Patterns were now being written and passed along with pride. It is interesting to note that the laces they made were from patterns of French, Greek and Italian design. the traditional Irish rose pattern, for example, was actually borrowed from Venetian lace.

It wasn't until the 19th century that crochet really came into its own. It was then that its full range of possibilities were explored. Wearing apparel, household items—all sorts of new uses for this art form—emerged. The Ursuline Sisters in Ireland taught crochet to children. It spread to become part of the curriculum in most Irish convents.

As time passed, styles changed and imaginations soared to produce the explosion of diversified designs available today.

Kitty-Cat Checkers

Curl up with Kitty for a relaxing game of checkers,
then keep the game board on the wall to decorate the room.

56

Let's Begin!

Experience Level: Beginner

Size: 17" long

Materials

☐ Bernat Berella® "4"® 4-ply yarn: 8 oz white #8942 and 3 oz arbutus #8922

☐ Size G/6 and F/5 crochet hook

☐ 25 (⅝") plastic rings

☐ 2 (12mm) black snap-on eyes

☐ ½"-thick 16" x 18" piece quilt batting

☐ Yarn needle

Gauge: 4 sc and 4 sc rows = 1" with G/6 hook

To save time, take time to check gauge.

Back

Row 1: With G hook and white, ch 65, sc in 2nd ch from hook, sc in each rem ch across, ch 1, turn. (64)

Row 2: Sc in each st across to within last st, 2 sc in last st, ch 1, turn. (65)

Row 3: Sc in each sc across, ch 1, turn.

Row 4: Dec 1 sc over next 2 sts, sc in each rem st across, ch 1, turn. (64)

Row 5: Sc in each st across to within last 2 sts, dec 1 sc over next 2 sts, ch 1, turn. (63)

Rows 6–8: Dec 1 sc over next 2 sts, sc in each st across to within last 2 sts, dec 1 sc over next 2 sts, ch 1, turn. (57)

Rows 9 & 10: Rep Rows 4 and 5. (55)

Rows 11–15: Rep Row 3.

Row 16: Rep Row 5. (54)

Row 17: Rep Row 3.

Row 18: Rep Row 5. (53)

Rows 19–25: Rep Row 3.

Row 26: Rep Row 5. (52)

Rows 27 & 28: Rep Row 3.

Row 29: Dec 1 sc over next 2 sts, sc in each st across to within last st, 2 sc in last st, ch 1, turn. (52)

Row 30: 2 sc in first st, sc in each rem st across, ch 1, turn. (53)

Rows 31–36: Rep Rows 29 and 3. (53)

Row 37: Rep Row 29.

Row 38: 2 sc in first st, sc in each rem st across to within last 2 sts, dec 1 sc over next 2 sts, ch 1, turn. (53)

Row 39: Rep Row 4. (52)

Row 40: Rep Row 3.

Row 41: Rep Row 29. (52)

Row 42: Rep Row 5. (51)

Row 43: Rep Row 4. (50)

Row 44: Rep Row 38. (50)

Rows 45 & 46: Rep Rows 5 and 4. (48)

Row 47: Rep Row 5. (47)

Row 48: Rep Row 6. (45)

Row 49: Draw up a lp in each of next 3 sts, yo and draw through all lps on hook (2-st dec over 3 sts), sc in each rem st across, ch 1, turn. (43)

Row 50: Dec 1 sc over next 2 sts, sc in each st across to within last 3 sts, dec 2 sc over next 3 sts, ch 1, turn. (40)

Row 51: Sl st in each of first 5 sts, ch 1, sc in each st across to within last 2 sts, dec 1 sc over next 2 sts, ch 1, turn. (34)

Row 52: Sc in each st across to within last 3 sts, turn, leaving rem 3 sts unworked. (31)

Row 53: Sl st in each of first 4 sts, ch 1, sc in each st across to within last st, 2 sc in last st, ch 1, turn. (28)

Rows 54 & 55: Rep Row 30. (30)

Row 56: 2 sc in first st, sc in each st across to within last st, 2 sc in last st, ch 1, turn. (32)

Row 57: Rep Row 30. (33)

Row 58: Sc in each st across to within last st, 2 sc in last st, ch 1, turn. (34)

Rows 59–62: Rep Row 3.

Row 63: Rep Row 6. (32)

Row 64: Rep Row 3.

Rows 65–68: Rep Row 5. (28)

Rows 69–73: Rep Row 3.

First ear

Row 74: Sc in each of next 10 sts, ch 1, turn, leaving rem 18 sts unworked. (10)

Row 75: Dec 1 sc over next 2 sts, sc in each rem st across, ch 1, turn. (9)

Row 76: Sc in each st across to within last 3 sts, dec 2 sc over next 3 sts, ch 1, turn. (7)

Rows 77 & 78: Dec 1 sc over next 2 sts, sc in each st across to within last 2 sts, dec 1 sc over next 2 sts, ch 1, turn. (3)

Row 79: Dec 2 sc over next 3 sts, fasten off. (1)

Second ear

Row 74: Sk next 8 sts of Row 73, attach white in next st, ch 1, sc in same st, sc in each of next 9 sts, ch 1, turn. (10)

Row 75: Sc in each st across to within last 2 sts, dec 1 sc over next 2 sts, ch 1, turn. (9)

Row 76: Dec 2 sc over next 3 sts, sc in each rem st across, ch 1, turn. (7)

Rows 77 & 78: Rep Rows 77 and 78 of first ear. (3)

Row 79: Dec 2 sc over next 3 sts, ch 1, turn. (1)

Rnd 80: Sc evenly sp around entire outer edge, with 3 sc on top of each ear, sl st to join, fasten off.

Front

Rows 1–8: Rep Rows 1–8 of back. (57)

Rows 9–40: Rep patt Rows 9–40 of back, following Chart for color changes. (52)

Rows 41–79: Rep Rows 41–79 of back.

Rnd 80: Rep Rnd 80 of back.

Padding

With WS of cat front next to padding, pin to padding from front side along bottom of Rnd 80. Using cat as a patt, cut padding. Do not remove pins.

Note: *Count the pins to assure that all will be removed later.*

Assembly

Place WS of back piece of cat on other side of padding, matching sts; attach white with sc in any st. Working through both thicknesses in back lps only, sc in each st around entire outer edge, sl st to join, fasten off.

Remove pins.

Finishing

Attach eyes to Row 65 of face with 10 sts between each.

With arbutus and yarn ndl, embroider nose in satin st over Rows 62 and 63 between eyes; embroider mouth in straight sts across Rows 62–59, as shown in photo.

Sew a plastic ring on back of cat in center of Rows 46 and 47 for hanging lp.

Playing Pieces *(Make 12 white & 12 arbutus)*

Rnd 1: Attach yarn over plastic ring, with F hook, ch 1, 14 sc over ring, sl st to join, fasten off.

Weave in loose ends.

String for playing pieces

With arbutus, leaving a 6" length at beg, ch 60, fasten off, leaving a 6" length.

Thread playing pieces onto string; place around cat's neck, with pieces on front. Tie 6" lengths tog in a bow at back of neck.

—Designed by Rosemarie Bitticks

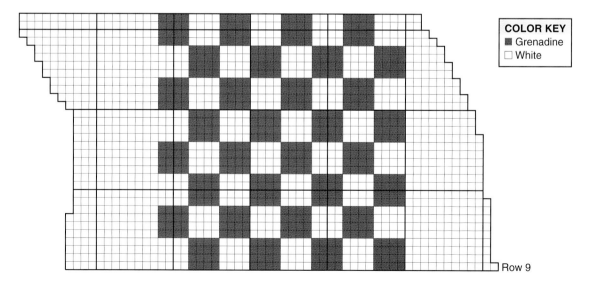

COLOR KEY
■ Grenadine
☐ White

Row 9

Mary's Little Lamb

Bring this favorite nursery rhyme to life for a child by making a cuddly little lamb of their own!

Let's Begin!

Experience Level: Intermediate

Size: Approximately 16" tall x 16" long

Materials
- ☐ 4-ply brushed acrylic yarn: 4½ oz white
- ☐ 4-ply acrylic yarn: small amount black
- ☐ Size G/6 crochet hook
- ☐ Polyester fiberfill
- ☐ Small bell
- ☐ 18" ½"-wide blue velvet ribbon
- ☐ Tapestry needle
- ☐ Scraps of black, white and blue felt
- ☐ Craft glue

Gauge: 5 sts = 1"

To save time, take time to check gauge.

Pattern Notes: This toy is not suitable for children under 3 years of age.

Do not join rnds unless indicated otherwise.

Weave in loose ends as work progresses.

Pattern Stitch
Lp st: Insert hook in st, wrap yarn over finger, catch yarn on hook, pull yarn through st, complete as a sc.

Body
Center
Row 1: Beg at center of body with white, ch 43, sc in 2nd ch from hook and in each of next 41 chs, ch 1, turn. (42 sts)

Row 2: Lp st in each st across, ch 1, turn. (42 sts)

Row 3: Sc in each st across, ch 1, turn. (42 sts)

Row 4: Lp st in each st across, ch 1, turn. (42 sts)

Rows 5–24: Rep Rows 3 and 4. At end of Row 24, fasten off.

Front
Rnd 1: With white, ch 2, 6 sc in 2nd ch from hook. (6 sts)

Rnd 2: 2 sc in each sc around. (12 sts)

Rnd 3: [Sc in next sc, 2 sc in next sc] 6 times. (18 sts)

Rnd 4: [Sc in each of next 2 sc, 2 sc in next sc] 6 times. (24 sts)

Rnd 5: [Sc in each of next 3 sc, 2 sc in next sc] 6 times. (30 sts)

Rnd 6: [Sc in each of next 4 sc, 2 sc in next sc] 6 times. (36 sts)

Rnd 7: [Sc in each of next 5 sc, 2 sc in next sc] 6 times. (42 sts)

Rnds 8–12: Sc in each sc around, at end of Rnd 12, fasten off, leaving 12" end for sewing. (42 sts)

Back
Rnds 1–7: Rep Rnds 1–7 of body front, at end of Row 7, fasten off. (42 sts)

Finishing
Fold center piece of body in half; st edges tog. St front piece to 1 end of center piece; stuff firmly with fiberfill. St back piece to other end of center piece.

Head
Rnds 1–3: With black, rep Rnds 1–3 of body

front. (18 sts)

Rnd 4: Sc in each sc around. (18 sts)

Rnd 5: [Sc in each of next 2 sc, sc in next sc] 6 times. (24 sts)

Rnd 6: Sc in each sc around, fasten off, attach white in next sc.

Rnds 7–9: Sc in each sc around. (24 sts)

Rnd 10: [Sc in each of next 3 sc, 2 sc in next sc] 6 times. (30 sts)

Rnds 11 & 12: Sc in each sc around. (30 sts)

Rnd 13: [Sc in each of next 4 sc, 2 sc in next st] 6 times. (36 sts)

Rnd 14: Sc in each sc around. (36 sts)

Rnd 15: [Sc in each of next 5 sc, 2 sc in next st] 6 times. (42 sts)

Rnds 16–18: Sc in each sc around. (42 sts)

Rnd 19: [Sc in each of next 5 sc, dec over next sc] 6 times. (36 sts)

Rnd 20: [Sc in each of next 4 sts, dec over next 2 sc] 6 times. (30 sts)

Rnd 21: [Sc in each of next 3 sc, dec over next 2 sc] 6 times. (24 sts)

Stuff firmly with fiberfill.

Rnd 22: [Sc in each of next 2 sc, dec over next 2 sc] 6 times. (18 sts)

Rnd 23: [Sc in next sc, dec over next 2 sc] 6 times. (12 sts)

Rnd 24: [Dec over next 2 sc] 6 times. (6 sts)

Rnd 25: Dec over next 2 sc, sl st to next sc, fasten off.

Head fleece

Row 1: With white, ch 4, sc in 2nd ch from hook and in each of next 2 chs, ch 1, turn. (3 sts)

Row 2: Lp st in each st across, ch 1, turn. (3 sts)

Row 3: 2 sc in next st, sc in next st, 2 sc in next st, ch 1, turn. (5 sts)

Row 4: Lp st in each st across, ch 1, turn. (5 sts)

Row 5: 2 sc in next st, sc in each of next 3 sts, 2 sc in next st, ch 1, turn. (7 sts)

Row 6: Lp st in each st across, ch 1, turn. (7 sts)

Row 7: 2 sc in next st, sc in each of next 5 sts, 2 sc in next st, ch 1, turn. (9 sts)

Row 8: Lp st in each st across, ch 1, turn. (9 sts)

Row 9: Sc in each st across, ch 1, turn. (9 sts)

Row 10: Lp st in each st across, ch 1, turn. (9 sts)

Row 11: [Sc in each of next 2 sts, 2 sc in next st] 3 times, ch 1, turn. (12 sts)

Row 12: Lp st in each st across, ch 1, turn. (12 sts)

Row 13: [Sc in each of next 3 sts, 2 sc in next st] 3 times, ch 1, turn. (15 sts)

Row 14: Lp st in each st across, ch 1, turn. (15 sts)

Row 15: Sc in each st across, ch 1, turn. (15 sts)

Row 16: Lp st in each st across, ch 1, turn. (15 sts)

Rows 17–24: Rep Rows 15 and 16. At end of Row 24, fasten off.

Center fleece on head so that Row 1 of fleece is in the center of the forehead; st in place.

Neck

With white, ch 25.

Row 1: Sc in 2nd ch from hook and in each of next 23 chs, ch 1, turn. (24 sts)

Row 2: Lp st in each st across, ch 1, turn. (24 sts)

Rows 3–6: Rep Rows 1 and 2. (24 sts)

At end of Row 6, fasten off, leaving 10" end for sewing.

Finishing

Fold neck in half; st edges tog. Position neck over front of body; st in place. Stuff neck firmly with fiberfill.

Position head over neck; st in place.

Legs (*Make 4*)

Rnd 1: With black, ch 2, 6 sc in 2nd ch from hook. (6 sts)

Rnd 2: 2 sc in each st around. (12 sts)

Rnd 3: [Sc in next st, 2 sc in next st] 6 times. (18 sts)

Rnd 4: Working in back lps, sc in each st around. (18 sts)

Rnd 5: Sc in each st around. (18 sts)

Rnd 6: [Sc in each of next 4 sts, dec over next 2 sts] 3 times. (15 sts)

Rnd 7: Sc in each st around, fasten off, attach white. (15 sts)

Rnds 8 & 9: Sc in each st around. (15 sts)

Rnd 10: [Sc in each of next 3 sts, dec over next 2 sts] 3 times. (12 sts)

Rnds 11 & 12: Sc in each st around. (12 sts)

Rnd 13: [Sc in each of next 3 sts, 2 sc in next st] 3 times. (15 sts)

Rnds 14–22: Sc in each st around, at the end of Rnd 22, fasten off. (15 sts)

Finishing

Stuff legs firmly with fiberfill; st to front and back of body.

Tail

Rnd 1: With black, ch 2, 6 sc in 2nd ch from hook. (6 sts)

Rnd 2: 2 sc in each sc around. (12 sts)

Rnds 3–5: Sc in each sc around. (12 sts)

At end of Rnd 5, fasten off. Stuff firmly with fiberfill; stitch to top back of body.

Ears

Row 1: With black, ch 7, sc in 2nd ch from hook and in each of next 4 chs, 3 sc in next ch, working down opposite side of ch, sc in each of next 5 chs, ch 1, turn. (13 sts)

Row 2: Sc in each of next 5 sc, [2 sc in next sc] 3 times, sc in each of next 5 sc, fasten off. St in place to top of head.

Face

From felt, cut 2 white eyes, 2 blue pupils, 2 black eyelashes and 2 black eyelids, using patts in Fig. 1.

Glue in place to front of face. String bell on velvet ribbon; tie around neck.

—Designed by Lee Ann Nolan

Fig. 1

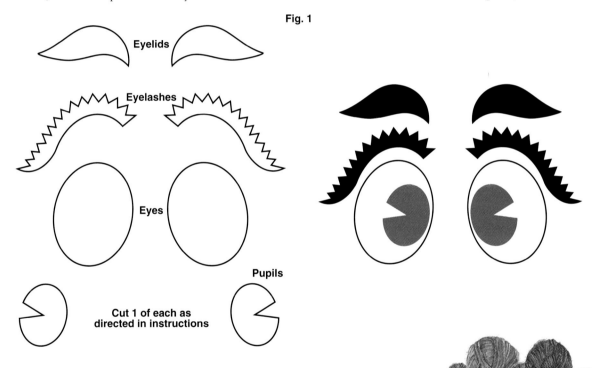

Eyelids

Eyelashes

Eyes

Pupils

Cut 1 of each as directed in instructions

Variations for Single Crochet Patterns

Work rows of single crochet in only the front loops of stitches to give a nice raised-rib effect.

A slightly different rib will form by working in only the back loops of stitches.

Still another easy variation is working 1 stitch in the front loop and the next in the back loop, alternating on each following row. This produces an interesting textured effect.

For a lacy look:

[Sc in 3 sc, ch 1, sk 1 st, 3 sc in next 3 sts] rep across.

For a basket weave effect, make a foundation row of single crochet, [sc in sc, ch 1, sk 1 st, sc in next sc] rep across. Rep for pattern, having sc in ch-1 sps on following rows.

Christmas Magic

Each evening after the little ones are tucked into bed, revel
in the stillnes of the house. Settle down with your favorite
afghan and a cup of spiced tea as you create holiday gifts
and decor to be cherished throughout the years.
From attractive home accents to delicate snowflakes
and elegant tree ornaments, each item will be
enjoyed throughout the Christmas season.

Christmas Past Stocking

Crochet this handsome folk-art style Santa stocking for hanging on your fireplace mantel.

Let's Begin!

Experience Level: Beginner

Size: 22" long

Materials
- 4-ply yarn: 5½ oz dark red, 3 oz white, small amounts each light pink and black and scrap of bright red
- Size H/8 crochet hook or size needed to obtain gauge
- 2 (12mm) sew-on eyes
- Yarn needle

Gauge: 4 sc and 4 sc rows = 1"

To save time, take time to check gauge.

Pattern Note: Join rnds with a sl st unless otherwise stated.

Pattern Stitch

Lp st: Insert hook in indicated st, wind yarn from back to front over finger, catch strand under finger with hook and draw through, drop lp from finger, yo and draw through lps on hook.

Front

Row 1: Beg at bottom with white, ch 37, sc in 2nd ch from hook, sc in each of next 14 chs, attach black, sc with black in each of next 6 chs, change to white, sc in each of next 15 chs, ch 1, turn. (36)

Row 2: Sc with white in each of next 16 sc, change to black, sc in each of next 4 sc, change to white, sc in each of next 16 sc, ch 1, turn.

Row 3: With white, dec 1 sc over next 2 sc, sc in each of next 15 sc, change to black, sc in each of next 2 sc, fasten off black, sc with white in each of next 15 sc, dec 1 sc over next 2 sc, ch 1, turn. (34)

Row 4: Sc in each sc across, draw up a lp of dark red, fasten off white, ch 1, turn. (34)

Row 5: Sc in each of next 11 sc, draw up a lp of white, sc with white in each of next 12 sc, change to dark red, sc in each of next 11 sc, ch 1, turn. (34)

Row 6: Sc with dark red in each of next 12 sc, change to white, sc in each of next 10 sc, change to dark red, sc in each of next 12 sc, ch 1, turn. (34)

Row 7: Sc with dark red in each of next 13 sc, change to white, sc in each of next 8 sc, change to dark red, sc in each of next 13 sc, ch 1, turn. (34)

Row 8: With dark red, dec 1 sc over next 2 sc, sc in each of next 11 sc, change to white, sc in each of next 8 sc, change to dark red, sc in each of next 11 sc, dec 1 sc over next 2 sc, ch 1, turn. (32)

Rows 9–14: Sc with dark red in each of next 12 sc, change to white, sc in each of next 8 sc, change to dark red, sc in each of next 12 sc, ch 1, turn. (32)

Row 15: With dark red, dec 1 sc over next 2 sc, sc in each of next 10 sc, change to white, sc in each of next 8 sc, change to dark red, sc in each of next 10 sc, dec 1 sc over next 2 sc, ch 1, turn. (30)

Rows 16–21: Sc with dark red in each of next 11 sc, change to white, sc in each of next 8 sc, change to dark red, sc in each of next 11 sc, ch 1, turn. (30)

Row 22: With dark red, dec 1 sc over next 2 sc, sc in each of next 9 sc, change to white, sc in each of next 8 sc, change to dark red, sc in each of next 11 sc, ch 1, turn. (29)

Row 23: Sc with dark red in each of next 11 sc, change to white, sc in each of next 8 sc, change to dark red, sc in each of next 10 sc, ch 1, turn. (29)

Row 24: Sc with dark red in each of next 10 sc, change to white, sc in each of next 8 sc, change to dark red, sc in each of next 11 sc, ch 1, turn. (29)

Row 25: With dark red, dec 1 sc over next 2 sc, sc in each of next 9 sc, change to white, sc in each of next 8 sc, change to dark red, sc in each of next 10 sc, ch 1, turn. (28)

Rows 26–35: Sc with dark red in each of next 10 sc, change to white, sc in each of next 8 sc, change to dark red, sc in each of next 10 sc, ch 1, turn. (28)

Row 36: With dark red, dec 1 sc over next 2 sc, sc in each of next 8 sc, change to white, sc in each of next 8 sc, change to dark red, sc in each of next 10 sc, ch 1, turn. (27)

Row 37: Sc with dark red in each of next 10 sc, change to white, sc in each of next 8 sc, change to dark red, sc in each of next 9 sc, ch 1, turn. (27)

Row 38: Sc with dark red in each of next 9 sc, change to white, sc in each of next 8 sc, change to dark red, sc in each of next 10 sc, ch 1, turn. (27)

Row 39: With dark red, dec 1 sc over next 2 sc, sc in each of next 8 sc, change to white, sc in each of next 8 sc, change to dark red, sc in each of next 9 sc, ch 1, turn. (26)

Rows 40–42: Sc with dark red in each of next 9 sc, change to white, sc in each of next 8 sc, change to dark red, sc in each of next 9 sc, ch 1, turn. (26)

Row 43: With dark red, sc in each of next 7 sc, change to white, sc in each of next 12 sc, change to dark red, sc in each of next 7 sc, ch 1, turn. (26)

Row 44: Sc with dark red in each of next 6 sc, change to white, sc in each of next 14 sc, change to dark red, sc in each of next 6 sc, ch 1, turn. (26)

Row 45: 2 sc with dark red in first sc, sc in each of next 6 sc, change to white, sc in each of next 3 sc, attach black, sc in each of next 6 sc, change to white, sc in each of next 3 sc, change to dark red, sc in each of next 6 sc, 2 sc in next sc, ch 1, turn. (28)

Row 46: With dark red, 2 sc in first sc, sc in each of next 7 sc, change to white, sc in each of next 3 sc, change to black, sc in each of next 2 sc, change to white, lp st in next sc, change to black, sc in each of next 3 sc, change to white, sc in each of next 3 sc, change to dark red, sc in each of next 7 sc, 2 sc in next sc, ch 1, turn. (30)

Row 47: Sc with dark red in each of next 9 sc, change to white, sc in each of next 3 sc, change to black, sc in each of next 2 sc, change to white, sc in each of next 2 sts, change to black, sc in each of next 2 sc, change to white, sc in each of next 3 sc, change to dark red, sc in each of next 9 sc, ch 1, turn. (30)

Row 48: Sc with dark red in each of next 9 sc, change to white, sc in each of next 3 sc, change to black, sc in each of next 2 sc, change to white, lp st in each of next 2 sc, change to black, sc in each of next 2 sc, change to white, sc in each of next 3 sc, change to dark red, sc in each of next 9 sc, ch 1, turn. (30)

Row 49: Sc with dark red in each of next 9 sc, change to white, sc in each of next 3 sc, change to black, sc in next sc, change to white, sc in each of next 4 sts, change to black, sc in next sc, fasten off black, change to white, sc in each of next 3 sc, change to dark red, sc in each of next 9 sc, ch 1, turn. (30)

Row 50: Sc with dark red in each of next 9 sc, change to white, sc in each of next 4 sc, lp st in each of next 4 sc, sc in each of next 4 sc, change to dark red, sc in each of next 9 sc, ch 1, turn. (30)

Row 51: Sc with dark red in each of next 12 sc, change to white, sc in each of next 6 sts, change to dark red, sc in each of next 12 sc, ch 1, turn. (30)

Row 52: Sc with dark red in each of next 12 sc, change to white, lp st in each of next 6 sts, change to dark red, sc in each of next 12 sc, ch 1, turn. (30)

Row 53: Sc with dark red in each of next 11 sc, change to white, sc in each of next 8 sts, change to dark red, sc in each of next 11 sc, ch 1, turn. (30)

Row 54: Sc with dark red in each of next 11 sc, change to white, lp st in each of next 8 sc, change to dark red, sc in each of next 11 sc, ch 1, turn.

Row 55: Sc with dark red in each of next 10 sc, change to white, sc in each of next 10 sts, change to dark red, sc in each of next 10 sts, ch 1, turn. (30)

Row 56: Sc with dark red in each of next 10 sc, change to white, lp st in each of next 10 sts, change to dark red, sc in each of next 10 sts, ch 1, turn. (30)

Row 57: Sc with dark red in each of next 8 sc, change to white, sc in each of next 14 sts, change to dark red, sc in each of next 8 sts, ch 1, turn. (30)

Row 58: Sc with dark red in each of next 8 sc, change to white, lp st in each of next 14 sts, change to dark red, sc in each of next 8 sts, ch 1, turn. (30)

Row 59: Sc with dark red in each of next 7 sc, change to white, sc in each of next 16 sts, change to dark red, sc in each of next 7 sc, ch 1, turn. (30)

Row 60: Sc with dark red in each of next 7 sc, change to white, lp st in each of next 16 sts, change to dark red, sc in each of next 7 sc, ch 1, turn. (30)

Row 61: With dark red, dec 1 sc over next 2 sc, sc in each of next 4 sc, change to white, sc in each of next 18 sts, change to dark red, sc in each of next 4 sc, dec 1 sc over next 2 sc, ch 1, turn. (28)

Row 62: With dark red, dec 1 sc over next 2 sc, sc in each of next 3 sc, change to white, lp st in each of next 18 sts, change to dark red, sc in each of next 3 sc, dec 1 sc over next 2 sc, ch 1, turn. (26)

Row 63: With dark red, sk first sc, sc in each of next 2 sc, change to white, sc in each of next 20 sts, change to dark red, sc in next sc, sk 1 sc, sc in last sc, fasten off dark red. (24)

Row 64: Draw up a lp of white in first white sc, ch 1, lp st in each of next 20 white sc sts, ch 1, turn. (20)

Row 65: 2 sc in first st, sc in each st across to

within last st, 2 sc in last st, ch 1, turn. (22)

Row 66: Lp st in each sc across, ch 1, turn. (22)

Row 67: 2 sc in first st, sc in each of next 8 sts, attach bright red, sc with bright red in each of next 4 sts, change to white, sc in each of next 8 sts, 2 sc in last st, ch 1, turn. (24)

Row 68: With white, lp st in each of next 10 sc, change to bright red, sc in each of next 4 sc, fasten off bright red, change to white, lp st in each of next 10 sc, ch 1, turn. (24)

Row 69: Sc with white in each of next 8 sts, attach light pink, sc with light pink in each of next 8 sts, change to white, sc in each of next 8 sts, ch 1, turn. (24)

Row 70: With white, lp st in each of next 8 sc, change to light pink, sc in each of next 8 sc, change to white, lp st in each of next 8 sc, ch 1, turn. (24)

Row 71: Sc with white in each of next 7 sts, change to light pink, sc in each of next 10 sts, change to white, sc in each of next 7 sts, ch 1, turn. (24)

Row 72: With white, lp st in each of next 7 sts, change to light pink, sc in each of next 10 sts, change to white, lp st in each of next 7 sts, ch 1, turn. (24)

Row 73: Sc with white in each of next 6 sts, change to light pink, sc in each of next 12 sts, change to white, sc in each of next 6 sts, ch 1, turn. (24)

Row 74: With white, lp st in each of next 6 sts, change to light pink, sc in each of next 12 sts, change to white, lp st in each of next 6 sts, ch 1, turn. (24)

Row 75: With white, dec 1 sc over next 2 sts, sc in each of next 4 sts, change to light pink, sc in each of next 12 sts, change to white, sc in each of next 4 sts, dec 1 sc over next 2 sts, ch 1, turn. (22)

Row 76: With white, lp st in each of next 5 sts, change to light pink, sc in each of next 12 sts, fasten off light pink, change to white, lp st in each of next 5 sts, ch 1, turn. (22)

Row 77: Sc in each st across, ch 1, turn. (22)

Row 78: Lp st in each st across, ch 1, turn. (22)

Rows 79–81: Sc in each st across, ch 1, turn, at end of Row 81, fasten off, do not turn. (22)

Row 82: Beg at beg of Row 81, attach dark red in 2nd sc, ch 1, sc in same sc, sc in each of next 19 sc, ch 1, turn. (20)

Row 83: Sk first sc, sc in each of next 17 sc, sk next sc, sc in last sc, ch 1, turn. (18)

Row 84: Sc in each sc across, ch 1, turn.

Row 85: Sk first sc, sc in each of next 15 sc, sk next sc, sc in last sc, ch 1, turn. (16)

Row 86: Rep Row 84.

Row 87: Sk first sc, sc in each of next 13 sc, sk next sc, sc in last sc, ch 1, turn. (14)

Row 88: Rep Row 84.

Row 89: Sk first sc, sc in each of next 11 sc, sk next sc, sc in last sc, ch 1, turn. (12)

Row 90: Rep Row 84.

Row 91: Sk first sc, sc in each of next 9 sc, sk next sc, sc in last sc, ch 1, turn. (10)

Row 92: Rep Row 84.

Row 93: Sk first sc, sc in each of next 7 sc, sk next sc, sc in last sc, ch 1, turn. (8)

Row 94: Rep Row 84.

Row 95: Sk first sc, sc in each of next 5 sc, sk next sc, sc in last sc, ch 1, turn. (6)

Row 96: Rep Row 84.

Row 97: Sk first sc, sc in each of next 3 sc, sk next sc, sc in last sc, ch 1, turn. (4)

Row 98: Rep Row 84.

Row 99: Sk first sc, sc in next sc, sk next sc, sc in last sc, ch 1, turn. (2)

Row 100: Rep Row 84.

Row 101: Sk first sc, sc in next sc, ch 1, turn. (1)

Row 102: Sc in sc, fasten off.

Back

Row 1: Beg at bottom with white, ch 37, sc in 2nd ch from hook and in each rem ch across, ch 1, turn. (36)

Row 2: Sc in each sc across, ch 1, turn.

Row 3: Dec 1 sc over next 2 sc, sc in each sc across to within last 2 sc, dec 1 sc over next 2 sc, ch 1, turn. (34)

Row 4: Sc in each sc across, attach dark red, fasten off white, ch 1, turn.

Rows 5–7: Sc in each sc across, ch 1, turn.

Row 8: Rep Row 3. (32)

Continued on Page 78

Angelina

With her graceful wings and delicate halo, Angelina will bring a serene and gentle beauty to your Christmas tree.

Skirt

Rnd 1: Ch 20, join to make ring, ch 3 (first dc), dc, ch 1, 2 dc in joining, sk next ch, *in next ch [2 dc, ch 1, 2 dc (shell made)], sk next ch, rep from * 8 times, join in top of beg ch-3. (10 shells)

Rnd 2: Sl st to ch-1 sp, rep Rnd 1 except make shells in ch-1 sps of shells.

Rnd 3: Rep Rnd 2.

Rnd 4: Rep Rnd 2, except ch 1 between shells.

Rnd 5: Sl st to ch-1 sp, ch 1, sc in same ch-1 sp, *7 dc in next ch-1, then sc in ch-1 sp of next shell, rep from * 9 times, join in beg sc.

Rnd 6: [Ch 3, sc in next dc] rep all around skirt, fasten off.

Rnd 7: Join crochet cotton in 5th lp (center) anywhere, then ch 3, dc, ch 1, 2 dc in same lp, ch 2, *shell in center lp of next fan, ch 2, rep from * 8 times, join last ch 2 in top of beg ch-3.

Rnd 8: Sl st to ch-1 sp of shell, ch 3, dc, ch 1, 2 dc in same ch-1 sp, ch 2, [shell of 2 dc, ch 1, 2 dc in next ch-1 sp, ch 2] rep around, join. (10 shells)

Rnd 9: Sl st to ch-1 sp of shell, ch 4 (first dc, ch 1), [dc, ch 1] 8 times in same sp, sc in ch-2 sp, ch 1, [dc, ch 1] 9 times in ch-1 sp, in next shell, sc in ch-2 sp, rep from * around, join last ch 1 in 3rd ch of beg ch-4.

Rnd 10: Sl st in ch-1 sp, ch 1, sc in same sp, *ch 4, sc in next ch-1 sp, rep from * around, join last ch 4 in beg sc, fasten off.

Rnd 11: Join in center lp of any fan, ch 3, dc, ch 1, 2 dc in same sp, ch 5, *2 dc, ch 1, 2 dc in center lp of each fan, ch 5, rep from * 8 times, join last ch 5 in top of beg ch-3.

Rnd 12: Sl st to ch-1 sp of shell, ch 3, dc, ch 1, 2 dc in same sp, ch 2, sk 2 ch, 2 dc, ch 1, 2 dc in next ch, sk next 2 ch and 2 dc, *2 dc, ch 1, 2 dc in next ch-1 sp, ch 2, sk next 2 ch, 2 dc, ch 1, 2 dc in next ch, ch 2, sk next 2 ch, rep from * around, join in top of beg ch-3.

Rnd 13: Sl st in ch-1 sp, ch 4 (first dc, ch 1), [dc, ch 1] 6 times in ch-1 sp, sc in ch-2 sp, ch 1, *[dc, ch 1] 7 times in next shell, sc in ch-2 sp, ch 1, rep from * around, join last ch 1 in 3rd ch of beg ch-4.

Rnd 14: Sl st in ch-1 sp, ch 1, sc in same sp, *ch 4, sc in next ch-1 sp, rep from * around, join last ch 4 in beg sc, fasten off.

Head

Rnd 1: Ch 4, 9 dc in 4th ch from hook, join in top of beg ch-4. (10)

Rnd 2: Ch 3 (first dc), 2 dc in next dc, *dc in dc, 2 dc in next dc, rep from * around, join in top of beg ch-3. (15)

Rnd 3: Ch 3, dc in dc, 2 dc in next dc, *dc in each of next 2 dc, 2 dc in next dc, rep from * around, join in top of beg ch-3. (20)

Rnd 4: Ch 3, dc in each dc around, join in top of beg ch-3.

Rnd 5: Ch 1, sc in same sp, sc in next dc, dec 1 st, [sc in next 2 dc, dec 1 st] rep around, join in beg sc.

Rnd 6: Ch 1, sc in same sp, dec 1 st, [sc in sc, dec 1 st] rep around, join in beg sc.

Rnd 7: Ch 1, sc in same sp, sc in each sc around (neck), join in beg sc.

Let's Begin!

Experience Level: Intermediate

Materials
- ☐ Size 10 white crochet cotton: 225 yds white
- ☐ Size 9 steel crochet hook
- ☐ Plastic funnel (widest opening, 4⅜" diameter; spout, ½" diameter; 4" high)
- ☐ Plastic wrap
- ☐ Heavy cardboard or large plastic-foam meat tray
- ☐ Inexpensive paintbrush
- ☐ Rustproof pins
- ☐ Tacky glue
- ☐ Fabric and lace stiffener

Gauge: 10 dc = 1" and 2 shell rows = 2"

To save time, take time to check gauge.

Pattern Note: Join rnds with a sl st unless otherwise stated.

Body

Rnd 8: Ch 4 (first dc, ch 1), [dc in next sc, ch 1] rep around, join in 3rd ch of beg ch-4.

Rnd 9: Ch 3, dc in ch-1 sp, [dc in dc, dc in ch-1 sp] rep around, join in top of beg ch-3.

Rnd 10: Ch 3, dc in each dc around, join in top of beg ch-3.

Rnd 11: Rep Rnd 10.

Rnd 12: Ch 1, sc in same sp, [ch 4, sk next dc, sc in next dc] rep around, join in beg ch-1.

Peplum

Rnd 13: Sl st in next ch, sl st in lp, ch 3, dc, ch 1, 2 dc in same lp, [2 dc, ch 1, 2 dc in next sp] rep around, join in beg ch-3, fasten off.

Stuff head with fiberfill; tie thread around neck to define.

Sleeves *(Make 2)*

Row 1: Ch 8, dc in 4th ch from hook, dc, ch 1, 2 dc in same sp, ch 1, 2 dc, ch 1, 2 dc in last ch, ch 1, turn, sl st to ch-1 sp.

Row 2: Ch 3, dc, ch 1, 2 dc in same sp, ch 2, 2 dc, ch 1, 2 dc in next ch-1 sp of shell, ch 3, turn.

Row 3: Dc, ch 1, 2 dc in same st, 2 dc, ch 1, 2 dc in next ch-1 sp of shell, ch 2, shell in shell, shell in top of last dc, ch 1, turn.

Row 4: Sl st to ch-1 sp of shell, ch 3, dc, ch 1, 2 dc in same sp, ch 1, shell in shell, ch 2, shell in shell, ch 1, shell in shell, ch 1, turn.

Row 5: Rep Row 4, fasten off, leaving 8" tail to sew sides tog.

Attach sleeves to body at shoulder edge on opposite sides, equally apart.

Halo

Rnd 1: Ch 4, join to form a ring, ch 2 (first hdc), 9 hdc in ring, join in top of beg ch-2.

Rnd 2: Ch 1, sc in same sp, [ch 5, sc in next hdc] rep around, join last ch-5 in base of beg ch-5, fasten off.

Wings *(Make 1)*

Row 1: Ch 5, join to form a ring, ch 3 (first dc), dc, ch 1, 2 dc in ring, ch 1, 2 dc, ch 1, 2 dc in ring, ch 1, turn.

Row 2: Sl st in dc and ch-1 sp, ch 1, [dc, ch 1] 7 times in ch-1 sp between shells, ch 1, sc in ch-1 sp of next shell, ch 1, sc in last sp, turn.

Row 3: [Ch 4, sc in next ch-1 sp] rep around, fasten off from last sc in last ch-1 sp.

Join crochet cotton in ring, rep Rows 1–3. Fasten off.

Braid for Head

Wrap crochet cotton over 4" x 6" piece cardboard 9 times in 6" lengths. Tie together at 1 end, cut, then place around a pin in pincushion to hold. Divide into 3 equal sections, then braid until length goes around head and meets at back. Tie crochet cotton around at end, clip, and glue to head.

Finishing

Wash crochet in mild detergent, except head and body part, towel-blot until almost dry. Cover cardboard or plastic foam with plastic wrap. Cover funnel with plastic wrap.

Stretch angel skirt over plastic-wrap–covered funnel, pin to cardboard in center lp of last rnd. Raise sides of fans upward. Place halo on cardboard, pin each lp out, stretching.

Pin wings to cardboard, pinning in each lp. When stiffener begins to set up, remove pins from lps,

Continued on Page 75

Down the Chimney!

How does Santa get down the chimney, anyway? This amusing tissue box cover is sure to bring a chuckle—or perhaps a hearty "Ho, ho, ho!"—from anyone with a case of the sniffles.

Let's Begin!

Experience Level: Beginner

Size: Fits boutique-style tissue box

Materials
- ☐ Bernat® Berella "4"® 4-ply yarn: 3 oz scarlet #8933 and 2 oz winter white #8941
- ☐ 3-ply sport weight yarn: 1 oz black
- ☐ Size F/5 crochet hook
- ☐ Size G/6 crochet hook or size needed to obtain gauge
- ☐ Yarn needle
- ☐ Fiberfill

Gauge: 4 sc and 4 sc rows = 1" with size G hook

To save time, take time to check gauge.

Pattern Notes: Weave in loose ends as work progresses.

Join rnds with a sl st unless otherwise stated.

Sides *(Make 4)*

Row 1: With larger hook and scarlet, ch 18, sc in 2nd ch from hook, sc in each rem ch across, turn. (17)

Row 2: Ch 1, sc in each sc across, changing to white in last step of last sc, fasten off scarlet, turn.

Row 3: Working in back lps for this row only, ch 1, sc in first st, [dc in next st 2 rows below, sk st directly behind dc, sc in each of next 3 sts] 4 times, dc in next st 2 rows below, sk st directly behind dc, sc in each of next 2 sts, changing to scarlet in last step of last sc (do not fasten off white; carry it behind and pick it up when needed), turn.

Row 4: Ch 1, sc in each sc across, turn.

Row 5: Ch 1, sc in each sc across, picking up white in last step of last sc, turn.

Row 6: Working in front lps for this row only, ch 1, [dc in st 2 rows below, sk st directly behind dc, sc in each of next 3 sts] 5 times, changing to scarlet in last step of last sc, turn.

Rows 7 & 8: Rep Rows 4 and 5.

Rows 9–20: [Rep Rows 3–8] twice.

Row 21: Rep Row 3, fasten off.

Top

Row 1: With scarlet yarn, ch 18, sc in 2nd ch from hook, sc in each rem ch across, turn. (17)

Rows 2–8: Ch 1, sc in each sc across, turn.

Row 9: Ch 1, sc in each of next 4 sts, ch 9, sk 9 sts, sc in each of next 4 sts, turn.

Row 10: Ch 1, sc in each of next 4 sc, sc in each of next 9 chs, sc in each of next 4 sc, turn.

Rows 11–16: Ch 1, sc in each sc across, turn, at end of Row 16, fasten off.

Boots *(Make 2)*

Rnd 1: With smaller hook and black, ch 9, 3 sc in 2nd ch from hook, sc in each of next 6 chs, 6 sc in last ch, working on opposite side of foundation ch, sc in each of next 6 chs, 3 sc in last ch, join in beg sc. (24)

Rnd 2: Ch 1, 2 sc in same sc as beg ch-1, 2 sc in next sc, sc in each of next 8 sc, 2 sc in each of next 4 sc, sc in each of next 8 sc, 2 sc in each of next 2 sc, join in beg sc. (32)

Rnd 3: Ch 1, working in back lps for this rnd only, sc in each st around, join in beg sc.

Rnd 4: Ch 1, sc in each sc around, join in beg sc.

Rnd 5: Ch 1, sc in each of next 8 sc, [dec 1 sc over next 2 sc, sc in next sc] 5 times, sc in each of next 9 sc, join in beg sc. (27)

Rnd 6: Ch 1, sc in each of next 7 sc, [dec 1 sc over next 2 sc, sc in next sc] 5 times, sc in each of next 5 sc, join in beg sc. (22)

Rnd 7: Ch 1, sc in each of next 7 sc, [dec 1 sc over next 2 sc, sc in next sc] 3 times, sc in each of next 6 sc, join in beg sc. (19)

Rnd 8: Ch 1, sc in each of next 7 sc, [dec 1 sc over next 2 sc, sc in next sc] twice, sc in each of next 6 sc, join in beg sc. (17)

Rnds 9–12: Ch 1, sc in each sc around, join in beg sc, at end of Rnd 12, fasten off, leaving a length of yarn.

Stuff each boot with fiberfill; set aside.

Finishing

With white yarn and yarn ndl, whipstitch all 4 sides tog. Sew top to sides. With toes pointing outward, sew boots to top on each side of opening.

—Designed by Kathleen Stuart

Rudolph's Christmas Cheer

Delight family and friends with this likeness of Rudolph leaping through a Christmas wreath. Large brass jingle bells provide seasonal sound effects, and a twinkling music box in Rudolph's red nose plays his famous song!

Wreath

Back

Rnd 1: With dark green, ch 90, join to form a ring, sc in each ch around.

Rnds 2 & 3: Sc in each sc around.

Rnd 4: Sc around, inc every 9th st. (100)

Rnd 5: Sc in each sc around.

Rnd 6: Sc around, inc every 5th st. (120)

Rnds 7–11: Rep Rnd 5.

Rnd 12: Sc around, inc every 6th st, fasten off. (140)

Front

Note: *Front of wreath is worked from WS.*

Rnd 1: With WS facing, work lp st in first st of beg ch-90, lp st in each st around. (90)

Rnd 2: Sc in each st around.

Rnd 3: Lp st in each st around.

Rnd 4: Sc around, inc every 9th st. (100)

Rnd 5: Rep Rnd 3.

Rnd 6: Sc around, inc every 5th st. (120)

Rnd 7: Rep Rnd 3.

Rnd 8: Rep Rnd 2.

Rnds 9–11: Rep Rnds 2 and 3 respectively, ending with a lp-st rnd.

Rnd 12: Sc in each st around, inc in every 6th st. (140)

Rnds 13–17: Rep Rnds 3 and 2 respectively, ending with a lp-st rnd, fasten off.

Finishing

Slip plastic foam ring over wreath back. With WS inside and lp sts outside, adjust back to cover the inside and back of ring.

Pull wreath front over ring. With yarn ndl and length of yarn, whipstitch back and front tog, matching sts.

Reindeer

Rnd 1: With brown, ch 4, 3 sc in 2nd ch from hook, sc in next ch, 3 sc in last ch, sc in first ch of beg ch-4, join in beg sc. (8)

Rnd 2: Ch 1, inc in first st, sc in next st, [inc in next st, sc in next st] 3 times, join in beg sc. (12)

Rnd 3: Ch 1, [inc in next st, sc in each of next 3 sts, inc in next st, sc in next st] twice, join in beg sc. (16)

Rnd 4: Ch 1, [sc in each of next 3 sts, inc in next st] 4 times. (20)

Rnd 5: Ch 1, sc in each of next 4 sts, inc in next st, sc in each of next 3 sts, inc in each of next 2 sts, [sc in each of next 4 sts, inc in next st] twice, join in beg sc. (25)

Rnds 6–13: Ch 1, sc in each st around, fasten off at end of Rnd 13.

Row 14: Sk 9 sts, join brown with sc in next st, sc in same st, inc in each of next 6 sts, sc in next st, ch 1, turn.

Row 15: [Sc in each of next 2 sts, inc in next st] 5 times, sc in next st of Rnd 13, fasten off.

Top of head

Rnd 16: Join brown with sc in first st, sc around, join in beg sc. (37)

Rnd 17: Ch 1, sc in each st around, join in beg sc.

Rnd 18: Ch 1, sc in each of first 17 sts, inc in next st, sc in next st, inc in next st, sc in each of last 17 sts, join in beg sc.

Rnd 19: Ch 1, sc in each of first 17 sts, inc in next st, sc in each of next 3 sc, inc in next sc, sc in each of last 17 sts, join in beg sc.

Rnd 20: Ch 1, sc in each of first 17 sts, inc in next st, sc in each of next 5 sts, inc in next st, sc in each of last 17 sts, join in beg sc.

Rnd 21: Ch 1, sc in each of first 17 sts, inc in next st, sc in each of next 7 sts, inc in next st, sc in each of last 17 sts, join in beg sc.

Let's Begin!

Experience Level: Intermediate

Size: 15" in diameter

Materials

- ☐ 4-ply worsted weight yarn (8 oz per skein): 1 skein each dark green and brown, and small amounts black, white, red, gold and light green
- ☐ Size G/6 crochet hook or size needed to obtain gauge
- ☐ Tapestry needle
- ☐ Fiberfill
- ☐ 6 (20mm) jingle bells
- ☐ 2 (12") lengths chenille stems
- ☐ Felt: black and white
- ☐ Glue
- ☐ 1½" red pompon
- ☐ 12" flat-backed plastic foam ring
- ☐ Music box with blinking red lights which plays *Rudolph the Red Nose Reindeer* (optional)

Gauge: 3 sts and 3 rnds = 1"

To save time, take time to check gauge.

Pattern Note: When working reindeer, join rnds with a sl st unless otherwise stated.

Pattern Stitch

Lp st: Insert hook in indicated st, wrap yarn around 2 fingers twice, pull 2 strands of yarn off fingers with hook, yo and draw through all 3 lps on hook.

Rnd 22: Ch 1, sc in each of first 17 sts, inc in next st, sc in each of next 9 sts, inc in next st, sc in each of last 17 sts, join in beg sc.

Rnd 23: Ch 1, sc in each of first 7 sts, inc in each of next 2 sts, sc around to within last 9 sts, inc in each of next 2 sts, sc in each of last 7 sts, join in beg sc.

Rnd 24: Ch 1, sc in each of first 7 sts, inc in next st, sc in each of next 2 sts, inc in next st, sc around to first st in inc section, inc in same st, sc in each of next 2 sts, inc in next st, sc in each of last 7 sts, join in beg sc.

Rnd 25: Ch 1, sc in each of first 7 sts, inc in next st, sc in each of next 4 sts, inc in next st, sc around to first st in inc section, inc in same st, sc in each of next 4 sts, inc in next st, sc in each of last 7 sts, join in beg sc.

Rnd 26: Ch 1, sc in each of first 7 sts, inc in next st, sc in each of next 6 sts, inc in next st, sc around to first st in inc section, inc in same st, sc in each of next 6 sts, inc in next st, sc in each of last 7 sts, join in beg sc.

Sides of head

Rnd 27: Ch 1, sc in each st around, join in beg sc. (63)

Find center of face for nose (pompon placement) on 4th rnd. Place music box inside head against Rnds 1 and 2, push light to marked place on Rnd 4. Place pompon over light, having light as close to center of pompon as possible. Stuff nose firmly.

Rnd 28: Ch 1, [sc in each of next 4 sts, dec in next st] rep around, join in beg sc.

Rnd 29: Ch 1, sc in each st around, join in beg sc.

Rnd 30: Ch 1, [sc in each of next 3 sts, dec in next st] rep around, join in beg sc.

Rnd 31: Ch 1, sc in each st around, join in beg sc.

Rnd 32: Ch 1, [sc in each of next 2 sts, dec in next st] rep around, join in beg sc.

Rnd 33: Ch 1, sc in each st around, join in beg sc.

Rnd 34: Ch 1, [sc in each of next 9 sts, dec in next st] rep around, join in beg sc.

Rnd 35: Ch 1, sc in each st around, join in beg sc.

Rnd 36: Ch 1, [sc in each of next 4 sts, dec in next st] rep around, join in beg sc.

Rnd 37: Ch 1, [sc in each of next 3 sts, dec in next st] rep around, join in beg sc.

Rnd 38: Ch 1, [sc in each of next 2 sts, dec in next st] rep around, join in beg sc.

Rnd 39: Ch 1, [sc in next st, dec in next st] rep around, join in beg sc, fasten off.

Stuff head firmly, pushing inc sections out at sides of head.

With running st, tightly gather sts at back of head.

Mouth

With black, sew mouth (Fig. 2) onto end of snout over Rnds 1–3, beg on Rnd 3 under nose.

Cut eyes from felt (Fig. 1); glue in place, using photo as a guide.

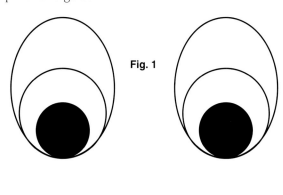

Fig. 1

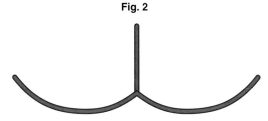

Fig. 2

Ear front *(Make 2)*

Rnd 1: With white, ch 12, dc in 4th ch from hook, dc in each of next 2 chs, hdc in each of next 3 chs, sc in each of next 3 chs, 3 sc in last ch, turn.

Working on opposite side of ch, sc in each of next 3 chs, hdc in each of next 3 chs, dc in each of last 3 chs, ch 3, turn.

Row 2: Working in back lps this row only, dc in each of next 2 dc, hdc in each of next 3 hdc, sc in each of next 4 sc, 3 sc in next sc, sc in each of next 4 sc, hdc in each of next 3 hdc, dc in each of last 3 dc, fasten off.

Ear back *(Make 2)*

Rnd 1: With brown, rep Rnd 1 for ear front.

Rnd 2: Working in both lps, rep Rnd 2 for ear front, do not fasten off, ch 1, turn.

With WS of ear front and back tog, working through both thicknesses, sc around sides with 3 sc in top of ear and 2 sc in each dc across bottom, join in beg sc, fasten off, leaving a 10" length of yarn.

With yarn ndl and running st, tightly gather sts at bottom.

Antlers *(Make 2)*

Rnd 1: With black, ch 5, join to form a ring, 5 sc in ring, join in beg sc.

Rnds 2–24: Ch 1, sc in each sc around, fasten off, leaving length for gathering.

Gather top 5 sts with yarn length and ndl.

Antler points *(Make 2)*

Rnd 1: With black, ch 5, join to form a ring, 5 sc in ring, join in beg sc.

Rnds 2–5: Ch 1, sc in each sc around, join in beg sc, fasten off.

Finishing

Sew each antler point to main antler 2½" from top.

Insert chenille stem into main antler, leaving 1" of stem to insert into head.

Center antlers 1½" apart on Rnds 26 and 27 of head. Sew ears 1" below antlers on each side of head on Rnds 25 and 26. Set aside.

Bridle

With gold, ch 30, join to form a ring, sc around in each free lp on back of ch, join in beg sc, fasten off.

Place over center of snout.

With gold, ch 65, sc in free lp of 2nd ch from hook and in each free lp across, fasten off.

Sew 1 end to bridle piece on snout, bring other

end around ears and antlers, sew opposite first end.

With length of yarn and yarn ndl, sew bells on each side of bridle as shown in photo, attaching bridle to head as you sew.

Legs
First Leg
Rnds 1–4: With black, rep Rnds 1–4 of head, fasten off.

Rnd 5: Attach white with sc, sc in each sc around, join in beg sc. (20)

Rnd 6: Ch 1, sc in each sc around, join in beg sc, fasten off.

Rnd 7: Attach brown, sc in each sc around, join in beg sc.

Rnds 8–20: Ch 1, sc in each sc around, join in beg sc.

Rnd 21: Ch 1, sc around, inc every 4th st, join in beg sc. (25)

Rnds 22–24: Rep Rnds 8–20.

Set aside.

Second Leg
Rnds 1–24: Rep Rnds 1–24 for First Leg, do not fasten off.

Row 25: Sl st in each of first 6 sc, ch 1, sc in each of next 13 sc, leave last 6 sts unworked, pick up first leg, sk first 6 sc, sc in next sc, sc in each of next 12 sc, leave last 6 sc unworked, ch 1, turn.

Row 26: Dec in first 2 sc, sc in each st across to within last 2 dc, dec in last 2 sc, ch 1, turn.

Rows 27–35: Rep Row 22, dec 5 sts at end of Row 35, fasten off.

Stuff legs firmly to Rnd 20; stuff remainder of leg lightly.

Assembly
Mark bottom center of wreath with length of yarn. Whipstitch on Rnd 35 of legs to inside of ring at back of wreath between Rnds 6 and 7.

Continue sewing toward front of wreath along straight sections on both sides of legs; stuff before closing.

Tack legs to wreath front.

Mark top center of wreath. Insert head, centering nose over legs; lay ears and antlers over wreath.

Tie antlers to wreath approximately 2" above head with piece of black yarn, using photo as a guide.

Tie ears to wreath with white yarn, using photo as a guide.

Carefully turn wreath over; sew back of head to top of leg section.

Finishing
Hanger
With dark green, ch 15. Sew to top of wreath at center back where lp sts and sc sts are joined.

Holly *(Make 3)*
With light green, ch 13, sl st in 2nd ch from hook, sl st in next ch, *sc in next ch, hdc in next ch, [dc, ch 3, sl st in 3rd ch from hook, dc in same st], hdc in next ch, sc in next ch, hdc in next ch, rep between [] once, hdc in next ch, sc in next ch*, sl st in last ch, turn, working on opposite side of beg ch, rep from * to * once, sl st in each of last 2 chs, sl st in turning ch, do not fasten off.

Second leaf
Ch 13, rep as for first leaf, except sl st in each of last 2 chs, do not turn.

Berries *(Make 9)*
Rnd 1: With red, ch 2, 6 sc in 2nd ch from hook, join in beg sc, ch 1.

Rnd 2: Sc in each sc around, join in beg sc.

Rnd 3: Ch 1, dec 3 times, fasten off.

Sew holly leaves and berries to wreath, using photo as a guide.

—Designed by Connie E. Clark

Angelina
Continued from Page 69

re-pin in base of each shell, pulling fan shape in 45-degree angle, pin on each side to hold in place. Allow to dry.

When each piece is stretched and pinned, paint stiffener on each piece, soaking well. Place head and body over spout, bringing sleeves to front of body. and pin in place (see photo), paint stiffener on, tilting head forward slightly. Allow to dry.

Twist pieces off funnel, glue body on top of skirt. Glue halo to top of head. Glue wings to back of body.

—Designed by Joan Glass

Bearly an Angel

Crochet this sweet angel to trim your Christmas tree
or to give as a special gift for an extra-special person.

Angel

Head

Rnd 1: Starting at top of head, with white yarn, ch 2, 6 sc in 2nd ch from hook. (6)

Rnd 2: Work 2 sc in each sc around. (12)

Rnd 3: [Sc in next sc, 2 sc in next sc] rep around. (18)

Rnd 4: [Sc in next 2 sc, 2 sc in next sc] rep around. (24)

Rnd 5: [Sc in next 3 sc, 2 sc in next sc] rep around. (30)

Rnd 6: Sc in each sc around.

Rnd 7: [Sc in next 4 sc, 2 sc in next sc] rep around. (36)

Rnds 8–14: Rep Rnd 6.

Rnd 15: [Sc in next 4 sc, dec 1 sc over next 2 sc] rep around. (30)

Rnd 16: Rep Rnd 6.

Rnd 17: [Sc in next 3 sc, dec 1 sc over next 2 sc] rep around. (24)

Rnd 18: Rep Rnd 6.

Rnd 19: [Sc in next 2 sc, dec 1 sc over next 2 sc] rep around. (18)

Stuff head with fiberfill.

Rnd 20: [Sc in next sc, dec 1 sc over next 2 sc] rep around. (12)

Rnds 21 & 22: Rep Rnd 6.

Finish stuffing head with fiberfill.

Upper Body

Rnd 23: Work 2 sc in each sc around. (24)

Rnd 24: Rep Rnd 5. (30)

Rnd 25: Rep Rnd 7. (36)

Rnds 26–32: Rep Rnd 6.

At the end of Rnd 32, sl st in next st, fasten off.

Skirt

Rnd 1 (RS): Working in front lps for this rnd only of Rnd 32, attach light seafoam yarn, ch 3 (first dc), work 2 dc in same st as beg ch-3, work 3 dc in each rem front lp around, sl st to join in top of beg ch-3, do not turn. (108)

Rnds 2–16: Ch 3 (first dc), dc in each dc around, sl st to join in top of beg ch-3, do not turn.

At the end of Rnd 16, fasten off.

Stuff upper body with fiberfill. Set aside.

Bottom Body

Rnd 1: With white yarn, leaving a 12"-length of yarn at beg, ch 36, sl st to join to form a ring, ch 1, sc in each ch around. (36)

Let's Begin!

Experience Level: Beginner

Size: 13" tall

Materials

- ☐ 4-ply yarn: 5 oz white, 3 oz light seafoam and a scrap of black
- ☐ Crochet hook size F/5
- ☐ 1¼ yds 8½"-wide white lace
- ☐ ⅔ yd 5"-wide double-sided white pre-gathered lace
- ☐ 1 yd ¹⁄₁₆"-wide aqua satin ribbon
- ☐ ½" white ribbon rose
- ☐ 7" aqua pearls on a string
- ☐ ½ sheet plastic canvas
- ☐ 3¾" x 3½" wooden heart
- ☐ Aqua metallic paint
- ☐ Black paint pen
- ☐ Glue
- ☐ Fiberfill
- ☐ Sewing needle and matching thread
- ☐ Paintbrush
- ☐ Yarn needle

Gauge: 4 sc and 4 sc rnds = 1"

To save time, take time to check gauge.

Pattern Notes: Weave in loose ends as work progresses.

Do not join rnds unless otherwise indicated. Use a scrap of CC yarn to mark rnds.

Rnds 2–5: Sc in each sc around.

First Leg

Rnd 6: Sc in next 2 sc, sk 18 sc, sc in next 16 sc. (18)

Rnds 7–23: Sc in each next 18 sc.

Rnd 24: [Sc in next sc, dec 1 sc over next 2 sc] rep around. (12)

Rnd 25: [Dec 1 sc over next 2 sc] rep around, sl st in next sc, leaving a length of yarn, fasten off. (6)

Sew bottom of leg opening closed.

Second Leg

Rnd 6: Attach white yarn in next unworked sc of

Rnd 6, ch 1, sc in same sc as beg ch-1, sc in each next 17 sc. (18)

Rnds 7–25: Rep Rnds 7–25 of first leg.

Stuff legs and bottom body with fiberfill. With yarn needle and rem length of yarn at beg of bottom body, sew opposite side of foundation ch of bottom body to rem back lp of Rnd 32 of upper body.

Muzzle

Rnd 1: With white yarn, ch 2, 6 sc in 2nd ch from hook. (6)

Rnd 2: Work 2 sc in each sc around. (12)

Rnd 3: [Sc in next sc, 2 sc in next sc] rep around. (18)

Rnd 4: Sc in each sc around, sl st in next sc, leaving a length of yarn, fasten off.

Sew muzzle to front of head over Rnds 13–19, stuffing with fiberfill before closing.

Ears *(Make 2)*

Rnd 1: With white yarn, ch 2, 6 sc in 2nd ch from hook. (6)

Rnd 2: Work 2 sc in each sc around. (12)

Rnd 3: [Sc in next sc, 2 sc in next sc] rep around. (18)

Rnds 4–7: Sc in each sc around.

Rnd 8: [Sc in next sc, dec 1 sc over next 2 sc] rep around, sl st in next sc to join, leaving a length of yarn, fasten off.

Sew ears to side of head.

Eyes

With yarn needle and black yarn, embroider eyes over Rnds 11 and 12 of head, 1½" apart.

Nose

With yarn needle and black yarn, embroider nose over Rnd 1 of muzzle.

Arms *(Make 2)*

Rnd 1: With white yarn, ch 2, 6 sc in 2nd ch from hook. (6)

Rnd 2: Work 2 sc in each sc around. (12)

Rnd 3: [Sc in next 3 sc, 2 sc in next sc] rep around. (15)

Rnds 4–22: Sc in each sc around.

At the end of Rnd 22, sl st in next st, leaving a length of yarn, fasten off.

Stuff arm with fiberfill, flatten top and sew across opening. Sew arms to side of body.

Wings (Make 2)

Row 1 (WS): Starting at top of wing, with white yarn, ch 23, sc in 2nd ch from hook, sc in each rem ch across, ch 1, turn. (22)

Rows 2–5: Work 2 sc in first sc, sc in each sc across to within last sc, work 2 sc in last sc, ch 1, turn. (30)

Rows 6 & 7: Sc in each sc across, ch 1, turn.

Rows 8–12: Dec 1 sc over next 2 sc, sc in each sc across to within last 2 sc, dec 1 sc over next 2 sc, ch 1, turn. (20)

Rows 13–15: Sc in each sc across, ch 1, turn.

Rows 16–19: Rep Rows 2–5. (28)

Rows 20 & 21: Sc in each sc across, ch 1, turn.

Rows 22–26: Rep Rows 8–12. (18)

At the end of Row 26, ch 1, do not turn.

Rnd 27: Sc evenly sp around entire outer edge of wing, sl st to join in beg sc, fasten off.

Using 1 wing section as pattern, place 1 wing section on plastic canvas, cut 1 piece of plastic canvas slightly smaller than wing section.

Holding WS of wing sections together and working through both thicknesses in back lps only, sl st in each st around, inserting plastic canvas before closing, fasten off.

Rnd 28: With RS facing, attach light seafoam with sl st in any back lp only of joining sl st, ch 2, [sl st in next back lp, ch 2] rep around, sl st to join in beg st, fasten off.

Finishing

With sewing needle and thread, run a gathering stitch at top of one long edge of flat white lace, gather around waist of bear and sew in place.

Run a gathering stitch on white 5" lace about 1" down from top edge, gather around neckline of bear and sew in place.

Cut 8" length of aqua satin ribbon and set aside.

Fold rem ribbon into an 8-loop bow. Glue to center front neckline of bear. Glue ribbon rose over center of bow.

Glue wings to back of bear, placing top edge of wings over Rnd 13 of head.

Allow to dry completely.

For halo, glue aqua pearl string in a circle to top of head.

Paint wooden heart with aqua paint. Allow to dry completely. Using paint pen, write "I Believe in Angels" on front. Allow to dry.

Glue rem 8" length of ribbon across upper back of heart.

Thread 1 end of ribbon onto tapestry needle and push needle through lower edge of 1 arm of bear. Tie into a triple knot on outside edge of arm, leaving about 1" of ribbon between inner arm and heart. Glue knot in place to secure. Thread rem edge onto needle, push through other arm and pull through until heart is centered between arms. Tie triple knot on outside of arm. Glue knot to secure. Trim ends of ribbon.

—*Designed by Jocelyn Sass*

Christmas Past Stocking

Continued from Page 67

Continued from Page 67

Rows 9–14: Rep Row 5.

Row 15: Rep Row 3. (30)

Rows 16–21: Rep Row 5.

Row 22: Sc in each sc across to within last 2 sc, dec 1 sc over next 2 sc, ch 1, turn. (29)

Rows 23 & 24: Rep Row 5.

Row 25: Rep Row 22. (28)

Rows 26–35: Rep Row 5.

Row 36: Rep Row 22. (27)

Rows 37 & 38: Rep Row 5.

Row 39: Rep Row 22. (26)

Rows 40–44: Rep Row 5.

Rows 45 & 46: 2 sc in first sc, sc in each sc across to within last sc, 2 sc in last sc, ch 1, turn. (30)

Rows 47–59: Rep Row 5.

Row 60: Attach dark red, sc in each of next 7 sc, change to white, lp st in each of next 16 sts, change to dark red, sc in each of next 7 sts, ch 1, turn. (30)

Row 61: With dark red, dec 1 sc over next 2 sc, sc in each of next 4 sc, change to white, sc in each of next 18 sts, change to dark red, sc in each of next 4 sc, dec 1 sc over next 2 sc, ch 1, turn. (28)

Row 62: With dark red, dec 1 sc over next 2 sc, sc in each of next 3 sc, change to white, lp st in each of next 18 sts, change to dark red, sc in each of next 3 sc, dec 1 sc over next 2 sc, ch 1, turn. (26)

Row 63: With dark red, dec 1 sc in next sc, change to white, sc in each of next 20 sts, change to dark red, sc in next sc, dec 1 sc over next 2 sc, fasten off dark red. (24)

Row 64: Beg in first white st, draw up a lp of white, ch 1, lp st in same st, lp st in each of next 19 sts, ch 1, turn. (20)

Row 65: 2 sc in first st, sc in each st across to within last st, 2 sc in last st, ch 1, turn. (22)

Row 66: Lp st in each st across, ch 1, turn.

Row 67: Rep Row 65. (24)

Row 68: Lp st in each st across, ch 1, turn.

Row 69: Sc in each st across, ch 1, turn.

Rows 70–74: Rep Rows 68 and 69.

Row 75: Dec 1 sc over next 2 sts, sc in each st across to within last 2 sts, dec 1 sc over next 2 sts, ch 1, turn. (22)

Row 76: Lp st in each st across, ch 1, turn.

Rows 77–102: Rep Rows 77–102 of front.

Face
Nose
Rnd 1: With light pink, ch 2, 6 sc in 2nd ch from hook, join to form a ring, ch 1. (6)

Rnd 2: Sc in each sc around, join in beg sc, ch 1.

Rnd 3: Sc in each sc around, join in beg sc, fasten off.

Sew nose to center of face over Rows 71 and 72.

Mustache
Row 1: With white, ch 13, sc in 2nd ch from hook and in each rem ch across, ch 1, turn. (12)

Row 2: Lp st in each sc across, fasten off, leaving a length of yarn.

Sew mustache below nose.

Sew eyes to face evenly sp apart over Rows 73 and 74.

Joining
With front and back tog, beg at Row 61 of shoulder, sew down side edge, across bottom and up opposite edge to Row 61 of shoulder.

Beg at Row 78 of cap, sew up to top and down opposite side to Row 78.

Santa's Bag
Row 1: With medium brown, ch 21, sc in 2nd ch from hook and in each rem ch across, ch 3, turn. (20)

Row 2: Dc in each st across, ch 1, turn.

Rows 3–44: Sc in each st across, ch 1, turn.

Row 45: Sc in each st across, ch 3, turn.

Row 46: Dc in each st across, ch 1, turn.

Row 47: Sc in each st across, fasten off.

Fold strip in half with dc rows matching. Sew down side to bottom; secure and fasten off.

With a length of medium brown yarn, beg at side seam of bag, weave through dc sts around edge of bag for drawstring.

Sew bag to left bottom of stocking.

Weave rem length of drawstring under gloves as if he is holding the drawstring. Secure ends and weave to inside of stocking.

Finishing
Make a white 1½" pompon; attach to top of cap.

With dark red, ch 10, fasten off, leaving a length of yarn.

Sew each end of ch to back top of cap below pompon for hanging lp.

—Designed by Marilyn Smith

Crocheted Coasters

For lacy crocheted coasters that can be wiped clean with a damp cloth, select a favorite motif pattern; crochet 1 motif for each coaster.

Block the motifs and paint 1 side with white glue. When thoroughly dry, turn over and paint 2nd side with glue. **Note:** *Blot lacy openings in motifs with soft paper towel to prevent glue from clogging them.*

When glue has dried, lightly spray-paint coasters in desired color by suspending them from a coat hanger on paper clips or thread. Allow plenty of drying time.

Enchanted Snowflakes

*Stitch a flurry of snowflakes, each as delicate and individual
as the marvelous works of nature that inspired them.*

Pictured clockwise from top left: Daisy Frost, Snow Princess, Snowy White, Frostbite, White Ice and Frozen Lace.

Daisy Frost

Rnd 1: Ch 5, join to form a ring, [ch 10, sl st in ring] 6 times. (6 lps)

Rnd 2: Ch 1, 12 sc over each ch-10 lp, join in beg sc.

Rnd 3: Sl st to 6th sc, ch 1, sc in same sc, [ch 8, sc in 6th sc of next lp] rep around, ending ch 8, join in beg sc.

Rnd 4: Ch 1, [6 sc, ch 4, 6 sc] in each ch-8 lp around, join in beg sc.

Rnd 5: Ch 1, sc in same sp, *ch 4, [sc, hdc, dc, ch 2, dc, hdc, sc] in next ch-4 lp, ch 4, sc in sp between 6th and 7th sc of next 12 sc, rep from * around, join in beg sc, fasten off.

Frozen Lace

Rnd 1: Ch 4, join to form a ring, ch 1, 12 sc in ring, join in beg sc.

Rnd 2: Ch 4 (counts as first dc, ch 1), [dc in next sc, ch 1] rep around, join in 3rd ch of beg ch-4.

Let's Begin!

Experience Level: Beginner

Size
Daisy Frost: 3¾" in diameter
Frozen Lace: 5" in diameter
Snowy White: 4" in diameter
Snow Princess: 3" in diameter
Frostbite: 4½" in diameter
White Ice: 5" in diameter

Materials
☐ Crochet cotton size 10: small amount white
☐ Size 1 steel crochet hook
☐ Fabric stiffener
☐ Plastic wrap
☐ Rustproof pins
☐ ¼" thick cardboard

Gauge: Work evenly and consistently

Pattern Notes: Work ends into WS of snowflakes.

Rnd 3: Ch 1, sc in same sp, [ch 6, sc in next dc] rep around, ending with ch 2, dc in first sc.

Rnd 4: Ch 1, sc in same sp, [ch 12, sc in 10th ch from hook, ch 7, sc in 7th ch from hook, ch 4, sc in 4th ch from hook, ch 5, sl st in last sc, ch 4, sl st in same sc, ch 1, sl st in next sc, ch 7, sl st in same sc, ch 1, sl st in next sc, ch 8, sl st in same sc, ch 2, sc in next ch-6 lp, ch 8, sc in 6th ch from hook, ch 2, sc in next ch-6 lp] rep around, join in beg sc, fasten off.

Snowy White

Rnd 1: Ch 6, join to form a ring, ch 3, 23 dc in ring, join in 3rd ch of beg ch-3. (24)

Rnd 2: Ch 1, sc in same sp, [ch 6, sk next dc, sc in next dc] rep around, ending with ch 2, dc in first sc to join.

Rnd 3: Ch 1, sc in same lp, [ch 8, sc in 6th ch from hook, ch 6, sl st in last sc, ch 6, sl st in same sc, ch 3, sc in next ch-6 lp, ch 7, sc in 5th ch from hook, ch 2, sc in next ch-6 lp] rep around, join in beg sc, fasten off.

Snow Princess

Rnd 1: Ch 4, join to form a ring, ch 1, 12 sc in ring, join in beg sc. (12)

Rnd 2: Ch 1, sc in same sp, [ch 10, sk next sc, sc in next sc] rep around, join.

Rnd 3: Ch 1, [3 sc, ch 4, 3 sc, ch 7 (tip of lp), 3 sc, ch 4, 3 sc] in each ch-12 lp around, join in beg sc, fasten off.

Frostbite

Rnd 1: Ch 6, join to form a ring, ch 2, [retaining last lp of each dc, work 3 dc in ring, yo and draw through all lps on hook, ch 3] 6 times, join.

Rnd 2: Sl st into next ch-2 sp, ch 1, sc in same sp, ch 10, [sc in next ch-2 sp, ch 10] rep around, join in beg sc.

Rnd 3: Ch 1, *[8 sc, ch 7, sc in 5th ch from hook, ch 6, sl st in same sc, ch 5, sl st in same sc, ch 3, 8 sc] in each ch-10 lp around, join in beg sc, fasten off.

White Ice

Rnd 1: Ch 6, join to form a ring, ch 1, sc in ring, [ch 4, sc in ring] 5 times, ch 2, join with a dc in beg sc. (6 lps)

Rnds 2 & 3: Ch 1, sc in same sp, [ch 6, sc in next ch lp] 5 times, ch 2, join with a tr in beg sc.

Rnd 4: Ch 1, [2 sc, 2 hdc, 2 dc, ch 3, 2 dc, 2 hdc, 2 sc] in each ch-6 lp around, join in beg sc.

Rnd 5: Sl st to ch-3 sp, ch 1, [sc in ch-3 sp, ch 6, sl st in 4th ch from hook, ch 6, sc in 4th ch from hook, ch 4, sl st in last sc, ch 3, sl st in same sc, ch 6, sl st in 4th ch from hook, ch 3, sl st in same ch-3 sp as beg sc, ch 8, sc in 4th ch from hook, ch 4, sl st in last sc, ch 4, sl st in same sc, ch 5] rep around, join in beg sc, fasten off.

Finishing

Saturate each snowflake with fabric stiffener; squeeze out excess. Lay snowflake flat on plastic–wrap–covered cardboard. Stretch out snowflake, placing a rustproof pin in each outside and inside point to bring out detail. Allow to dry completely before removing pins.

—Designed by Cindy Harris

Victorian Ornaments

*A trio of delicately stitched ornaments will grace
your Christmas tree with Victorian elegance.*

Basket

Rnd 1: Ch 5, join to form a ring, ch 3 (counts as
first dc), 19 dc in ring, join in 3rd ch of beg ch-3.
(20 dc)

Rnd 2: Working in back lps, ch 3 (counts as first
dc), dc in same sp, [dc in next st, 2 dc in next st]
rep around, join in 3rd ch of beg ch-3.

Rnd 3: Ch 8 (counts as first dtr, ch 2), work dtr,
ch 2 in each st around, join in 6th ch of beg ch-8.

Rnd 4: Ch 3 (counts as first dc), work dc, ch 2, dc
in same sp, dc in same sp, draw through 2 lps only,
dc in next dtr, work off 2 lps only, yo and draw
through 3 lps (counts as 2 dc tog), shell in each dtr
with 2 dc tog between each shell, on last dc work
off 2 lps, join in 3rd ch of beg ch-3, draw through
lps, fasten off.

Base

Join in front lps of Row 1, ch 3, [2 dc in next st, dc
in next st] rep around, join in 3rd ch of beg ch-3,
fasten off.

Handle

Ch 41, dc in 4th ch from hook and in each ch
across, fasten off.

Finishing

Starch and dry flat, pinning in shell sps. Remove
pins when almost dry and fold sides over plastic
foam form covered with plastic wrap; pin in place
until completely dry.

Stiffen handle and lay flat until almost dry. Shape
over plastic foam form to dry completely. Glue
handle to sides of basket. (See photo.)

Cut 2 pieces pink ribbon each 6" and 2 pieces aqua
ribbon each 1". Make a double bow with pink
ribbon. Glue to side of basket where handle joins.
Make individual loops from aqua ribbon; glue in
center of double bow.

Rep for opposite side.

Glue ⅜" blue ribbon roses in center of bows.

Glue length of pink ribbon around base of basket.

Parasol

Rnd 1: Ch 4, join to form a ring, ch 5 (counts as
first tr, ch 1), [tr, ch 1] 15 times in ring, join in 4th
ch of beg ch-5.

Rnd 2: Ch 1, sc in same sp, ch 3, [sc, ch 3] in each
tr around, join in beg sc.

Let's Begin!

Experience Level: Advanced beginner

Size
Basket: Approximately 4" tall x 4¾" long
Parasol: Approximately 5" tall x 4½" in diameter
Ruffled Angel: Approximately 5" tall x 4½" wide

Materials
- ☐ Crochet cotton size 10: small amount ecru
- ☐ Size 5 steel crochet hook
- ☐ 5"-long cylindrical plastic foam form
- ☐ 1½"-diameter plastic foam ball
- ☐ Cotton balls
- ☐ Small funnel
- ☐ 3½"-wide piece of cardboard
- ☐ 5"-wide piece of cardboard
- ☐ Plastic wrap
- ☐ Hot-glue gun
- ☐ ⅛"-wide satin ribbon: 30" pink, 10" teal, 6" burgundy and 4" aqua
- ☐ ⅔ yd ⅜"-wide mauve double-faced feather-edge ribbon
- ☐ 6mm x 12mm pearl drop
- ☐ 4½" length gold metallic embroidery floss
- ☐ 6½" length of wire
- ☐ 4" gold cording
- ☐ 9 (¼") blue ribbon roses
- ☐ 2 (⅜") blue satin ribbon roses
- ☐ 1½" mauve silk poinsettia
- ☐ 1" mauve silk poinsettia
- ☐ Starch

Gauge: To save time, take time to check gauge.

Pattern Note: Join rnds with a sl st unless otherwise stated.

Pattern Stitch
Shell: [2 dc, ch 2, 2 dc] in indicated st.

Rnd 3: Sl st to center of next ch-3 sp, ch 1, sc in same sp, ch 4, [sc, ch 4] in each ch-3 sp around, join in beg sc.

Rnd 4: Sl st to center of next ch-4 sp, sc and ch 4 in each ch-4 sp around, join in beg sc.

Rnd 5: Sl st to 2nd ch of next ch-4 sp, ch 2 (counts as first hdc), hdc in same sp, ch 2, 2 hdc in next ch (shell made), [ch 2, sc, ch 2 in next lp, shell in 2nd and 3rd chs of next lp] rep around, join in 2nd ch of beg ch-2.

Rnd 6: Ch 5 (counts as first dc, ch 2), *dc and ch 2 in next hdc, [dc, ch 2] 5 times in ch-2 sp, dc and ch 2 in next hdc, dc in next hdc, sc in sc, dc and ch 2 in first hdc of next shell, rep from * around, join in 3rd ch of beg ch-5.

Rnd 7: Ch 1, sc and ch 3 in same sp, sc and ch 3 in each of next 6 dc, *sc in last dc of scallop, sk sc, [sc, ch 3 in next dc] 7 times, rep from * around, join in beg sc, fasten off.

Finishing
Cut plastic foam ball in half. Starch crocheted piece and shape to dry over half of ball, pinning in scs.

Weave ⅜"-wide mauve ribbon through shell sps; trim ends and secure with glue. (See photo.)

Glue 8 (¼") blue ribbon roses evenly sp over ribbon.

Cut 10" piece of ⅛"-wide teal ribbon into 1" lengths. Form into individual loops and glue 1 loop at each rose.

Cover wire with ⅜"-wide mauve ribbon, securing ends with glue. Curve 1 end of covered wire to form parasol handle; glue opposite end in center of stiffened crocheted piece. Roll small piece of ribbon and glue to top center.

Glue rem 2 lps of ⅛"-wide teal ribbon to handle approximately ¾" from bottom.

Thread pearl drop onto 1" length of gold embroidery floss; double floss and glue ends over ribbon lps on handle. Glue ¼" blue ribbon rose over floss.

Ruffled Angel
Rnd 1: Ch 3, 19 hdc in 3rd ch from hook, join in 2nd ch of beg ch-3. (20 hdc)

Rnds 2–6: Ch 2 (counts as first hdc), hdc in each st around, join in 2nd ch of beg ch-2.

Rnd 7: Ch 1, sc in same sp, [sk 1 st, sc in next st]

rep around, join in beg sc. (10 sc)

Rnd 8: Sc, ch 3 in each st around, ch 1 and hdc in beg sc to join.

Rnd 9: Sc, ch 3 in each lp around, ch 1 and hdc in beg sc to join.

Rnds 10–15: Sc, ch 4 in each lp around, ch 1 and dc in beg sc to join.

Rnd 16: [Sl st to 2nd ch of next ch-4 lp, [sc, picot (ch 4, sl st in same sp), ch 5] in each lp around, ch 5, join in beg sc.

Rnd 17: Sl st to 3rd ch of next ch-5 lp, in 3rd ch of each ch-5 lp, [ch 3, sl st in same ch, ch 5, sl st in same ch, ch 3, sl st in same ch, ch 3, sl st in 3rd ch of next ch-5 lp] rep around, join in beg ch.

Rnd 18: Ch 10 (counts as first dc, ch 7), dc and ch 7 in each ch-3 sp around, join in 3rd ch of beg ch-10.

Rnd 19: Ch 5 (counts as first dc, ch 2), *dc and ch 2 in 5 more chs, dc in next ch, dc and ch 2 in first ch of next lp, rep from * around, join in 3rd ch of beg ch-5.

Rnd 20: Ch 1, sc in same sp, *[ch 3, sc in next dc] 6 times, sc in first dc of next scallop, rep from * around, join in beg sc, fasten off.

Arms

Ch 4, join to form a ring, ch 28, sl st in 4th ch from hook, work 5 sc in ch-3 sp just made, work 11 hdc in each ch to next ch-3 sp, 5 sc in ch-3 sp, join in sl st sp, fasten off.

Wings

Row 1: Ch 4, join to form a ring, ch 3 (counts as first dc), 6 dc, ch 1, 7 dc in ring, turn.

Row 2: Ch 8 (counts as first dc, ch 5), sk 1 st, sc in next st, [ch 5, sk 1 st, sc in next st] twice, sc in ch-1 sp, sc in next dc, rep between [] across, ch 5, dc in 3rd ch (counts as last dc), ch 1, turn.

Row 3: Sc in same sp, [sl st to 3rd ch of next ch-5 lp, work ch 3, sl st in 3rd ch, ch 5, sl st in same sp, ch 3, sl st in same sp, sl st in each of next 2 chs, sc in sc] 3 times, sc in each of next 2 sc, rep between [] 3 times, sc in 3rd ch at end, turn.

Row 4: Ch 10 (counts as first dc, ch 7), dc and ch 7 in each of next 2 sc, dc in next sc, hdc in next sc, dc and ch 7 in each of next 3 sc, dc in last sc at end, ch 1, turn.

Row 5: Sc in same sp, ch 2, dc and ch 2 in each of next 6 chs, [dc in last ch of lp, dc and ch 2 in first ch of next lp, dc and ch 2 in each of next 5 chs] twice, ch 2, sc and ch 2 in center hdc, [dc and ch 2 in first ch of next lp, dc and ch 2 in each of next 5 chs, dc in next ch] 3 times, ch 2, sc in sc at end, ch 1, turn.

Row 6: Sc in same sp, [ch 3 and sc in next dc] 7 times, sc in next dc, *rep between [] 6 times, sc in next dc *, rep between [] 6 times, work ch 2, sc and ch 2 in center sc, sc in next dc, rep from * to * across, ch 3, sc in sc at end, fasten off.

Finishing

Stuff head with cotton and cinch neck.

Insert arms through first row of ch-4 lps on angel, sk 4 lps, insert arms through next row of ch-4 lps.

Starch angel and shape over funnel to dry, shaping ruffled edge and joining arms at hands in front.

Starch wings and pin to blocking board to dry, shaping ruffled edge. Glue stiffened wings to back of angel.

Hair

Wrap crochet cotton around 3½"-wide piece of cardboard 75 times; cut at 1 end; lay aside.

Wrap crochet cotton around 5"-wide piece of cardboard 75 times; cut at 1 end.

Comb thread. Glue short piece to top of head so that it hangs down the back. Glue long piece over top of head from side to side.

Use a long straight pin dipped in water and glue to make part in center of head. Let dry.

Braid a small section of hair on each side of face and pull to back. Glue ends.

Glue 4" piece of gold cording around top of head to form halo. Secure ends with glue in back.

Glue 1" silk poinsettia to angel's hands.

Cut 4½" length of burgundy ribbon and tie into bow. Glue to lower right front of skirt. Glue 1½" silk poinsettia over bow.

Tie rem burgundy ribbon into bow and glue over braid ends.

Form loop from 3½"-length of gold metallic embroidery floss and glue to top of head at back of halo for hanging.

—Designed by Jo Ann Maxwell

Satin Elegance

*Add a dramatic accent to any holiday decor with
this set of four delicately crocheted designs.*

Let's Begin!

Experience Level: Advanced beginner

Size: 2½" in diameter

Materials
- ☐ Crochet cotton size 10: 25 yds red
- ☐ Crochet cotton size 20: 150 yds white
- ☐ Size 8 steel crochet hook
- ☐ 2½"-diameter satin Christmas ornaments: 1 each white, blue, gold and red

Gauge: Work evenly and consistently throughout.

Pattern Note: Join rnds with a sl st unless otherwise stated.

Pattern Stitches
V-st: [Dc, ch 2, dc] in indicated st.
Beg shell: [2 dc, ch 2, 3 dc] in indicated st.
Shell: [3 dc, ch 2, 3 dc] in indicated st.

Poinsettia White Ball

Rnd 1: With size 10 crochet cotton, ch 6, join to form a ring, ch 1, 12 sc in ring, join in beg sc.

Rnd 2: Working in back lps, *ch 9, sk next st, sl st in next st, rep from * around, join in beg st. (6 lps)

Rnd 3: Ch 1, *15 sc in lp, sl st in sl st, rep from * around, join in beg sl st, fasten off.

Rnd 4: Working in back lps, join cotton with a sl st in 8th sc of lp, *ch 8, sl st in 8th sc of next lp, rep from * around, join in beg st.

Rnd 5: Ch 3, *8 dc in next lp, dc in sl st, rep from * around, join in 3rd ch of beg ch-3.

Rnd 6: Ch 5, dc in same sp, *sk 2 dc, V-st in next st, rep from * around, ending with sl st in 3rd ch of beg ch-5.

Rnd 7: Ch 3, *2 dc in next ch-2 sp, sk next dc, dc in next dc, rep from * around, join in 3rd ch of beg ch-3.

Rnd 8: *Ch 15, sk 5 dc, sl st in next st, rep from * around, ending with ch 5, tr in first sl st.

Place on white ball.

Rnd 9: Ch 1, 2 sc in same sp, *2 sc in next lp, rep

from * around, join in beg sc.

Rnd 10: *Ch 3, sk next st, sl st in next st, rep from * around, join in beg sl st.

Rnd 11: Sl st to center of next lp, ch 1, sc in same sp, *sc in next lp, rep from * around, join, fasten off.

Shell Star Christmas Ball

Rnd 1: With size 20 crochet cotton, ch 10, join to form a ring, ch 1, 16 sc in ring, join in beg sc.

Rnd 2: Ch 3, 2 dc in same sp, [ch 2, sk next sc, 3 dc in next sc] 7 times, ch 2, join in 3rd ch of beg ch-3.

Rnds 3 & 4: Sl st in each of next 2 sts, sl st in lp, ch 3, beg shell in same sp, [shell in next shell lp] 7 times, join in 3rd ch of beg ch-3, fasten off after Rnd 4.

Rnd 5: Working in ch-2 lps of Rnd 4, attach cotton in any shell, ch 3, beg shell in same sp, *ch 3, shell in ch-2 sp of next shell, rep from * around, ch 3, join in 3rd ch of beg ch-3, fasten off.

Rnd 5A: Attach cotton with shell st in any ch-3 sp of Rnd 5, *ch 3, sk next shell, shell in next ch-3 sp, rep from * around, ch 3, join in beg dc, fasten off.

Rnd 6: Pull shells of Rnd 5 forward with ch-3 lps behind, attach cotton with shell st in any shell of Rnd 5, ch 3, *shell in shell, ch 3, rep from * around, join in beg dc.

Rnd 7: Pull all shells of Row 5A forward with ch-3 lps behind, join with [shell in shell lp, ch 3] rep around, join in beg dc, fasten off.

Rnd 8: Pull shell forward with ch-3 lps behind shells of Row 6, join with [shell in shell, shell in next ch-3] rep around, join in beg dc.

Rnd 9: Sl st to next lp, ch 3, 2 dc in same sp, *ch 2, 3 dc in next shell lp, rep from * around, ch 2, join in 3rd ch of beg ch-3.

Rnd 10: Ch 3, dc in each of next 2 dc, *ch 1, sk next lp, dc in each of next 3 dc, rep from * around, ch 1, join in 3rd ch of beg ch-3.

Rnd 11: Ch 3, dc in each of next 2 dc, *sk ch-1, dc in each of next 3 dc, rep from * around, join in 3rd ch of beg ch-3.

Rnd 12: Ch 2, dc in each of next 2 sts, *dc 2 dc tog, dc in next st, rep from * around.

When ⅔ of way around Rnd 12, place on blue ball, join.

Rnd 13: Ch 3, beg shell in same sp, [sk 4 sts, shell in next st] 5 times, join in 3rd ch of beg ch-3, fasten off.

Cross Christmas Ball

Note: *Beg ch-3 counts as first dc throughout.*

Rnd 1: With size 20 crochet cotton, ch 10, join to form a ring, ch 3, 29 dc in ring, join in 3rd ch of beg ch-3. (30 dc)

Rnd 2: Ch 1, sc in same st, sc in each of next 29 sts, join in beg sc.

Rnd 3: Ch 6, *sk next 2 sts, dc in next st, ch 3, rep from * around, join in 3rd ch of beg ch-6.

Rnd 4: Ch 3, *6 dc in next ch-3 sp, dc in next dc, ch 4, sk next ch-3 sp, dc in next dc, rep from * around, 6 dc in next ch-3 sp, dc in next dc, ch 4, join in 3rd ch of beg ch-3.

Rnd 5: Ch 3, dc in each of next 7 dc, *ch 4, sk next ch-4 sp, dc in each of next 8 dc, rep from * around, ch 4, join in 3rd ch of beg ch-3.

Rnd 6: Ch 3, dc in same st, *dc in each of next 2 dc, ch 4, sk 2 sts, dc in each of next 2 sts, 2 dc in next st, ch 4, sk next ch-4 sp, 2 dc in next st, rep from * around, dc in each of next 2 sts, ch 4, sk 2 sts, dc in each of next 2 sts, 2 dc in next st, ch 4, join in 3rd ch of beg ch-3.

Rnd 7: Ch 3, dc in same st, 2 dc in next st, *ch 2, sk next st, dc in next dc, ch 4, sk next ch-4 sp, dc in next dc, ch 2, sk next st, 2 dc in each of next 2 dc, ch 4, sk next ch-4 sp, 2 dc in each of next 2 dc, rep from * around, ch 2, sk next st, dc in next dc, ch 4, sk next ch-4 sp, dc in next dc, ch 2, sk next st, 2 dc in each of next 2 dc, ch 4, join in 3rd ch of beg ch-3.

Rnd 8: Ch 3, dc in each of next 3 sts, *2 dc in next ch-2 sp, dc in next dc, ch 3, sk next ch-4 sp, dc in next dc, 2 dc in next ch-2 sp, dc in each of next 4 sts, ch 3, sk next ch-4 sp, dc in each of next 4 dc, rep from * around, 2 dc in next ch-2 sp, dc in next dc, ch 3, sk next ch-4 sp, dc in next dc, 2 dc in next ch-2 sp, dc in each of next 4 sts, ch 3, join in 3rd ch of beg ch-3.

Rnd 9: Ch 3, dc in each of next 6 sts, *3 dc in next ch-3 sp, dc in each of next 7 sts, sk next ch-3 sp, dc in each of next 7 sts, rep from * around, 3 dc in next ch-3 sp, dc in each of next 7 sts, sk next st, join in 3rd ch of beg ch-3.

Rnd 10: Ch 2, dc 2 dc tog, *ch 2, sk next 2 sts, dc 3 dc tog, rep from * around, ch 2, join in 2nd ch of beg ch-2.

Rnd 11: Ch 6, *sk next ch-2 sp, sl st in next st, ch 6, rep from * around, ending with [ch 3, dc] in beg st (this sets up for next row).

Place over yellow ball.

Rnd 12: Ch 3, *sl st in next ch-6 lp, ch 3, rep from * around, join in beg sl st.

Rnd 13: Sl st to center of next lp, *ch 5, sl st in next ch-3 lp, rep from * around, join with [ch 2, dc] in beg sl st.

Rnd 14: *Ch 2, sl st in next ch-5 lp, rep from * around, join in beg sl st.

Rnd 15: Ch 1, sc in same st, *sc next ch-2 lp, sc in sl st, rep from * around, join in beg sc.

Rnd 16: Ch 1, sc in same st, *sk 2 sts, 6 dc in next st, sk 2 sts, sc in next st, rep from * around, join in beg sc, fasten off.

Eyelet Star Christmas Ball

Rnd 1: With size 20 crochet cotton, ch 10, join to form a ring, ch 1, 21 sc in ring, join in beg sc.

Rnd 2: Ch 5, dc in same sp, [sk 2 sts, V-st in next st] 6 times, join in 3rd ch of beg ch-5. (7 V-sts)

Rnd 3: Ch 3, [sk next 2 chs, dc in next dc, ch 3, dc in next dc] 6 times, ch 3, join in 3rd ch of beg ch-3.

Rnd 4: Ch 3, dc in next dc, [ch 5, sk next ch-3 sp, dc in each of next 2 dc] 6 times, ch 5, join in 3rd ch of beg ch-3.

Rnd 5: Ch 2, dc in next dc, [ch 7, sk next ch-5 lp, dc 2 dc tog] 6 times, ch 7, join in 2nd ch of beg ch-2.

Rnd 6: Ch 13, [sk next ch-7 sp, dc in next st, ch 10] 6 times, join in 3rd ch of beg ch-13.

Rnd 7: Ch 8, dc in same sp, ch 5, dc in same sp, [sl st in next ch-10 sp, {dc, ch 5} 3 times, dc in same sp] 6 times, sl st in next st, [dc, ch 5] in same st as beg st, join in 3rd ch of beg ch-8.

Rnd 8: Ch 8, [{dc, ch 5, dc} in 3rd ch of next lp, ch 5, dc in next dc, sk 2 ch-5 lps, dc in next dc, ch 5] 6 times, [dc, ch 5, dc] in 3rd ch of next lp, ch 5, dc in next dc, join in 3rd ch of beg ch-8.

Rnd 9: *6 sc in next ch-5 lp, sl st in next st, rep from * around, join in beg sc, fasten off.

Rnd 10: Working in back lps, sk next 6-sc lp, attach cotton with a sl st in 3rd st of next lp, [ch 4, tr in 4th st of next lp, tr in 3rd st of next lp, ch 4, sl st in 3rd st of next lp] 6 times, ch 4, tr in 4th st of next lp, tr in 3rd st of next lp, ch 4, join in beg sl st.

Note: *Place over red ball halfway around Rnd 11.*

Rnd 11: Ch 11, [dc in next sl st, {sk ch-4 lp, 2 tr, ch-4 lp}, ch 8] 6 times, sl st in 3rd ch of beg ch-11.

Rnd 12: Ch 3, dc in same st, [ch 4, 2 dc in next dc] 6 times, ch 4, join in 3rd ch of beg ch-3.

Rnd 13: Ch 4, dc in next dc, *ch 1, dc in next dc, rep from * around, ch 1, join in 3rd ch of beg ch-4.

Rnd 14: Ch 1, sc in same st, sc in each dc around, skipping each ch-1 sp, join in beg sc, fasten off.

—Designed by Sandra Jean Smith

Tips for Completing Crocheted Projects

Time is at a premium for many of us today, but if we use the time we have and choose our projects carefully, we can enjoy our craft and the lovely, original things we create for ourselves and others.

• Don't bite off more than you can chew. If you don't have much time for crochet, don't try to tackle an afghan or a tablecloth. Choose a place mat or doily instead, or some quick and easy bazaar items.

• Budget your crochet time. Resolve to work one or two rows or motifs on your project each day. You'll be amazed at how fast your project will take shape.

• Try using a jumbo hook for large projects. Working with 2–3 strands of yarn and a jumbo hook, you can make a lovely pillow cover in one sitting, and an entire afghan in next to no time.

Most important of all, don't become discouraged. Once you have completed something, your crochet confidence will be bolstered enough to spur you on to bigger and better projects!

BAZAAR
AT
5:00

Bazaar Fun

You'll not lack for quick and easy ideas to help boost your organization's profits at it's next fundraiser or bazaar. Choose from this fun mix of decorative, versatile and useful items that can be stitched in record time and minimal materials. They'll help make your booth one of the most successful ever!

Easter Plant Pokes

Add them to a spring flower arrangement, poke them into an Easter basket or brighten up a potted plant! These quick and easy characters will add a cheerful touch anywhere you choose to use them.

Ears (Make 2)

Row 1: Ch 4, sc in 2nd ch from hook, sc in each of next 2 chs, ch 1, turn. (3)

Rows 2–6: Sc in each sc across, ch 1, turn.

Row 7: Dec 1 sc over next 2 sc, sc in next sc, ch 1, turn. (2)

Row 8: Dec 1 sc over next 2 sc, ch 1, turn. (1)

Rnd 9: 4 sc in tip of ear, sc in each rem sc evenly sp around, join in beg sc, fasten off.

Finishing

Whipstitch head sections tog, stuffing with fiberfill before closing.

Sew eyes ½" apart at center of head. Glue white pompons side by side below eyes, as shown in photo; glue pink pompon for nose above white pompons.

Place a small amount of glue on skewer and insert into center bottom of head. Tie length of lavender ribbon in a bow. Glue to skewer below head.

Duck

Head (Make 2)

Rnds 1–7: With baby yellow, rep Rnds 1–7 of Bunny.

Mark 1 of 2-sc sections in each of next 4 sts of Rnd 5 for center bottom of head.

Bill Top

Row 1: With dark peach, ch 4, sc in 2nd ch from hook, sc in each of next 2 chs, ch 1, turn. (3)

Rows 2 & 3: Sc in each sc across, ch 1, turn.

Row 4: Dec 1 sc over next 2 sc, sc in next sc, ch 1, turn. (2)

Rnd 5: Sc evenly sp around beak, join, fasten off.

Bill Bottom

Row 1: With dark peach, ch 3, sc in 2nd ch from hook, sc in next ch, ch 1, turn. (2)

Row 2: Sc in each sc across, ch 1, turn.

Row 3: Dec 1 sc over next 2 sc, ch 1, turn. (1)

Rnd 4: Sc evenly sp around outer edge, join in beg sc, fasten off.

Finishing

Whipstitch head sections tog, stuffing with fiberfill before closing.

Continued on Page 93

Let's Begin!

Experience Level: Beginner

Size
Bunny: Approximately 3" in diameter
Duck: Approximately 2½" in diameter
Egg: Approximately 2½"-tall x 1½"-wide

Materials
☐ Bernat® Berella "4"® 4-ply yarn: small amounts each pale damson #8853, baby yellow #8945, dark peach #8979 and baby green #8948

☐ Size F/5 crochet hook

☐ 4 (8mm) black shank buttons

☐ 2 (½") white pompons

☐ ¼" pink pompon

☐ 3 bamboo skewers

☐ Pastel ribbon: white, 12" each lavender, yellow

☐ Fiberfill

☐ Fabric glue

☐ 2" square of cardboard

☐ Yarn needle

Gauge: 4 sc and 4 sc rnds = 1"

To save time, take time to check gauge.

Pattern Note: Do not join rnds; use yarn marker to mark rnds.

Bunny

Head (Make 2)

Rnd 1: With pale damson, ch 2, 6 sc in 2nd ch from hook. (6)

Rnd 2: 2 sc in each sc around. (12)

Rnd 3: [Sc in next sc, 2 sc in next sc] rep around. (18)

Rnd 4: [Sc in each of next 2 sc, 2 sc in next sc] rep around. (24)

Rnd 5: [2 sc in each of next 4 sc, sc in each of next 8 sc] twice. (32)

Mark 1 of the 8-sc sections as the bottom of head.

Rnds 6 & 7: Sc in each sc around, fasten off at end of Rnd 7.

Heart Pincushion

Stitch more than one of these easy-to-make pincushions—then give your heart to a friend! It will be fondly appreciated whenever it is used.

Let's Begin!

Experience Level: Beginner

Size: Approximately 5½" tall x 4¾" wide

Materials

☐ Bernat® Berella "4"® 4-ply yarn: small amounts each rose #8921 and winter white #8941

☐ Size F/5 crochet hook

☐ Polyester fiberfill

Gauge: 4 sc and 4 sc rows = 1"

To save time, take time to check gauge.

Pattern Note: For larger heart, use size G crochet hook.

Heart *(Make 2)*

Row 1: Beg at point with rose, ch 2, sc in 2nd ch from hook, ch 1, turn.

Row 2: 2 sc in next st, ch 1, turn. (2 sc)

Row 3: 2 sc in each of next 2 sts, ch 1, turn. (4 sc)

Row 4: Sc in each st across, ch 1, turn.

Row 5: 2 sc in first st, sc in each st across to within last st, 2 sc in last st, ch 1, turn. (6 sc)

Rows 6–16: Rep Rows 4 and 5, do not fasten off after Row 16.

First side

Row 17: Sc in each of next 6 sts, dec 1 sc over next 2 sc, ch 1, turn. (7)

Row 18: Sc in each st across, turn.

Row 19: Sc in next st, hdc in each of next 2 sts, dc in next st, hdc in each of next 2 sts, sc in last st, fasten off.

Second side

Row 1: Join rose in same sc as last sc of first side, ch 1, dec 1 sc over next 2 sc, sc in each st across, ch 1, turn.

Rows 2 & 3: Rep Rows 18 and 19 of first side, fasten off at end of Row 3.

Finishing

With winter white, embroider one side following Fig. 1.

Edging

Rnd 1: Holding both hearts tog, join winter white at bottom point, ch 4, working through both thicknesses, sc in same place as joining, *ch 4, sc in end of next row, rep from * to top, [ch 4, sc] in

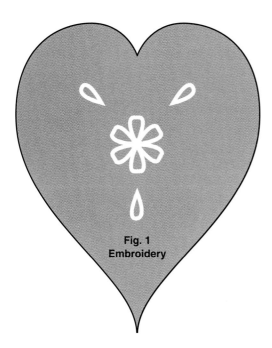

**Fig. 1
Embroidery**

each st across top and in end of each row down to other side of top, rep from * down to point. Stuff before completing Rnd 1.

—Designed by Mildred Joplin

Easter Plant Pokes

Continued from Page 91

Sew bills to head front between Rnds 3 and 4. Sew eyes above bill.

Wrap baby yellow around 2" piece of cardboard 8 times. Slip off cardboard; tie at center and cut ends. Separate plies of yarn; fluff. Trim ends. Sew to top of head.

Place glue on skewer; insert into center bottom of head. Tie length of yellow ribbon in a bow; glue to skewer just below head.

Egg
Rnd 1: With baby green, ch 2, 6 sc in 2nd ch from hook. (6)

Rnd 2: 2 sc in each sc around. (12)

Rnd 3: Sc around, inc 3 sc evenly sp around. (15)

Rnds 4 & 5: Sc in each sc around.

Rnd 6: Sc around, inc 2 sc evenly sp around. (17)

Rnds 7 & 8: Sc in each sc around.

Rnd 9: [Sc in each of next 2 sc, dec 1 sc over next

2 sc] 4 times, sc in next sc. (13)

Rnd 10: Sc in each sc around.

Stuff with fiberfill as work progresses.

Rnd 11: Sc in next sc, [dec 1 sc over next 2 sc, sc in next sc] 4 times. (9)

Rnd 12: [Sc in next sc, dec 1 sc over next 2 sc] rep around. (6)

Rnd 13: [Dec 1 sc over next 2 sc] rep around, fasten off. (3)

Finishing
Place glue on skewer; insert into center bottom of egg. Tie length of white ribbon in a bow; glue to skewer at base of egg.

—Designed by Glenna Robinson

Putting a Price on Your Work

When you decide to sell your crocheted items, here are some guidelines for setting a fair price:

Take into consideration the materials you use. Figure the cost of materials for each item you wish to sell by keeping a notebook record of everything—not just the yarn or cotton—used for the item.

Decide how much you want to make per hour for your labor and add this to the price of the materials.

If the figure you arrive at seems too steep for the item you're selling, you must make a few adjustments.

Try to reduce your cost by stocking up on materials when the price is down.

Choose wisely the items you plan to sell. It's better to be known for one special crocheted item than to offer a mishmash of different items that are time-consuming to make and may not sell well.

Start out with one or two items, then gradually add to your list of salable items.

In a nutshell, offer a customer something special at an affordable price while making a profit on your investment.

Country Bumpkins

*In just a couple of hours, you can add two whimsical
critters to your warm and cozy country decor!*

Let's Begin!

Experience Level: Beginner

Gauge: 4 sc = 1"

To save time, take time to check gauge.

Pattern Note: Join rnds with a sl st unless
otherwise stated.

Udderly Scentsational

Hat Preparation

With black paint and sponge, sponge on spots
randomly around hat. Set aside.

Nose

Rnd 1: With rose, ch 2, 6 sc in 2nd ch from hook,
join.

Rnd 2: 2 sc in each st around, join.

Rnd 3: *2 sc in each of next 3 sc, sc in each of

Let's Begin!

Materials
- ☐ 4-ply yarn: 1 oz each rose, tan, black and red
- ☐ Size F/5 crochet hook
- ☐ 6" white doll hat
- ☐ Small amount black paint
- ☐ Sponge
- ☐ Glue
- ☐ 2 (15mm) brown animal eyes
- ☐ 1 cup potpourri
- ☐ 6" x 6" piece lace or sheer fabric
- ☐ Yarn needle
- ☐ ⅞" copper bell
- ☐ Silk sunflower

next 3 sc, rep from * around, join.

Rnd 4: Sc in each of next 2 sc, 2 sc in each of next 3 sc, sc in each of next 6 sc, 2 sc in each of next 3 sc, sc in each of next 4 sc, join.

Rnds 5–8: Sc in each st around, join.

Rnd 9: *Sc in each of next 6 sc, [dec 1 sc over next 2 sc] twice, rep from * around, sc in each of next 5 sc, fasten off, leaving a length of yarn for sewing to hat.

Stuff nose. With black, straight-stitch nostrils on Rnd 2 with 3 sc between. Push top of hat crown down so it is indented. Sew nose onto 1 side of indented portion, not the center. Glue eyes above nose about 1" apart.

Horns
Rnd 1: With tan, ch 2, 6 sc in 2nd ch from hook, join.

Rnd 2: [Sc in next sc, 2 sc in next sc] rep around, join.

Rnds 3–13: Sc in each st, fasten off, leaving a length of yarn for sewing.

Stuff lightly. Sew to sides by eyes.

Ears (Make 2)
Rnd 1: With black, ch 2, 6 sc in 2nd ch from hook, join.

Rnd 2: 2 sc in each sc around, join.

Rnd 3: [Sc in next sc, 2 sc in next sc] rep around, join.

Rnds 4–8: Sc in each sc around, join.

Rnd 9: [Sc in each of next 2 sc, dec 1 sc over next 2 sc] rep around, join.

Rnd 10: Sc in each sc around, join.

Sl st opening closed. Fold in ½", sl st in first sl st, fasten off, leaving a length of yarn for sewing. Sew below horns.

Collar
Rnd 1: With red, ch 50, hdc in 3rd ch from hook and each ch across, fasten off, leaving a length of yarn for sewing.

Place collar behind ears on rim of hat with ends meeting under nose. Sew in place, working through both ends and bell.

Finishing
Fill inside of hat with potpourri. Glue lace over opening. Fold brim down between horns; glue in place. Glue sunflower at top.

Scarecrow Potpourri Hat

Let's Begin!

Materials
- ☐ 3-ply acrylic yarn: 1 oz each orange, tan and red; small amount black
- ☐ Size E/4 crochet hook
- ☐ 6" tan doll hat
- ☐ 2 (15mm) wiggly eyes
- ☐ Craft glue
- ☐ Yarn needle
- ☐ 6" x 6" piece lace
- ☐ 1 cup potpourri
- ☐ Silk sunflower
- ☐ 12" ruler

Hair
Wrap tan yarn around 12" ruler 20 times. Slip off lps; sew to brim of hat. Fold brim down over hair

Continued on Page 111

Grandma's Paddle

"Spare the rod and spoil the child" as they say! And who better to spoil them than Grandma? This softly padded paddle says it all.

Continued on Page 98

Let's Begin!

Experience Level: Beginner

Size: 7½" wide x 8½" long without handle

Materials
- ☐ Bernat® Berella "4"® 4-ply yarn: 3 oz arbutus #8922
- ☐ 2-ply yarn: small amount white
- ☐ Size G/6 crochet hook
- ☐ 1 yd 2"-wide gathered white eyelet
- ☐ 1 yd ¼"-wide white satin ribbon
- ☐ Wire-handled flyswatter
- ☐ ½" plastic ring
- ☐ Fiberfill
- ☐ ¼ yd quilt batting
- ☐ Rose sewing thread
- ☐ Sewing needle
- ☐ Yarn needle

Gauge: 4 sc and 4 sc rows = 1"

To save time, take time to check gauge.

Heart *(Make 2)*

Row 1: Beg at top of heart with arbutus, ch 23, sc in 2nd ch from hook, hdc in next ch, dc in each of next 6 chs, hdc in next ch, sc in next ch, sl st in each of next 2 chs, sc in next ch, hdc in next ch, dc in each of next 6 chs, hdc in next ch, sc in last ch, turn. (22)

Rows 2–5: Ch 1, 2 sc in first st, sc in each st across to within last st, 2 sc in last st, turn. (30)

Rows 6–11: Ch 1, sc in each sc across, turn.

Row 12: Ch 1, sc in each sc across, turn.

Row 13: Ch 1, dec 1 sc over next 2 sc, sc in each sc across to within last 2 sc, dec 1 sc over next 2 sc, ch 1, turn. (28)

Row 14: Rep Row 12.

Row 15: Rep Row 13. (26)

Rows 16 & 17: Rep Row 12.

Row 18: Rep Row 13. (24)

Rows 19 & 20: Rep Row 12.

Row 21: Rep Row 13. (22)

Pretty Hair Ties

Thrill a little girl with this colorful assortment of hair ties.
Patterns are given for four bright and cheerful ties.

Let's Begin!

Experience Level: Advanced beginner

Finished Size: 26"

Materials

☐ Brunswick® Windrush® 4-ply worsted weight yarn: small amounts each of flame red #9026, Christmas green #9043, Christmas red #90017, white #9010, medium powder blue #90112, saffron yellow #9008, sour apple green #90049 and burnt orange #90611

☐ Size H/8 crochet hook

☐ Tapestry needle

Gauge: Work evenly and consistently throughout.

Cherry Hair Tie

Cherries *(Make 2)*

Row 1: With flame red, ch 2, 6 sc in 2nd ch from hook, ch 1, turn. (6 sc)

Row 2: Work 2 sc in each st around, sl st in last sc. (12 sc)

Sl st in center ch, join with sl st in beg sc, fasten off.

Stem & Leaves

Join Christmas green with sl st in center sl st of cherry, ch 7, *sc in 2nd ch from hook, sc in next ch, sl st in next ch (first leaf made)*, ch 106, rep from * to * once (2nd leaf made), ch 4, sl st in center of 2nd cherry, working back along ch and at the same time working through 2 lps of foundation ch instead of 1, sl st in 2nd ch from hook and in next ch, ch 4, rep from * to * once (3rd leaf made), sl st in each ch to within last 2 chs, ch 4, rep from * to * once (4th leaf made), sl st in each ch to end, fasten off.

Weave in loose ends.

Hearts Hair Tie

Hearts *(Make 4)*

With white, ch 2, [sc, hdc, dc, 2 tr, ch 2, sl st, ch 2, 2 tr, dc, hdc, sc] in 2nd ch from hook, ch 2, join with sl st in beg sc, fasten off.

Weave in loose ends.

Tie

Join Christmas red in sl st between 2 curves of heart, ch 10, sl st in next heart, ch 90, sl st in next heart, ch 10, sl st in next heart, working back along ch and at the same time drawing through 2 lps of foundation ch, sl st in each ch to beg ch, fasten off.

Weave in loose ends.

Spiral Hair Tie

With medium powder blue, ch 12, *4 sc in 2nd ch from hook and in each of next 10 chs *, ch 110, rep from * to * once, working back along ch and at the same time drawing through 2 lps of foundation ch, sl st in each ch to first ch, fasten off.

Weave in loose ends.

Rainbow Hair Tie

Rainbows *(Make 2)*

Note: *Leave ½" of yarn on each end of each row.*

Row 1: With flame red, ch 2, 5 sc in 2nd ch from hook, fasten off. (5 sc)

Row 2 (RS): Join burnt orange in first sc, [ch 1, sl st] in same st and in each st across, fasten off. (13 sts and chs)

Row 3 (RS): Working in back lps only, join saffron yellow in beg sl st, sl st in each st and ch across, fasten off. (13 sl sts)

Row 4: With sour apple green rep Row 2. (23 sts and chs)

Row 5: With medium powder blue rep Row 3. (23 sl sts)

Handy Gauge Measure

Tired of rooting through your supplies for your ruler whenever you have to stop and check your gauge? Here's a way to keep it at your fingertips—literally:

Using craft paint or permanent markers, score off 1" on the ends of your crochet hooks. The search is over. All you'll ever need to do is lay your hook alongside the stitches to be measured and you'll see if your gauge is correct instantly.

Tie

With RS facing, join medium powder blue in center st of Row 5, ch 110, sl st in center ch of 2nd rainbow, working back along ch and at the same time drawing through 2 lps of foundation ch, sl st in each ch to beg ch, fasten off.

Weave in loose ends.

—Designed by Maggie Weldon for Designs for America

Grandma's Paddle

Continued from Page 96

Row 22: Rep Row 12.

Row 23: Rep Row 13. (20)

Row 24: Rep Row 12.

Rows 25–32: Rep Row 13. (4)

Row 33: Ch 1, [dec 1 sc over next 2 sc] twice, turn. (2)

Row 34: Ch 1, dec 1 sc over next 2 sc, turn. (1)

Trim

Rnd 35: Ch 1, work 3 sc in 1 rem sc of Row 34, working around entire outer edge, sc in each row and sc in each ch on opposite side of foundation ch, except, sl st in 2 sl sts at center top of heart, join with a sl st in beg sc, fasten off.

Embroidery

Thread yarn ndl with length of white 2-ply yarn. Working in straight sts, embroider "GRANDMA'S PADDLE" on each heart.

Finishing

Using heart as patt, cut 4 quilt batting hearts ¼" smaller. Baste flyswatter between layers of batting, stuffing with small amount of fiberfill before closing.

Beg at bottom point of heart, baste eyelet to WS of 1 heart. Place heart sections tog with flyswatter in middle. With rose thread and sewing ndl, sew tog, working through all thicknesses.

Make 4 bows from white ribbon; attach 1 to top and bottom of each side of paddle.

Attach arbutus to plastic ring, ch 1, work 20 sc over ring, join with a sl st in beg sc, fasten off.

Sew hanging lp to back top of heart.

—Designed by Rose Weibling

Sunny Fridgie

Bring a little sunshine in! This cheerful refrigerator magnet will brighten your day.

Let's Begin!

Experience Level: Beginner

Size: 4½" in diameter

Materials
- ☐ Bernat® Berella "4"® 4-ply yarn: small amounts each banana #8900 and rose #8921
- ☐ Size F/5 crochet hook
- ☐ 3 (7mm) glue-on eyes
- ☐ 1½" magnetic strip
- ☐ Glue

Gauge: 5 sc and 5 sc rows = 1"

To save time, take time to check gauge.

Pattern Note: Do not join rnds unless otherwise stated; mark with yarn marker.

Front Piece

Rnds 1–5: Rep Rnds 1–5 of back piece, do not fasten off at end of Rnd 5.

With yarn ndl and rose, embroider mouth between Rnds 2 and 3 as shown in photo.

Joining Front & Back

Rnd 6: With WS tog, working through both thicknesses, sl st, ch 1, 2 sc in same st, sc in each of next 5 sts, [2 sc in next st, sc in each of next 5 sts] rep around, join in beg st. (35 sc)

Rnd 7: [Ch 4, sl st in 2nd ch from hook, sc in next ch, hdc in last ch, sk 1 st, sl st in next st] rep around, join in first ch of beg ch-4, fasten off.

Finishing

Glue eyes in place as shown in photo. For nose, glue 3rd eye in center of face with black side showing.

Glue magnetic strip to back.

—Designed by Irene G. Charette

Back Piece

Rnd 1: With banana, ch 2, 6 sc in 2nd ch from hook, do not join. (6 sc)

Rnd 2: 2 sc in each sc around. (12 sc)

Rnd 3: [2 sc in next st, sc in next st] rep around. (18 sc)

Rnd 4: [2 sc in next st, sc in each of next 2 sts] rep around. (24 sc)

Rnd 5: [2 sc in next st, sc in each of next 3 sts] rep around, fasten off. (30 sc)

Balloon Chalkboard

Make this decorative chalkboard to accent a child's room or to give to a favorite teacher. It even makes a great memo pad for the kitchen or another room.

Let's Begin!

Experience Level: Advanced beginner

Finished Size: Approximately 15" x 12"

Materials
☐ Brunswick® Windrush® 4-ply worsted weight yarn: small amounts each of flame red #9026, Christmas green #9043, saffron yellow #9008 and bright royal blue #90012

☐ Size I/9 crochet hook

☐ Tapestry needle

☐ 8½" x 11½" framed chalkboard

☐ Hot-glue gun

Gauge: Work evenly and consistently throughout.

Ruffles
Rnd 1: With bright royal blue, ch 110, being careful not to twist ch, join with sl st in beg ch to form a ring, ch 3 (counts as dc throughout), 4 dc in same ch as joining, *dc in each of next 22 chs, 5 dc in next ch, dc in each of next 31 chs *, 5 dc in next ch, rep from * to * once, join with sl st in 3rd ch of beg ch-3. (126 dc)

Rnd 2: Working in front lps only, sl st to center dc of 5-dc group, ch 1, [sc, ch 5, sc] in same sp, ch 5, sk 1 st, [sc in next st, ch 5, sk 1 st] rep across to next center dc, *[sc, ch 5, sc] in center dc, ch 5, sk 1 st, [sc in next st, ch 5, sk 1 st] rep across to next corner, rep from * around, join with sl st in beg sc, fasten off. (67 ch-5 lps)

Rnd 3: Working in unused lps of Rnd 2, RS facing, join saffron yellow in any corner center dc, ch 2 (counts as hdc), 4 hdc in same st, hdc in each st to next corner, *5 hdc in center dc, hdc in each st to next corner, rep from * around, join with sl st in top of beg ch-2. (142 hdc)

Rnd 4: Rep Rnd 2. (75 ch-5 lps)

Rnd 5: Working in unused lps of Rnd 4 with Christmas green, rep Rnd 3. (158 hdc)

Rnd 6: Working in both lps, rep Rnd 2. (83 ch-5 lps)

Balloons *(Make 4: 1 each Christmas green, bright royal blue, saffron yellow and flame red)*

Rnd 1: Ch 1 (center ch), ch 3 (counts as dc), 11 dc in center ch, join with sl st in 3rd ch of beg ch-3, ch 3. (12 dc)

Rnd 2: Dc in same st as joining, 2 dc in each st around, join. (24 dc)

Balloon stem
Ch 3, work 2 dc in same st as joining, ch 1, turn, sl st in beg and next st, fasten off leaving 10" length for balloon string.

Weave in loose ends.

Large Bow
With flame red, ch 50, fasten off. Tie into bow.

Small Bow
With flame red, ch 25, fasten off. Tie into bow.

Finishing
Glue RS of crocheted ruffle to back edge of chalkboard.

Glue balloons in upper left corner with strings hanging down.

Draw balloon strings tog and glue large bow over them approximately 3" from ends.

Glue small bow at lower right corner of chalkboard.

—Designed by Maggie Weldon for Designs for America

Cornucopia Centerpiece

Decorate your Thanksgiving table with a beautiful
cornucopia, complete with a garden harvest.

Let's Begin!

Skill Level: Intermediate

Size
Cornucopia: 6" in diameter x 9" long
Pumpkin: 5" x 5"
Corn: 2" x 8"
Pear: 2½" x 3½"
Apple: 2½" x 2¾"
Bunch of Grapes: 2" x 4"

Materials
- □ 4-ply acrylic yarn: 5 oz warm brown, 2 oz tangerine, 1½ oz each grass green and purple, 1 oz each yellow, jockey red and honey gold
- □ Size G/6 crochet hook
- □ Small amount quilt batting, cut in ¾"-wide strips
- □ Fiberfill
- □ Yarn needle

Gauge: 9 dc = 2"; 2 dc rnds = ¾"

To save time, take time to check gauge.

Pattern Note: Weave in loose ends as work progresses.

Cornucopia

Notes: Two rnds of each inner and outer sections are worked separately and then crocheted together every 3rd rnd. Use separate balls of warm brown yarn, each about 2½ oz.

Ch 2 at beg of rnds helps to fill in the area at joining, but does not count as 1 dc.

Inside
Starting with first ball of warm brown yarn, ch 3, work 12 dc in first ch, sl st to join in first dc, draw up a lp, remove hook and set aside. (12)

Outside
Rnd 1: With 2nd ball of warm brown yarn, ch 3, work 9 dc in first ch, sl st to join in top of first dc. (9)

Rnd 2: Ch 2, 2 dc in first st, [dc in each next 2 sts, 2 dc in next st] twice, dc in last 2 sts, sl st to join in top of first dc. (12)

Rnd 3: Hold RS of inside section against WS of outside section and match first sts, using yarn from outside section and being careful not to catch inside yarn and lp, ch 1 and sc both sections together through both lps of each st, inserting a small amount of fiberfill before closing, join with sl st through front lp only of first sc, draw up a lp, remove hook and drop outside yarn.

Pull lp of inside yarn through back lp only of first sc of Rnd 3 and adjust lp to working length.

Rnd 4: Ch 2, working in back lps only with inside yarn, work 2 dc in first st, dc in next st, 2 dc in next st, dc in next st, hdc in next st, sc in next 2 sts, hdc in next st, [dc in next st, 2 dc in next st] twice, join. (12 dc, 2 hdc and 2 sc = 16 sts)

Rnd 5: Ch 2, working through both lps, dc in first 2 sts, 2 dc in next st, dc in next 2 sts, 2 dc in next st, hdc in next st, sc in next 2 sts, hdc in next st, [2 dc in next st, dc in next 2 sts] twice, join, draw up a lp and drop inside yarn. (20 sts)

Pick up outside yarn and adjust lp, rep Rnds 4 and 5 with outside yarn, working Rnd 4 in front lps of Rnd 3.

Insert a strip of quilt batting between inner and outer sections and trim length to fit.

Rnd 6: Holding sections tog and matching sts, with outside yarn, ch 1 and sc sections tog as before.

Mark center 4 sts with a piece of CC yarn. These 4 sts (1 hdc, 2 sc and 1 hdc) will be worked on the rnds worked separately through Rnd 26.

Rnds 7–12: Continue in established pattern, working 2 increases before and 2 increases after the 4 center sts of each rnd worked separately, varying position of increases. Insert quilt batting and sc sections together every 3rd rnd with outside yarn.

At the end of Rnd 12 there is a total of 36 sts.

Rnd 13: Rep pattern, working 2 inc before and after 4 center sts. (40)

Rnd 14: Rep pattern, working 1 inc before and after 4 center sts. (42)

Rnd 15: Insert quilt batting and sc sections tog as before.

Rnds 16–27: Rep Rnds 13–15, varying positions of inc. (66)

Rnds 28 & 29: Rep Rnds 13 and 14, but hdc in each of the 4 center sts. (72)

Rnd 30: Rep Rnd 15.

Rnds 31 & 32: Keeping in pattern, dc in each st around, join.

At the end of Rnd 32, leaving a 2-yd length of both yarns, fasten off.

Insert quilt batting, matching sts and working with both yarn lengths on yarn needle, overcast sts tog around edge, fasten off.

Pumpkin

Blossom End
Rnd 1: With tangerine yarn, ch 2, work 8 sc in 2nd ch from hook, sl st to join in beg sc, fasten off and set aside. (8)

Body
Row 1: With tangerine yarn, ch 29, sc in 2nd ch from hook, sc in next 4 chs, hdc in next 18 chs, sc in next 5 chs, turn.

Rows 2–40: Working in back lps only, ch 1, sc in next 5 sts, hdc in next 18 sts, sc in next 5 sts, turn.

At the end of Row 40, leaving a length of yarn, fasten off.

Weave yarn through ends of rows and pull tight to gather, secure and sew blossom end piece to ends of rows at bottom of pumpkin. Sew side seam.

Stuff pumpkin with fiberfill.

With yarn needle and length of tangerine yarn, gather end of rows at top of pumpkin, pull tight and fasten off. Stem will cover top hole.

Stem
Rnd 1: With brown yarn, ch 4, 3 sc in 2nd ch from hook, sc in next ch, 3 sc in last ch, working on opposite side of foundation ch, sc in next ch, do not join. (8)

Rnd 2: [2 sc in each of next 3 sts, sc in next st] twice, sl st to join in beg sc. (14)

Rnd 3: Ch 1, working in back lps for this rnd only, sc in first st, [dec 1 sc over next 2 sc] twice, sc in next 9 sts, do not join. (12)

Rnd 4: Sc in next st, dec 1 sc over next 2 sts, sc in next 9 sts, do not join. (11)

Rnds 5–7: Sc in each sc around, do not join.

At the end of Rnd 7, sl st in next sc, leaving a length of yarn, fasten off.

Stuff stem with fiberfill and sew to top of pumpkin.

Leaves & Tendrils *(Make 2)*
Rnd 1: With grass green yarn, ch 4, 2 sc in 2nd ch from hook, sc in next ch, 3 sc in last ch, working on opposite side of foundation ch, sc in next ch, sc in same ch as beg sc sts, sl st to join in beg sc. (8)

Rnd 2: Ch 1, sc in first 2 sts, *in next st work hdc, dc, ch 3, sl st in first ch, dc and hdc, sl st in next st, rep from * twice, but work sc in last st instead of sl st, sl st to join, ch 20 for tendril, sl st in 2nd ch from hook, [sc and sl st in next ch] rep across, ending with sl st in last ch, sl st in sc at base of ch, fasten off.

Sew leaves to base of pumpkin stem.

Corn

Cob
Row 1: With yellow yarn, ch 31, sc in 2nd ch from hook, sc in next 3 chs, hdc in each next 24 chs, sc in next 2 chs, turn. (30)

Row 2: Ch 1, working in back lps only, sc in next 2 sts, working in both lps, hdc in next 24 sts, working in back lps only, sc in next 4 sts, turn.

Row 3: Working in back lps only, sc in next 4 sts, working in both lps, hdc in next 24 sts, working in back lps only, sc in next 2 sts, turn.

Rows 4–13: Rep Rows 2 and 3.

Row 14: Rep Row 2, leaving a length of yarn, fasten off.

Weave yarn through ends of rows and pull tight to gather, knot to secure and sew side seam, knot to secure, stuff cob with fiberfill, weave rem length through ends of rows at top and pull tight, knot to secure, fasten off.

Husk
Rnd 1: With grass green yarn, ch 2, 8 sc in 2nd ch from hook, sl st to join in beg sc. (8)

Rnd 2: Ch 1, working in back lps for this rnd only, sc in each st around, do not join.

Rnds 3 & 4: Sc in each sc around.

Rnd 5: Ch 1, work 2 dc in each sc around, sl st to join in top of beg dc. (16)

Rnd 6: Ch 2 (does not count as a st), dc in first st, 2 dc in next st, [dc in next st, 2 dc in next st] rep around, sl st to join in first dc. (24)

Rnd 7: Ch 2 (does not count as a st), dc in each next 24 dc, sl st to join in first dc.

Row 8: Ch 2 (counts as first dc), sk first st, dc in next 23 sts, dc in same st as joining, turn. (25)

Rows 9–12: Ch 2 (first dc), dc in next 24 dc, turn.

First leaf

Row 13: Ch 2 (first dc), sk first st, dc in next 8 sts, do not work rem sts, turn. (9)

Rows 14–16: Ch 2, sk first st, dc in next 8 sts, turn.

Rows 17–19: Ch 2, sk first st, dec 1 dc over next 2 sts, dc across to within last 2 sts, dec 1 dc over next 2 sts, turn. (3)

Row 20: Ch 2, sk first st, dec 1 dc over next 2 sts, fasten off.

Second & third leaves

Row 13 (WS): Attach grass green yarn to same st as last dc of Row 13 of previous leaf, ch 2, dc in next 8 sts, turn.

Rows 14–20: Rep Rows 14–20 of first leaf.

Stuff stem of husk with fiberfill, insert top of cob into husk (end with 2 sc sts), tack husk to cob at center front and at Row 12 between each leaf.

Pear

Notes: *Do not join rnds unless otherwise indicated. Use a scrap of CC yarn to mark rnds.*

WS of sc sts is the RS of pear.

Rnd 1: Starting at top of pear, with honey gold yarn, ch 2, 8 sc in 2nd ch from hook. (8)

Rnd 2: Work 2 sc in each sc around. (16)

Rnd 3: [2 sc in next sc, sc in each next 3 sc] 4 times. (20)

Rnds 4–9: Sc in each sc around.

Rnd 10: Sc around, inc 4 sc evenly sp around. (24)

Rnd 11: Sc in each sc around.

Rnds 12–15: Rep Rnds 10 and 11, varying positions of inc sts. (32)

Rnds 16–18: Sc in each sc around.

Rnds 19 & 20: Sc around, dec 4 sc evenly sp around. (24)

Rnds 21–23: Sc around, dec 6 sc evenly sp around varying positions of decreases. (6)

At the end of Rnd 23, sl st in next st, leaving a length of yarn, fasten off.

Stuff pear with fiberfill. Weave rem length of yarn through rem sts, pull tightly to close securely, fasten off.

Stem

With brown yarn, leaving a 5"-length at beg, ch 5, sl st in 2nd ch from hook, sl st in each rem ch across, leaving a 5"-length, fasten off.

Sew stem to top center of pear.

Apple

Note: *Do not join rnds unless otherwise indicated. Use scrap of CC yarn to mark rnds.*

Rnd 1: Starting at center top of apple, with jockey red yarn, ch 2, work 6 sc in 2nd ch from hook. (6)

Rnd 2: Work 2 sc in each sc around. (12)

Rnds 3–6: Sc around, inc 6 sc evenly and varying position of increases on each rnd. (36)

Rnds 7–12: Sc in each sc around.

Rnd 13: Sc around, dec 6 sc evenly sp around. (30)

Rnd 14: Sc in each sc around.

Rnds 15 & 16: Rep Rnds 13 and 14. (24)

Rnd 17: [Sc in next st, sk next st, 3 dc in next st, sk next st] 6 times, sl st to join in beg sc, fasten off.

Blossom End

Rnd 1: With jockey red yarn, ch 2, 6 sc in 2nd ch from hook. (6)

Rnd 2: Work 2 sc in each sc around. (12)

Rnd 3: [Sc in next sc, 3 dc in next sc] 6 times, sl st to join in beg sc, leaving an 8"-length of yarn, fasten off.

Stuff apple with fiberfill. With yarn needle and rem length of yarn, matching sts, sew blossom end to bottom of apple. Insert yarn needle and length of yarn through center of apple from bottom to top and back to bottom, secure at bottom to dimple top, fasten off.

Stem

Rep stem for pear. Attach to top of apple.

Bunch of Grapes

Note: *Pattern makes 2 bunches of grapes.*

Grapes *(Make 36)*

Rnd 1: With purple yarn, ch 3, work 8 hdc in first ch, sl st to join in beg hdc.

Rnd 2: Ch 2, hdc in each st around, join, leaving a

Continued on Page 106

Pretzel Magnet

It's guaranteed low in calories and fat-free!

Let's Begin!

Experience Level: Beginner

Size: 3" x 4"

Materials

☐ Bernat® Berella "4"® 4-ply yarn: ¼ oz oak #8796 and scraps of winter white #8941

☐ Size G/6 crochet hook

☐ Yarn needle

☐ 2 (½") magnetic strips

Gauge: 4 sc = 1"

Pretzel

Row 1: With oak, ch 51, sc in 2nd ch from hook, sc in each rem ch across, ch 1, turn. (50)

Rows 2–6: Sc in each sc across, ch 1, turn, at end of Row 6, fasten off, leaving a length of yarn.

With yarn ndl and length of yarn, fold crocheted piece in half lengthwise, holding Row 6 to opposite side of foundation ch, whipstitch edge closed.

Shaping

Lay piece flat horizontally in front with sewn edge facing away. Mark center of piece with yarn marker. Curl right-hand edge ¼" to left of center mark. Sew end in place. Curl left-hand edge over top of right-hand edge and sew ¼" to right of center mark.

Salt

With yarn ndl and winter white, stitch 11 French knots as desired on top of pretzel.

Finishing

Attach magnetic strips to back of pretzel.

—Designed by Rita Thatcher

Cornucopia Centerpiece

Continued from Page 105

length of yarn, fasten off.

Stuff grape with fiberfill. With yarn needle and rem length of yarn, weave through front lps only of each st, pull tight, secure, fasten off.

With yarn needle and length of yarn, thread yarn through tops of grapes to form 8 circles as follows: Make 2 circles of 3 grapes, 2 circles of 4 grapes and 4 circles of 5 grapes, secure each ring of grapes and fasten off. Thread a 12"-length of purple yarn through the top of 1 of the rem grapes and center grape on length of yarn, remove needle.

Thread the double strand of yarn through 4 circles in the following order: 3 grapes, 5 grapes, 5 grapes and 4 grapes. Snuggle circles together and fasten yarn at top of last circle. Rep with rem grapes.

Leaves & Tendrils *(Make 4)*

Rnd 1: With grass green yarn, ch 4, 2 sc in 2nd ch from hook, sc in next ch, 3 sc in last ch, working on opposite side of foundation ch, sc in next ch, sc in same ch as beg 2 sc, sl st to join. (8)

Rnd 2: Ch 1, sc in each next 2 sc, *in next st work dc, ch 3, sl st in first ch and dc, sc in next st, rep from * 2 more times, sl st to join in beg sc, ch 17, fasten off. Twist ch sts to curl.

Stems *(Make 2)*

With grass green yarn, rep stem pattern for pear.

Sew 1 stem to base of 2 leaves and tack unit to top of 1 bunch of grapes. Rep for rem bunch.

—Designed by Sharon Volkman

Halloween Jar Covers

Delight Halloween party-goers with these clever jar covers!
Filled with candy corn or other treats, covered jars make festive decorations!

Basic Cover

Rnd 1: Ch 4, 11 dc in first ch, join in top of beg ch. (12)

Rnd 2: Ch 3 (first dc), dc in same st as beg ch-3, 3 dc in next st, [2 dc in next st, 3 dc in next st] rep around, join in top of beg ch-3. (30)

Rnd 3: Ch 3, dc in next dc, 2 dc in next dc, [dc in each next 2 dc, 2 dc in next dc] rep around, join in top of beg ch-3. (40)

Rnd 4: Ch 3, 2 dc in next dc, [dc in next dc, 2 dc

Let's Begin!

Skill Level: Easy

Size: Fits 3" lid

Materials
☐ Crochet cotton size 10; 1 ball each orange and ecru; small amount white, green and black

☐ Size 7 steel crochet hook

☐ 20" ⅛"-wide orange satin ribbon

☐ 40" ⅛"-wide black satin ribbon

☐ 2 sets 6mm wiggle eyes

☐ Black plastic spider

☐ Hot-glue gun

☐ Tapestry needle

Gauge: 5 dc = ½"; 2 dc rnds = ½"

To save time, take time to check gauge.

Pattern Notes: Weave in loose ends as work progresses.

Join rnds with a sl st unless otherwise stated.

in next dc] rep around, join in top of beg ch-3. (60)

Rnd 5: Ch 3, dc in next dc, 2 dc in next dc, [dc in each next 2 dc, 2 dc in next dc] rep around, join in top of beg ch-3. (80)

Rnds 6–9: Ch 3, dc in each dc around, join in top of beg ch-3.

Rnd 10: Ch 3, dc in next 2 dc, ch 1, sk 1 dc, [dc in next 3 dc, ch 1, sk 1 dc] rep around, join in top of beg ch-3, fasten off.

Tie
Cut a 20"-length of satin ribbon. Weave ribbon through ch-1 sps of Rnd 10.

Cat Jar Cover
Make Basic Cover with orange cotton and a black tie.

Head
Rnds 1–3: With black cotton, rep Rnds 1–3 of Basic Cover. (40)

At the end of Rnd 3, do not fasten off.

Ears
*Ch 5, 3 dtr in same st as beg ch-5, sk 2 dc *, sl st in next 5 dc, rep from * to * once, sl st in next dc, fasten off.

Facial Features
With tapestry needle and length of white cotton, embroider smiling mouth with ch sts. Cut 3 strands of white cotton each 2"-long; tie together at center with overhand knot. Glue in place at center of head. Glue eyes in place.

Glue head to center of cover.

Pumpkin Cover
Make Basic Cover with ecru cotton and an orange tie.

Pumpkin
Rnds 1 & 2: With orange cotton, rep Rnds 1 and 2 of Basic Cover. (30)

Rnd 3: Ch 3 (first dc), dc in next dc, 2 dc in next dc, [dc in next 2 dc, 2 dc in next dc] 7 times, changing to green cotton in last step of last dc, [dc in next 2 dc, 2 dc in next dc] twice, join in top of beg ch-3, turn. (40)

Stem
Row 4: Sl st in first 5 green dc, ch 6, sc in 2nd ch from hook, sc in each next 4 chs, sl st in same dc as last sl st, sl st in each rem green dc, fasten off.

Facial Features
With tapestry needle and length of black cotton, embroider triangle-shaped nose over lower section of Rnd 1 and embroider smiling mouth between Rnds 2 and 3, centered below nose. Glue eyes in place.

Glue pumpkin to center of cover.

Spiderweb Cover
Make Basic Cover with orange cotton and a black tie.

Spiderweb
Rnd 1: With white cotton, ch 5, join to form a ring, ch 5 (first dc, ch 2), [dc in ring, ch 2] 5 times, join in 3rd ch of beg ch-5. (6 ch-2 sps)

Rnd 2: Ch 9 (first dc, ch 6), [dc in next dc, ch 6] 5 times, join in 3rd ch of beg ch-9.

Rnd 3: Ch 7 (first dc, ch 4), dc in next ch-6 sp, ch 4, [dc in next dc, ch 4, dc in next ch-6 sp, ch 4] 5 times, join in 3rd ch of beg ch-7. (12 ch-4 sps)

Continued on Page 111

Catnip Mouse

The scent of dried catnip will bring out the kitten in any cat, so pamper your pet with this fun-loving feline toy.

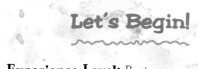

Let's Begin!

Experience Level: Beginner

Size: 2" x 2" x 4"

Materials:
- ☐ Bernat® Berella "4"® 4-ply yarn: 1 oz pearl gray #8912 and small amounts each black #8994 and rose #8921
- ☐ Crochet cotton size 3: small amount ecru
- ☐ Size G/6 crochet hook
- ☐ Fiberfill
- ☐ 1 tablespoon dried catnip
- ☐ Yarn needle

Gauge: 4 sc and 4 sc rows = 1"

To save time, take time to check gauge.

Body Side *(Make 2)*

Row 1: With pearl gray, ch 20, sc in 2nd ch from hook, sc in each rem ch across, ch 1, turn. (19 sts)

Row 2: Sc in each sc across to within last 2 sc, sk next sc (mark this end as nose end of mouse), sc in last sc, ch 1, turn. (18 sts)

Row 3: Sk first sc, sc in each sc across to within last 2 sc, sk next sc, sc in last sc, ch 1, turn. (16 sts)

Row 4: Sk first sc, sc in each of next 10 sc, [dec 1 sc over next 2 sc] twice, ch 1, turn. (13 sts)

Rows 5 & 6: Rep Row 3. (11, 9 sts)

Row 7: Sk first sc, sc in each rem sc across, ch 1, turn. (8 sts)

Row 8: Sc in each sc across, fasten off.

Body Bottom

Row 1: With pearl gray, ch 4, sc in 2nd ch from hook, sc in each of next 2 chs, ch 1, turn. (3 sts)

Row 2: 2 sc in first sc, sc in next sc, 2 sc in next sc, ch 1, turn. (5 sts)

Rows 3–15: Sc in each sc across, ch 1, turn.

Row 16: Dec 1 sc over next 2 sc, sc in next sc, dec 1 sc over next 2 sc, ch 1, turn. (3 sts)

Row 17: Sc in each sc across, ch 1, turn.

Row 18: Sc in first sc, sk next sc, sc in last sc, ch 1, turn. (2 sts)

Row 19: Dec 1 sc over next 2 sc, fasten off. (1 st)

Note: *Row 19 is nose end of mouse.*

Assembly

Holding sides tog, attach pearl gray at nose end. Working through both thicknesses, sc across from nose, over back to opposite end, fasten off.

Turn mouse so seam is inside. Match edges of bottom piece and sides. Attach pearl gray, sc bottom and sides tog, leaving a small opening; do not fasten off. Place a small amount of fiberfill in mouse, then catnip; finish stuffing with fiberfill. Crochet rem opening closed, fasten off.

Tail

Attach rose to back of body, ch 15, fasten off.

Nose

With yarn ndl and rose, overcast area at nose end.

Eyes *(Make 2)*

With yarn ndl and black, make 1 French knot for each eye about ½" above nose.

Continued on Page 111

Pumpkin Candy Basket

Fill this cute candy basket to the brim with sweet treats for Halloween! It's quick and easy to stitch.

Let's Begin!

Skill Level: Easy

Size: 2½" x 3½"

Materials
- ☐ 4-ply yarn: 1 oz orange, ¼ oz grass green, ¼ oz bronze
- ☐ Size E/4 crochet hook
- ☐ 24" ¼"-wide green satin ribbon
- ☐ Yarn needle

Gauge: Rnds 1 and 2 = 1½"

To save time, take time to check gauge.

Pattern Notes: Weave in loose ends as work progresses.

Join rnds with a sl st unless otherwise stated.

Pumpkin

Rnd 1: With orange yarn, ch 4, join to form a ring, ch 1, work 8 sc in ring, join in beg sc. (8)

Rnd 2: Ch 1, work 2 sc in each sc around, join in beg sc. (16)

Rnd 3: Ch 1, [sc in next sc, 2 sc in next sc] rep around, join in beg sc. (24)

Rnd 4: Ch 1, [sc in next 2 sc, 2 sc in next sc] rep around, join in beg sc. (32)

Rnd 5: Ch 1, [sc in next 7 sc, 2 sc in next sc] rep around, join in beg sc. (36)

Rnd 6: Ch 1, sc in first sc, sk 2 sc, 5 dc in next sc, sk 2 sc, [sc in next sc, sk 2 sc, 5 dc in next sc, sk 2 sc] rep around, join in beg sc.

Rnd 7: Ch 3 (first dc), 6 dc in same sc as beg ch-3, sc in center dc of next 5-dc group, [7 dc in next sc, sc in center dc of 5-dc group] rep around, join in top of beg ch-3, sl st to center dc of 7-dc group.

Rnd 8: Ch 1, sc in same dc as beg ch-1, 7 dc in next sc, [sc in center dc of 7-dc group, 7 dc in next sc] rep around, join in beg sc.

Rnd 9: Ch 3 (first dc), 4 dc in same sc as beg ch-3, sc in center dc of 7-dc group, [5 dc in next sc, sc in center dc of 7-dc group] rep around, join in top of beg ch-3, fasten off.

Rnd 10: Draw up a lp of bronze yarn in center dc of any 5-dc group of Rnd 9, ch 1, sc in same dc as beg ch-1, sc in next dc, [hdc in next dc, dc in next sc, hdc in next dc, sc in next 3 dc] rep around, ending with on last rep, sc in last dc instead of 3 dc, join in beg sc, fasten off.

Rnd 11: Draw up a lp of grass green in first sc of previous rnd, ch 1, sc in each st around, join in beg sc, fasten off. (36)

Finishing

Cut ribbon in half. Attach first length of ribbon around the post of first sc of Rnd 11, tie ends in bow. Sk next 17 sc sts of Rnd 11, attach 2nd length of ribbon around post of 18th sc, tie ends in a bow.

—Designed by Katherine Eng

Halloween Jar Covers

Continued from Page 108

Rnd 4: Ch 8 (first dc, ch 5), [dc in next dc, ch 5] 5 times, sl st to join in 3rd ch of beg ch-8.

Rnd 5: Ch 10 (first dc, ch 7), [dc in next dc, ch 7] 5 times, sl st to join in 3rd ch of beg ch-10, fasten off.

Finishing
Glue spiderweb to center top of cover. Glue spider to spiderweb.

—Designed by Angela Tate

Catnip Mouse

Continued from Page 109

Ears *(Make 2)*
With yarn ndl and black, make large lps above eyes for ears.

Whiskers
Cut 2 (2½") lengths of ecru crochet cotton; fold each piece in half. Pull center lp through mouse where whiskers would be; pull ends through lp and tighten. Rep for other side.

—Designed by Carol Mittal

Country Bumpkins

Continued from Page 95

and stitch for added hold. Place a few drops of glue under hair; snip lps open. Sew hanging lp directly behind folded-down brim. Set aside.

Carrot Nose
Rnd 1: With orange, ch 2, 6 sc in 2nd ch from hook, join.

Rnd 2: [Sc in each of next 2 sc, 2 sc in next sc] rep around, join.

Rnd 3–7: Sc in each sc, fasten off, leaving a length of yarn for sewing.

Stuff lightly. Sew to center of hat top.

Mouth
With black, ch 15, hdc in 3rd ch from hook and

each ch across, fasten off. Sew under nose.

Bow Tie
Row 1: With red, ch 15, hdc in 3rd ch from hook and each ch across, ch 2, turn.

Rows 2–5: Hdc in each hdc, at end of Row 5 do not turn, sc around entire piece, fasten off.

Bow tie middle
Row 1: Ch 5, hdc in 3rd ch from hook and each ch across, ch 2, turn.

Rows 2–8: Hdc in each hdc, ch 2, turn, fasten off, leaving a length for sewing.

Wrap around center of bow tie. Sew Row 1 to Row 8. Sew or glue to rim of hat under mouth.

Finishing
Glue eyes above nose. Glue flower to folded brim. Place potpurri in back of hat and glue lace over opening.

—By Denise Rothberg

Crocheting with Embroidery Floss

When crocheting with embroidery floss, be sure to purchase enough for your project. There are only approximately 6 yards of floss in most skeins, and that won't go a long way when working in crochet.

Before you begin, unwrap the skeins and wind the floss on small pieces of cardboard for ease in handling.

Many items may be crocheted from embroidery floss. here are just a few ideas:

• Light, delicately finished to-scale dollhouse miniatures may be crocheted using embroidery floss and a size 3 steel crochet hook.

• The wide variety of shades floss offers can be used to create lovely and unusual edgings.

• Create jewelry by crocheting small motifs from embroidery floss. Stiffen and lacquer, then glue to pin and earring findings.

• For an eye-catching personal touch, glue tiny, lacy motifs crocheted from embroidery floss to place cards and invitations.

Kitchen Fixin's

The kitchen is the heart of the home, and certainly not to be overlooked when creating crocheted accents. Hot pads and place mats may be practical necessities, but they can also provide attractive decorative touches which allow you to make your house into a home!

Blueberry Delight

Give your kitchen a fresh look with this sunny ensemble. Set includes a pot holder, a dishcloth, an oven mitt and a dish detergent bottle apron.

Pot Holder

First Side

Rnd 1: With larger hook and marine blue, ch 4, join in beg first ch to form ring, ch 1, 8 sc in ring, join in beg ch.

Rnd 2: Ch 1, 2 sc in each sc around, join in first sc. (16 sts)

Rnd 3: Ch 1, sc in first sc, 2 sc in next sc, [sc in next sc, 2 sc in next sc] rep around, join in first sc. (24 sts)

Rnd 4: Ch 1, sc in each of first 2 sc, 2 sc in next sc, [sc in each of next 2 sc, 2 sc in next sc] rep around, join with a sl st in first sc. (32 sts)

Rep Rnd 4, having 1 more sc between incs every rnd until there is a total of 104 sts, fasten off. Circle should measure 6½" in diameter.

Second Side

Work as for first side, *do not fasten off*. Set work aside.

Center

Cut a piece of batting in a 6¼" circle. Cut 2 (6½") circles of blue fabric. Place fabric circles on each side of batting, RS facing out, and zigzag around entire outside edge twice. Trim edges.

Place this center between 2 crocheted sides of pot holder, with unfinished yarn side on top.

Outside Edging

With larger hook and working through both thicknesses, sc around outside edge of pot holder sides, fasten off.

Leaves *(Make 2 sets)*

With larger hook and 2 strands myrtle green cotton held tog, ch 3, sc in 2nd ch from hook and in next ch, ch 1, turn. (2 sts)

Inc 1 st at both ends of every row until there is a total of 8 sts, work evenly on these 8 sts for 6 rows, dec 1 st at both ends of every row until 2 sts rem, work 1 row sc even on these 2 sts, fasten off.

Make another leaf in same manner, *do not fasten off*.

Leaf edging

Change to smaller hook, ch 1.

Holding 2 leaf pieces with WS held tog and working through both thicknesses, sc around entire leaf edge, join, fasten off.

Let's Begin!

Experience Level: Intermediate

Size

Pot Holder: 6½" in diameter
Dishcloth: Approximately 10½" square
Oven Mitt: Approximately 5½" at bottom x 11" long
Dish Detergent Apron: Fits standard 22-oz detergent bottle

Materials (for all items)

☐ Patons® Weekender® 100 percent cotton yarn (1¾ oz/50 grams per ball): 4 balls marine blue #5806 and 3 balls white #5801

☐ South Maid crochet cotton size 10 (350 yds/ball): 1 ball myrtle green #484

☐ Size F/5 crochet hook

☐ Size G/6 crochet hook or size needed to obtain gauge

☐ ⅓ yd polyester batting

☐ ⅓ yd marine blue cotton fabric

☐ Sewing thread to match fabric

☐ Large-eyed, blunt-tipped tapestry needle

☐ Sewing needle

☐ Sewing machine with zigzag stitch

Gauge: Pot Holder: 9 sts = 2"; 13 rnds = 3" with larger hook over sc

Dishcloth, Oven Mitt and Dish Detergent Apron: 9 sts = 2"; 15 rows = 3" with larger hook over blueberry patt or sc

To save time, take time to check gauge.

Pattern Notes: Dishcloth is double-faced.

Instructions are given for right-handed oven mitt; reverse shapings for left-handed mitt. Lining will slightly stretch mitt.

Join rnds with a sl st unless otherwise stated.

Pattern Stitch

Mbb (marine blue bobble): Change color from white to marine blue in last sc before bobble, in next sc [yo, draw up lp] 3 times, yo with white and draw through all lps on hook (bobble made). Work over color not in use.

Stem

Note: *The stem is the pot holder hanger.*

With larger hook and 2 strands myrtle green held tog, attach yarn in last st of pot holder edging, ch 20.

Sc in 2nd ch from hook, [remove hook from lp, draw lp through joining sl st of 1 leaf, sc in each ch of stem] rep across until last 2 chs, rep between [], fasten off.

Sew loose end of stem to pot holder edge, sew stem tog approximately ½". Sew leaves to pot holder as shown in photo.

Dishcloth

Front

Base Row: With larger hook and white, ch 48, sc in 2nd ch from hook and in each ch across, ch 1, turn. (47 sts)

Rows 1 & 2: Sc in each st across, ch 1, turn.

Row 3 (WS): Sc in each of first 7 sc, [mbb in next sc, sc in each of next 7 sc] rep across, ch 1, turn.

Rows 4–6: Sc in each st across, ch 1, turn.

Row 7 (WS): Sc in each of first 3 sc, [mbb in next sc, sc in each of next 7 sc] rep across, ending with sc in each of last 3 sc, ch 1, turn.

Row 8: Sc in each st across, ch 1, turn.

Rep Rows 1–8 for patt until there is a total of 51 rows, fasten off.

Work lazy-daisy leaves with 2 strands of myrtle green around bobbles as shown in the photo, set aside.

Back

Row 1: With larger hook and marine blue, ch 48, sc in 2nd ch from hook and in each ch across, ch 1, turn. (47 sts)

Work even in sc until piece is 50 rows, ch 1, *do not fasten off.*

Joining Front & Back

Holding top and bottom WS tog with marine blue piece on bottom and working through both thicknesses, work 3 sc in first sc (corner), sc across top edge, 3 sc in corner st, sc in corresponding rows along left edge, 3 sc in corner st, sc across bottom edge, 3 sc in corner st, sc in corresponding rows along right edge, join to beg sc, do not turn.

Picot edging

Change to smaller hook, [ch 2, sl st in 2nd ch from hook, sk next sc, sl st in next sc] rep around entire outside edge, ending with ch 14, sl st to last sc to form hanging lp.

Finishing

Work half-cross sts with 2 strands myrtle green around entire sc rnd.

Oven Mitt

Back

With larger hook and marine blue, ch 26, sc in 2nd ch from hook and in each ch across, ch 1, turn. (25 sts)

Work even in sc until there is a total of 24 rows.

Thumb Inc: [2 sc in first sc at beg of next row, ch 1, turn, 2 sc in last sc at end of next row, ch 1, turn] 5 times. (35 sts)

Thumb

Sc in each of next 9 sts *only* for 2 rows, dec 1 st at both ends of next 3 rows, fasten off. (3 sts)

Hand

Skipping thumb area just worked, join yarn with a sc, sk 1 sc, sc in rem 24 sts. (25 sts)

Work even in sc until there is a total of 10 rows from beg of hand, dec 1 st at both ends of every row until 11 sts rem, fasten off.

Front

With larger hook and white, work as for back until there is a total of 3 rows.

Bobble placement

Row 1 (WS): Sc in each of first 6 sc, [mbb in next sc, sc in each of next 7 sc] twice, ending mbb in next sc, sc in each of last 2 sc], ch 1, turn.

Rows 2–4: Sc across all sts, ch 1, turn.

Row 5 (WS): Sc in each of first 2 sc, [mbb in next sc, sc in each of next 7 sc] twice, ending mbb in next sc, sc in each of last 6 sc, ch 1, turn.

Rows 6–8: Sc in each st across, ch 1, turn.

Continue in est bobble patt, when there is a total of 24 rows, work thumb inc.

Thumb Inc: [2 sc in last sc at end of next row, ch 1, turn, 2 sc in first sc at beg of next row, ch 1, turn] 5 times, *at the same time maintain est bobble patt,* ch 1, turn. (35 sts)

Hand

Work across first 25 sts *only* for hand. Work as for hand back, keeping to est bobble patt.

Thumb

Re-join yarn with a sc at thumb by skipping hand sts, sk 1 sc, sc across 8 rem sc, ch 1, turn. (9 sts)

Thumb Dec: Work 1 row even. Dec 1 st at both ends of next 3 rows, fasten off. (3 sts)

Finishing

Work lazy-daisy leaves with 2 strands myrtle green around bobbles as shown in photo.

Joining front & back

Place front and back tog with WS facing and working through both thicknesses, beg at right wrist edge of front with front facing, with larger hook and marine blue, attach yarn with a sc and work in sc in corresponding rows all around to left wrist edge, fasten off.

Re-join marine blue at right side as before with smaller hook, work picot edging around sc as for dishcloth, fasten off.

Wrist edging

With larger hook and marine blue yarn, join with a sl st at thumb side of front with RS facing, sc into edging, sc across opposite side of front foundation ch, sc into edging, sc across opposite side of back foundation ch, join with a sl st in first sc.

Change to smaller hook and work picot edging all around with RS facing, ending with ch 14, sl st to first st to form hanger, fasten off.

Lining

Using the crocheted mitt bottom as a pattern, cut 2 pieces of batting and 4 pieces of fabric in the shape of the mitt, reversing 2. For each side of mitt, sandwich a piece of batting between 2 pieces of fabric, with RS of fabric facing out. Pin tog, zigzag around edges 3 times.

Turn crocheted mitt inside out. Sew edges of linings around edges of each side of mitt separately. Turn RS out.

With myrtle green, work half-cross sts on sc row in every other st of all *top* edgings as per photo.

Dish Detergent Apron

Row 1: With larger hook and white, ch 18, sc in 2nd ch from hook and in each ch across, ch 1,

turn. (17 sts)

Row 2: Sc in each st across, ch 1, turn.

Row 3 (RS): 2 sc in first sc, sc across to last sc, 2 sc in last sc, ch 1, turn. (19 sc)

Row 4 (WS): Sc in each of first 5 sc, mbb, sc in each of next 7 sc, mbb, sc in each of rem 5 sc.

Row 5: Rep Row 3, ch 1, turn. (21 sc)

Rows 6 & 7: Rep Row 2.

Row 8 (WS): Sc in each of first 2 sc, mbb, [sc in each of next 7 sc, mbb] twice, ending with sc in each of last 2 sc, ch 1, turn.

Rows 9–11: Rep Row 2.

Row 12: Sc in each of first 6 sc, mbb, sc in each of next 7 sc, mbb, sc in each of last 6 sc, ch 1, turn.

Rows 13–15: Rep Row 2.

Row 16: Rep Row 8.

Rows 17–19: Work first 2 sc tog, sc in each sc across to last 2 sc, work last 2 sc tog, ch 1, turn. (19, 17, 15 sc)

Row 20: Work first 2 sc tog, sc in next sc, mbb, sc in each of next 7 sc, mbb, sc in next sc, sc last 2 sc tog, ch 1, turn. (13 sts)

Row 21: Rep Row 17. (11 sts)

Rows 22 & 23: Sc in each st across, ch 1, turn.

Row 24: Sc in each of first 5 sc, mbb, sc in each of rem 5 sc, ch 1, turn.

Rows 25–27: Rep Row 3. (13, 15, 17 sc)

Row 28: Sc in each of first 4 sc, mbb, sc in each of next 7 sc, mbb, sc in each of rem 4 sc, ch 1, turn.

Row 29: Rep Row 3. (19 sc)

Rows 30 & 31: Rep Row 2.

Row 32: Sc in first sc, mbb, [sc in each of next 7 sc, mbb] twice, sc in last sc, ch 1, turn.

Rows 33–35: Rep Row 17. (17, 15, 13 sc)

Row 36: Sc in each of first 4 sc, mbb, sc in each of next 7 sc, mbb, sc in each of rem 2 sc, ch 1, turn.

Rows 37 & 38: Rep Row 17, fasten off. (11, 9 sc)

Finishing

Work lazy-daisy sts with 2 strands myrtle green around bobbles as shown in photo.

Edging

With larger hook and marine blue, beg at bottom edge, attach yarn with a sc in any st and work

Continued on Page 127

Pot Holder Magic

Add zip to your kitchen decor with any of these bright and cheerful
pot holders! You're sure to find a style to suit your taste and decor.

Cookie Pot Holder

Let's Begin!

Experience Level: Beginner

Size: 7¼" in diameter

Materials
☐ Bernat® Berella "4"® 4-ply yarn: 2 oz pale tapestry gold #8887, small amount walnut #8916

☐ Size G/6 crochet hook

☐ Yarn needle

Gauge: 4 dc and 2 dc rnds = 1"

To save time, take time to check gauge.

Pattern Note: Join rnds with a sl st unless otherwise stated.

Front & Back *(Make 2)*
Rnd 1: With pale tapestry gold, ch 4, join to form a ring, ch 3, 7 dc in ring, join in 3rd ch of beg ch-3. (8)

Rnd 2: Ch 3, dc in same st as ch-3, 2 dc in each dc around, join in 3rd ch of beg ch-3. (16)

Rnd 3: Ch 3, 2 dc in next dc, [dc in next dc, 2 dc in next dc] rep around, join in 3rd ch of beg ch-3. (24)

Rnd 4: Ch 3, dc in same st as ch-3, 2 dc in each rem dc around, join in 3rd ch of beg ch-3. (48)

Rnd 5: Ch 3, dc in each of next 2 dc, 2 dc in next dc, [dc in each of next 3 dc, 2 dc in next dc] rep around, join in 3rd ch of beg ch-3. (60)

Rnd 6: Ch 3, dc in each of next 3 dc, 2 dc in next dc, [dc in each of next 4 dc, 2 dc in next dc] rep around, join in 3rd ch of beg ch-3. (72)

Rnd 7: Ch 3, dc in each of next 5 dc, 2 dc in next dc, [dc in each of next 6 dc, 2 dc in next dc] rep around, ending with dc in each of last 2 dc, join in 3rd ch of beg ch-3, fasten off. (82)

Chocolate Chips *(Make 7)*
With walnut, ch 4, join to form a ring, ch 1, 8 sc in ring, join in beg sc, fasten off, leaving a 6" length of yarn.

Finishing
Sew chocolate chips onto front of pot holder.

With WS of front and back held tog, attach pale tapestry gold in any st, ch 1, working in both lps of each piece, sc in each dc around, join in beg sc, ch 15 (hanging lp), join to beg ch, fasten off.

—Designed by Becky Adams

Daisy Pot Holder

Let's Begin!

Experience Level: Beginner

Size: 7½" in diameter

Materials
☐ Bernat® Berella "4"® 4-ply yarn: 1 oz each gold #0007, green #0002 and white #0001

☐ Size G/6 crochet hook

Gauge: 4 sc and 3 sc rows = 1"

To save time, take time to check gauge.

Pattern Note: Join rnds with a sl st unless otherwise stated.

Front & Back *(Make 2)*
Rnd 1: With gold, ch 2, 6 sc in 2nd ch from hook, mark for beg of rnd.

Rnd 2: 2 sc in each st around, join in beg sc, fasten off. (12 sts)

Rnd 3: Attach white in last st made, working in back lps only, *ch 4, [tr, ch 4, sl st] in same st, sl st in next st, rep from * around, join in base ch of beg ch-4.

Rnd 4: Sl st in each ch of beg ch-4 (to top of first tr), [ch 3, sl st in next tr] rep around, join in base of beg ch-3.

Rnd 5: Sl st to next ch-3 sp, *[ch 4, tr, ch 4, sl st] in same ch-3 sp, sl st in next sl st, sl st in next ch-3 sp, [ch 4, tr, ch 4, sl st, ch 4, tr, ch 4, sl st] in same ch-3 sp, sl st in next sl st, sl st in next ch-3 sp, rep from * around, join in base of beg ch-4. (18 petals)

Rnd 6: Sl st in each ch of beg ch-4, [ch 3, sl st in next tr] rep around, join in base of beg ch-3, fasten off.

Rnd 7: Attach green in any ch-3 sp, 4 sc in same sp, [sk next sl st, 5 sc in next ch-3 sp] rep around, join in beg sc.

Continued on Page 126

Gingham Kitchen Set

Make this cheerful four-piece kitchen set in a charming gingham pattern to brighten up your kitchen!

Place Mat

Row 1: With true blue and size G hook, ch 67, sc in 2nd ch from hook, sc in each of next 4 chs, to change color on next sc, work sc with true blue until 2 lps rem on hook, yo with blue jewel to complete sc, working over yarn not in use, sc in each of next 6 chs, changing back to true blue on 6th sc, laying old color over new before yo with new color, continue across, alternating 6 sc with true blue and 6 sc with blue jewel, do not change color on last sc of row, carry yarn not in use up side by laying it over yarn in use, ch 1, turn.

*Work a total of 6 rows, alternating 6 sc true blue

with 6 sc blue jewel for a total of 11 blocks across.

Change to blue jewel on last sc of Row 6, fasten off true blue at end of Row 6.

Work next 6 rows alternating 6 sc with blue jewel and 6 sc with white, working color changes as before and working over yarn not in use.

Rep from * for block colors and changes, work 7 sets of blocks in length, 11 blocks wide.

At end of last row, fasten off.

Edging

Rnd 1: Attach white yarn to first sc worked on last row worked, ch 1, sc in same st as ch-1, [sc in each

Let's Begin!

Experience Level: Beginner

Size
Place Mat: 13½" x 18"
Pot Holder: 6½" square
Towel Topper: fits towel 16" wide
Napkin Ring: 2½" wide x 2" in diameter

Materials
☐ Bernat® Nice 'n Soft® 4-ply yarn (3½ oz per skein): 1 skein each blue jewel #4634 and white #4711 and true blue #4641

☐ Crochet cotton size 10: small amounts each hunter's green, Spanish red, lemon peel and peach

☐ Size 7 steel crochet hook

☐ Size G/6 crochet hook or size needed to obtain gauge

☐ 16"-wide terry kitchen towel, cut in half

☐ ⅝"-diameter light blue shank button

☐ White sewing thread

☐ Sewing needle

☐ Yarn needle

☐ Tapestry needle

Gauge: 4 sc and 4 sc rows = 1" with size G crochet hook

To save time, take time to check gauge.

Pattern Note: Join rnds with a sl st unless otherwise stated.

st across, with {sc, ch 1, sc} in last st to turn corner] rep around, join in beg sc. (43 sc on short sides between each corner ch-1 sp; 67 sc on long sides)

Rnds 2–4: Ch 1, sc in same st as ch-1, [sc in each st around, with sc, ch 1, sc in corner ch-1 sp] rep around, join in beg sc, at end of Rnd 4, fasten off.

Rnd 5: Sk first 3 sc after ch-1 sp on long side, attach white to next sc, *sk next 2 sc, 6 dc in next sc, sk next 2 sc, sl st in next sc *, rep from * to * for 11 scallops total, sk next 2 sc, 3 dc in next sc, 3 dc in ch-1 sp, 3 dc in next sc, sk next 2 sc, sl st in next sc (corner scallop), rep from * to * for 7 scallops total, work corner scallop, complete rem in

same manner, join in beg st, fasten off.

Rnd 6: Attach true blue to first dc on first scallop, ch 1, sc in same st as ch-1 and in each of next 5 dc, *sl st in next sl st, sc in each of next 6 dc, rep from * across, sl st in next sl st, sc in each of first 3 dc of corner scallop, [2 sc in next dc] 3 times, sc in each of next 3 dc, rep from * to complete rnd in same manner, join in beg st, fasten off.

Pot Holder
Beg with ch 21, work as for place mat, except blocks consist of 4 sc by 4 rows, making 5 blocks wide x 5 blocks in length.

Edging
Rnd 1: Attach white to first sc worked on last row of pot holder, ch 1, sc evenly sp around entire outer edge, with [sc, ch 1, sc] in each corner st, join in beg sc.

Rnd 2: Sl st in next sc, ch 1, sc in same st as ch-1, *ch 2, yo, insert hook from front to back around post of last sc worked, complete a hdc st, sk next st, sc in next st (the sc is vertical and the hdc ends up being horizontal over the post of the sc st)*, rep from * to * across edge, ending with sc in last sc on side, ch 10 for hanging lp, sl st in 10th ch from hook, sk ch-1 sp, sc in next sc, rep from * to * around, join in beg st, fasten off.

Towel Topper
Scallop Edging
Row 1: With white, ch 37, 2 sc in 2nd ch from hook, sc in each rem ch across, ch 1, turn. (37)

Row 2: Sl st in first sc, *sk next 2 sc, 6 dc in next sc, sk 2 sc, sl st in next sc, rep from * across for a total of 6 scallops, do not turn, fasten off.

Row 3: Attach true blue to first sl st on Row 2, *sc in each of next 6 dc, sl st in next sl st, rep from * across, fasten off.

Towel Preparation
Cut kitchen towel in half width-wise. Fold raw edge under; sew with sewing ndl and thread.

Row 1: With white and WS of sewn edge of towel facing, work 36 sc evenly sp across edge of towel, ch 1, turn.

Row 2: With RS of towel facing, place opposite side of foundation ch of scallop edge to sts of Row

1 of towel preparation, working through both thicknesses, work 36 sc sts across, fasten off.

Gingham Topper

Row 1: Working in gingham patt for rem of piece, attach blue jewel to first sc, dec 1 sc over this and next sc, work 1 more sc with blue jewel, then 6 sc true blue, 6 sc blue jewel, 6 sc true blue, 6 sc blue jewel, 6 sc true blue, sc with blue jewel, dec 1 sc over next 2 sc with blue jewel, ch 1, turn. (34)

Rows 2–8: Keeping in gingham patt, dec 1 sc at beg and end of row, ch 1, turn. (At the end of Row 8, 20 sc will rem)

Rows 9–17 (odd rows): Sc in each st across, ch 1, turn.

Rows 10–18 (even rows): Dec 1 sc over next 2 sc, sc across in patt to within last 2 sc, dec 1 sc over next 2 sc, ch 1, turn. (At end of Row 18, 10 sc will rem)

Rows 19–33: Work even in gingham patt.

Row 34: Working in gingham patt, sc in each of first 4 sc, ch 2, sk next 2 sc (buttonhole), sc in each of next 4 sc, ch 1, turn.

Rows 35 & 36: Dec 1 sc over next 2 sc, sc in each st across to within last 2 sts, dec 1 sc over next 2 sts, ch 1, turn, at end of Row 36, fasten off.

Sew button at center front sc of Row 21.

Napkin Ring

Row 1: With true blue, ch 5, sc in 2nd ch from hook, sc in each rem ch across, turn. (4)

Rows 2–4: Ch 1, sc in each sc across, turn.

Rows 5–8: With blue jewel, ch 1, sc in each sc across, turn.

Rows 9–12: With true blue, ch 1, sc in each sc across, turn.

[Rep Rows 5–12] twice.

[Rep Rows 5–8] once.

At end of last rep, fasten off.

Sew last row to opposite side of foundation ch.

Trim

Note: *Trim is worked on each edge of rows.*

Rnd 1: Attach white, ch 1, 24 sc evenly sp around, join in beg sc.

Rnd 2: Ch 1, sc in same st as ch-1, *ch 2, yo,

insert hook from front to back around post of last sc worked, complete a hdc st, sk next st, sc in next st, rep from * around, join in beg st, fasten off.

Flowers & Leaves

Large Flower *(Make 5)*

Rnd 1: With yellow crochet cotton and size 7 steel crochet hook, ch 4, 9 dc in 4th ch from hook, drop yellow, join with red or peach cotton in 4th ch of beg ch-4, fasten off yellow. (10)

Rnd 2: [Ch 4, hdc in 2nd ch from hook, hdc in each of next 2 chs, sl st in next dc] 10 times, fasten off, leaving a length of crochet cotton.

Small Flower *(Make 6)*

Rnd 1: With size 7 steel crochet hook and yellow crochet cotton, ch 3, 8 hdc in 3rd ch from hook, drop yellow, join with red or peach crochet cotton in 3rd ch of beg ch-3, fasten off yellow. (9)

Rnd 2: [Ch 3, hdc in 2nd ch from hook, hdc in next ch, sl st in next hdc] 9 times, fasten off, leaving a length of crochet cotton.

Leaf *(Make 22)*

Row 1: With size 7 steel crochet hook and hunter's green crochet cotton, ch 9, dc in 3rd ch from hook, tr in each of next 3 chs, dc in each of next 2 chs, sc, ch 2 and sc in last ch, working on opposite side of foundation ch, dc in each of next 2 chs, tr in each of next 3 chs, dc in next ch, ch 2, sl st in same st, fasten off, leaving a length of cotton.

Finishing

Note: *When sewing flowers and leaves to each piece in set, backstitch around center of each flower and down center of each leaf.*

With tapestry ndl, sew 1 large flower, 1 small flower and 2 leaves for each to center of napkin ring.

Sew 1 large flower, 2 small flowers and 2 leaves for each to center front of towel topper.

Sew 1 large flower, 1 small flower and 2 leaves for each to pot holder in same corner as hanging lp.

Sew 1 large flower, 1 small flower and 2 leaves each in lower left corner of place mat.

Sew rem large flower, small flower and 2 leaves each to upper right corner of place mat.

—Designed by Rosanne Kropp

Lacy Luncheon Set

*Serve up a special ladies' luncheon or Sunday
brunch with this pretty place mat and napkin ring set!*

Let's Begin!

Experience Level: Beginner

Size
Place Mat: 12" x 17"
Napkin Ring: 2½" wide x 6" in diameter

Materials
☐ Bernat® Handicrafter® crochet cotton size 10:
400 yds white #500, and small amount pale
pink #514
☐ Size 7 steel crochet hook
☐ Starch

Gauge: 7 dc and 3 dc rows = ¾"

To save time, take time to check gauge.

Pattern Note: Join rnds with a sl st unless
otherwise stated.

Place Mat

Row 1: With white, ch 102, dc in 4th ch from
hook, dc in each of next 2 chs, [ch 4, sk 4 chs, dc in
each of next 4 chs] 12 times, turn. (13 4-dc groups)

Row 2: Ch 3, dc in each of next 3 dc, [ch 3, sc in
next ch-4 sp, ch 3, dc in each of next 4 dc] 12
times, turn.

Row 3: Ch 3, dc in each of next 3 dc, [ch 4, dc in
each of next 4 dc] 12 times, turn.

Row 4: Ch 7 (counts as first dc, ch 4), sk 4 dc, [4
dc in ch-4 sp, ch 4, sk 4 dc] 11 times, 4 dc in next
ch-4 sp, ch 4, sk 3 dc, dc in next dc, turn.

Row 5: Ch 6 (counts as first dc, ch 3), sc in ch-4 sp,
ch 3, dc in each of next 4 dc, [ch 3, sc in next ch-4
sp, ch 3, dc in each of next 4 dc] 11 times, ch 3, sc
in next ch-4 sp, ch 3, dc in 3rd ch of ch-7, turn.

Row 6: Ch 7, [dc in each of next 4 dc, ch 4] 12

times, dc in 3rd ch of ch-6, turn.

Row 7: Ch 3, dc in each of next 3 chs, [ch 4, sk 4
dc, dc in each of next 4 chs] 12 times, turn.

Rows 8–55: Rep Rows 2–7.

Rows 56 & 57: Rep Rows 2 and 3, at end of Row
57, fasten off.

Edging
Rnd 1: Attach pale pink in end of Row 57, ch 3,
dc evenly sp around entire outer edge, join in 3rd
ch of beg ch-3, fasten off.

Rnd 2: Attach white in any dc, ch 1, sc in same dc,
ch 4, sk 2 dc, [sc in next dc, ch 4, sk 2 dc] rep
around, join in beg sc.

Rnd 3: Sl st into ch-4 sp, ch 1, in same ch-4 sp,
sc, ch 6, sc in 3rd ch from hook, ch 3, sc in same
ch-4 sp, ch 2, [in next ch-4 sp, sc, ch 6, sc in 3rd
ch from hook, ch 3, sc in same ch-4 sp, ch 2] rep

Continued on Page 131

Pretty Petals

*This toaster cover with matching pot holders will
add a pretty touch of freshness to your summertime kitchen.*

Let's Begin!

Experience Level: Beginner

Size
Toaster Cover: Fits 2-slice toaster
Round Pot Holder: 6½"in diameter
Square Pot Holder: 7" square

Materials
☐ 4-ply acrylic or cotton yarn: 9 oz rose pink, 3 oz off-white and small amount olive green

☐ Size G/6 crochet hook or size needed to obtain gauge

☐ 2 plastic ⅝" rings

☐ 15 straight pins

☐ Yarn needle

Gauge: 7 sc and 8 sc rows = 2"

To save time, take time to check gauge.

Pattern Notes: Weave in loose ends as work progresses.

Join rnds with a sl st unless otherwise stated.

Toaster Cover

Center Panel
Row 1: With rose pink yarn, ch 17, sc in 2nd ch from hook, sc in each rem ch across, ch 1, turn. (16)

Rows 2–80: Sc in each sc across, ch 1, turn.

At the end of Row 80, fasten off, leaving a long length of yarn.

Side Panels (Make 2)
Row 1: With rose pink yarn, ch 30, sc in 2nd ch from hook, sc in each rem ch across, ch 1, turn. (29)

Rows 2–25: Sc in each sc across, ch 1, turn.

At the end of Row 25, fasten off.

Matching Row 1 and Row 80 of center panels to each end of Row 1 of first side panel, pin pieces together with straight pins. With yarn needle and rem length of rose pink, sew pieces together. Remove pins. Rep in same manner on opposite edge of center panel with 2nd side panel.

Ruffle Trim (Make 3)
Row 1: With off-white yarn, ch 65, sc in 2nd ch from hook, 3 dc in next ch, [sc in next ch, 3 dc in next ch] rep across, fasten off leaving a long length of yarn.

Using straight pins, pin ruffle trim over joining seam of side panel and center panel. With rem length of off-white yarn, sew ruffle to cover.

Rep in same manner on opposite joining seam with 2nd ruffle piece.

Flowers (Make 3)
Rnd 1: With rose pink yarn, ch 2, 6 sc in 2nd ch from hook, join in front lps only, do not turn. (6)

Rnd 2: Working in front lps only, ch 1, work 5 sc in same st as beg ch-1, work 5 sc in each rem front lp around, join in beg sc, fasten off. (30)

Rnd 3: Working in rem free back lps of Rnd 1, attach off-white yarn in any st, ch 3 (first dc), work 7 dc in same st as beg ch-3, work 8 dc in each rem st around, join in top of beg ch-3, fasten off. (48)

Sew 1 flower centered on top of center panel of cover. Sew 1 flower centered on each side of side panels.

Leaves (Make 6)
Row 1: With olive green yarn, ch 5, sc in 2nd ch from hook, sc in each next 2 chs, 3 sc in last ch, working on opposite side of foundation ch, sc in each next 3 chs, leaving a length of yarn, fasten off.

With yarn needle and rem length of yarn, sew 1 leaf to cover to both sides of each flower.

Square Pot Holder

Back
Row 1: With rose pink yarn, ch 24, sc in 2nd ch from hook, sc in each rem ch across, ch 1, turn. (23)

Rows 2–24: Sc in each sc across, ch 1, turn.

At the end of Row 24, fasten off.

Front
Rows 1–23: Rep Rows 1–23 of back.

Row 24: Sc in each sc across, ch 1, turn.

Rnd 25: Holding front and back of pot holder together and working through both thicknesses, sc evenly sp around entire outer edge, join in beg sc, fasten off.

Ruffle Trim
Rnd 1: Attach off-white yarn in any sc of Rnd 25,

ch 3 (first dc), 2 dc in same sc as beg ch-3, work 3 dc in each sc around entire outer edge, join in 3rd ch of beg ch-3, fasten off.

Finishing

Make 1 flower and 2 leaves for toaster cover. Sew flower and leaves to the center front of pot holder.

Sew 1 plastic ring to back of pot holder in any corner of Rnd 25.

Round Pot Holder

Back

Note: Do not join rnds unless otherwise indicated. Use a scrap of CC yarn to mark rnds.

Rnd 1: With rose pink yarn, ch 2, 6 sc in 2nd ch from hook. (6)

Rnd 2: Work 2 sc in each sc around. (12)

Rnd 3: [Sc in next sc, 2 sc in next sc] rep around. (18)

Rnd 4: [Sc in each of next 2 sc, 2 sc in next sc] rep around. (24)

Rnd 5: [Sc in each of next 3 sc, 2 sc in next sc] rep around. (30)

Rnd 6: Sc in each sc around.

Rnd 7: [Sc in each of next 4 sc, 2 sc in next sc] rep around. (36)

Rnd 8: [Sc in each of next 5 sc, 2 sc in next sc] rep around. (42)

Rnd 9: Rep Rnd 6.

Rnd 10: [Sc in each of next 6 sc, 2 sc in next sc] rep around. (48)

Rnd 11: [Sc in each of next 7 sc, 2 sc in next sc] rep around. (54)

Rnd 12: Rep Rnd 6.

Rnd 13: [Sc in each of next 8 sc, 2 sc in next sc] rep around. (60)

Rnd 14: [Sc in each of next 9 sc, 2 sc in next sc] rep around, sl st in next sc, fasten off. (66)

Front

Rnds 1–14: Rep Rnds 1–14 of back.

Ruffle Trim

Rnd 1: Holding front and back of pot holder tog and working through both thicknesses, attach off-white yarn, ch 3, 2 dc in same st as beg ch-3, work 3 dc in each sc around, join in 3rd ch of beg ch-3, fasten off.

Finishing

Make 1 flower and 2 leaves as for toaster cover. Sew flower and leaves to center front of pot holder.

Sew 1 plastic ring to back of pot holder over Rnd 14.

—Designed by Barbara Badde

Pot Holder Magic

Continued from Page 119

Rnds 8 & 9: Ch 1, sc in each st around, join in beg sc, fasten off at end of Rnd 9.

Center

Working in front lps only, attach white in any st on Rnd 2, [ch 2, hdc, ch 2, sl st] in same st, *sl st in next st, [ch 2, hdc, ch 2, sl st] in same st, rep from * around, join, fasten off.

Finishing

With WS tog, attach green through both thicknesses in any st of last rnd, ch 10, sl st in base st where yarn was attached, 15 sc in ring (forms hanging ring), sc in next st of pot holder through both thicknesses and in each st around, join in beg sc, fasten off.

—Designed by Eileen Duffield

Mother's Rose Pot Holder

Body

Row 1: With China rose, ch 31, sc in 2nd ch from hook, sc in each rem ch across, ch 1, turn. (30)

Let's Begin!

Experience Level: Beginner

Size: 6¾" x 5¾"

Materials
- [ ] Bernat® Berella "4"® 4-ply yarn: small amounts each China rose #8923 and pale tapestry gold #8887
- [ ] Size G/6 crochet hook
- [ ] Large yarn needle

Gauge: 4 sc and 5 sc rows = 1"

To save time, take time to check gauge.

Pattern Note: Each square of graph is 1 sc.

Rows 2–29: Sc in each sc across, ch 1, turn.

Row 30: Sc in each sc across, ch 10 (hanging lp), sl st in beg ch, fasten off.

Finishing

With yarn ndl and pale tapestry gold, working in cross-st, embroider rose patt on front of pot holder following graph.

Work all loose ends into piece.

—Designed by Brenda Neely

CHART A

COLOR KEY
☐ China rose   ☒ Pale tapestry gold

Scrap Yarn Pot Holders

Motif *(Make 18)*

Rnd 1: With blue, ch 5, join to form a ring, ch 3 (counts as first dc), 15 dc in ring, join in 3rd ch of beg ch-3, fasten off.

Rnd 2: With yellow, join with sc in first st, ch 1, [dc in sp between next 2 dc, ch 1, sk next st, sc in next st, ch 1] rep around, join to beg sc, do not fasten off. (16 ch-1 lps)

Rnd 3: [Sc in next ch-1 sp, ch 2] rep around, join to beg sc, fasten off.

Rnd 4: With red, join with sl st in any ch-2 sp, [ch 3 (counts as first dc), 2 dc] in same sp, 3 dc in each ch-2 sp around, join in 3rd ch of beg ch-3, fasten off. (48 dc)

Rnd 5: Working in back lps only, with green, join with sc in first st, [hdc in each of next 2 sts, dc in each of next 2 sts, 2 tr in next st, ch 2, 2 tr in next st, dc in each of next 2 sts, hdc in each of next 2 sts, sc in each of next 2 sts] rep around, ending

Let's Begin!

Experience Level: Beginner

Size: 7½" square

Materials
☐ Crochet cotton size 10: 30 yds blue, 60 yds yellow, 60 yds red and 70 yds green *or* 220 yds assorted colors
☐ Size 4 hook

Gauge: 1 motif = 2¼"

To save time, take time to check gauge.

Pattern Note: Join rnds with a sl st unless otherwise stated.

with sc in last st, join in beg hdc, fasten off.

Rnd 6: With yellow, join with sc in first st, sc in each st around with [sc, ch 2, sc] in each ch-2 corner sp, fasten off.

Joining Motifs

Sew 3 rows of 3 squares each tog for each side.

Border

Rnd 1: With WS tog, join with sc in any corner ch-2 sp, ch 25, sk 2 sc, sc in next st, sc in each st around with 3 sc in each corner, join to beg sc.

Rnd 2: Sl st in each ch of hanging lp and each sc around, fasten off.

—Designed by Pamela McKee

Blueberry Delight

Continued from Page 117

evenly in sc around entire apron, join with a sl st in first sc, fasten off.

Change to smaller hook and marine blue, attach yarn on underside of both sides of waist, work an 11" ch, fasten off.

Backing

Using crochet apron as a pattern, cut a piece of fabric the shape of apron. Fold edges under ¼" and, with WS tog, sew onto back of apron just under the edging.

—Designed by Michele Maks Thompson for Coats & Clark

Old-Fashioned Pot Holders

Stitch this trio of pot holders to add to your kitchen decor. Work them in pastels for a soft, delicate look or brighter colors for a more vibrant look.

Round Pot Holder

Center (*Make 2*)

Rnd 1: With creme, ch 4, join to form a ring, ch 3 (counts as first dc), 15 dc in ring, join in beg dc, ch 1. (16)

Rnd 2: [Sc in sc, 3 dc in next sc] rep around, join in beg sc, fasten off.

Rnd 3: Attach aqua in any center dc of 3-dc group, ch 1, sc in same dc, 5 dc in next sc, [sc in center dc of next 3-dc group, 5 dc in next sc] rep around, join in beg sc.

Rnd 4: Ch 4 (counts as first dc, ch 1), [ch 1, sc in center dc of next 5-dc group, ch 1, 1 dc, ch 1 and 1 dc in next sc] rep around, ending with dc in same st as beg ch-4, ch 1, join in 3rd ch of beg ch-4.

Let's Begin!

Experience Level: Beginner

Size
Round Pot Holder: 7" in diameter
Square Pot Holder: 6" square
Hexagonal Pot Holder: 6" in diameter

Materisals
☐ Bernat® Tradition® crochet cotton size 10 (150 yds per ball):
  Round Pot Holder: 1 ball each aqua #528 and creme #502
  Square Pot Holder: 1 ball each amethyst #523, French Pink #515, mint green #530 and creme #502
  Hexagon Pot Holder: 1 ball each amethyst #523, true blue #527 and creme #502

☐ Size 10 steel crochet hook

Gauge
Round Pot Holder: Rnds 1–3 = 1½"
Square Pot Holder: 3 rnds of front = 1"
Hexagonal Pot Holder: Rnds 1–3 = 1½"

Pattern Note: Join rnds with a sl st unless otherwise stated.

Rnd 5: Sl st to ch-1 sp between dc sts, ch 3 (counts as first dc), dc, ch 2, 2 dc in same ch-1 sp between dc sts, [2 dc, ch 2, 2 dc in next sc st and in next ch-1 sp between dc sts] rep around, join in beg dc. (16 shells)

Rnd 6: Sl st in ch-2 sp of shell, ch 3, 2 dc, ch 2, 3 dc in same ch-2 sp, [3 dc, ch 2, 3 dc in next ch-2 sp of shell] rep around, join in beg dc.

Rnd 7: Sl st in ch-2 sp of shell, ch 3, 3 dc, ch 2, 4 dc in same ch-2 sp, [4 dc, ch 2, 4 dc in next ch-2 sp of shell] rep around, join in beg dc.

Rnd 8: Sl st in ch-2 sp of shell, ch 3, 4 dc, ch 2, 5 dc in same ch-2 sp of shell, [5 dc, ch 2, 5 dc in next ch-2 sp of shell] rep around, join in beg dc, sl st in next dc, ch 1.

Rnd 9: [Sc in each of next 4 dc, sc, ch 2 and sc in ch-2 sp, sc in each of next 4 dc, ch 2, sk 2 dc] rep around, join in beg sc, fasten off.

Border
Rnd 10: With WS tog, working through both thicknesses, draw up a lp of creme through ch-2 sps of both sides at ch-2 point of shell, ch 1, [sc, ch 2 and sc in ch-2 sp of point of shell, ch 3, sc in next ch-2 sp between shells, ch 3] rep around, join in beg sc, sl st in ch-2 sp at point of shell.

Rnd 11: Ch 4 (counts as first tr), 6 tr in same ch-2 sp, ch 3, sc in next sc, ch 3, [7 tr in next ch-2 sp at point of shell, ch 3, sc in next sc, ch 3] rep around, join in beg tr, fasten off.

Rnd 12: Draw up a lp of aqua in first tr of tr group, ch 3 (counts as first dc), dc in each of next 2 tr, 3 dc in center tr, dc in each of next 3 tr, 2 dc in each of next 2 ch-3 sps, [dc in each of next 3 tr, 3 dc in center tr, dc in each of next 3 tr, 2 dc in each of next 2 ch-3 sps] rep around, join in beg dc, ch 1.

Rnd 13: Sc in each dc around, join in beg sc, fasten off.

Rnd 14: With creme, draw up a lp in any sc above 2nd dc in ch-3 sp to left of any shell, ch 1, [sc in 2 sc, ch 2, sk 2 sc, sc in next sc, ch 2, sk 2 sc, sc, ch 3 and sc in next sc (point of shell), ch 2, sk 2 sc, sc in next sc, ch 2, sk 2 sc] rep around, working hanging lp at any point of shell with sc, ch 18, sc in 2nd ch from hook, sc in each rem ch across, turn ch to right and in back of first sc to form lp, sl st in end ch, sc in same sc, join at end of rnd, fasten off.

Square Pot Holder
Front
Rnd 1 (RS): With French pink, ch 4, join to form a ring, ch 1, 8 sc in ring, join in beg sc, ch 1. (8)

Rnd 2: Sc in same sc as ch-1, ch 2, [sc in next sc, ch 2] rep around, join in beg sc, ch 1.

Rnd 3: [Sc in sc, 3 dc in next ch-2 sp] rep around, join in beg sc, ch 1.

Rnd 4: [Sc in sc, ch 2 behind group of 3 dc sts] rep around, join in beg sc, ch 1.

Rnd 5: [Sc in sc, 5 dc over ch-2 sp] rep around, join in beg sc, ch 1.

Rnd 6: [Sc in sc, ch 3 behind 5-dc group] rep around, join in beg sc, ch 1.

Rnd 7: [Sc in sc, 7 dc over ch-3 sp] rep around, join in beg sc, ch 1.

Rnd 8: [Sc, ch 2 and sc in sc, ch 2, sk 3 dc, sc, ch 2 and sc in next dc, ch 2, sk 3 dc] rep around, join in beg sc, sl st in ch-2 sp.

Rnd 9: Ch 4 (counts as first tr), 8 tr in same ch-2

129

sp, sc in next ch-2 sp, [9 tr in next ch-2 sp, sc in next ch-2 sp] rep around, join in beg tr, fasten off.

Rnd 10: With amethyst, draw up a lp in 5th tr of any 9-tr group, ch 4 (counts as first tr), retaining last lp of each tr on hook, 2 tr in same st, yo and draw through all lps on hook, [ch 2, retaining last lp of each tr on hook, 3 tr in same st, yo, draw through all lps on hook] twice in same st as first tr cluster (corner), ch 4, dc in next sc, ch 4, sc in 5th tr of 9-tr group, ch 4, dc in next sc, ch 4, *3-tr cluster in 5th tr of 9-tr group, [ch 2, 3-tr cluster in same dc as previous cluster] twice, ch 4, dc in next sc, ch 4, sc in 5th tr of 9-tr group, ch 4, dc in next sc, ch 4, rep from * around, join in 4th ch of beg ch-4, fasten off.

Rnd 11: Attach creme in ch-4 sp to the left of any corner on edge (first ch-4 sp beyond last corner cluster), ch 3, 4 dc in same ch-4 sp, [5 dc in each ch-4 sp across to within first corner cluster, 5 dc in next ch-2 sp, tr, ch 2 and tr in top of next center cluster, 5 dc in next ch-2 sp] rep around, join in 3rd ch of beg ch-3.

Rnd 12: Ch 3 (counts as first dc), dc in each st around with [3 dc, ch 2, 3 dc] in each corner ch-2 sp, join in 3rd ch of beg ch-3, sl st in each of next 2 dc.

Rnd 13: Ch 3 (counts as first dc), 2 dc in same dc, sk 2 dc, [3 dc in next dc, sk 2 dc] rep around, with [3 dc, ch 2, 3 dc] in each corner ch-2 sp, join in 3rd ch of beg ch-3.

Rnd 14: Ch 3 (counts as first dc), dc in each dc around, with [3 dc, ch 2, 3 dc] in each corner ch-2 sp, join in 3rd ch of beg ch-3, ch 1, turn.

Rnd 15 (WS): [Sc between next 2 dc, ch 3, sk 3 dc] rep around, with [sc, ch 2, sc] in each corner ch-2 sp, join in beg sc, fasten off.

Back

Rnd 1: With mint green, ch 4, join to form a ring, ch 3 (counts as first dc), 3 dc in ring, ch 2, [4 dc in ring, ch 2] 3 times, join in beg dc.

Rnd 2: Ch 1, sc in each dc around, with [2 sc, ch 2, 2 sc] in each corner ch-2 sp, join in beg sc.

Rnd 3: Ch 3, dc in each sc around, with [2 dc, ch 2, 2 dc] in each corner ch-2 sp, join in beg dc.

Rnds 4–9: Rep Rnds 2 and 3, at end of Rnd 9, fasten off mint.

Draw up a lp of creme in 7th dc to left of any corner ch-2 sp, ch 1.

Rnds 10 & 11: Rep Rnds 2 and 3.

Rnd 12: Ch 3, dc in each dc around, with [2 dc, ch 2, 2 dc] in each corner ch-2 sp, join, ch 1, turn.

Rnd 13 (WS): Rep Rnd 15 of front, working ch 2 instead of ch 3.

Border

Rnd 1: With WS tog and front facing, draw up a lp of French pink in 5th sp to the right of any corner ch-2 sp, ch 1, working through ch sps of both thicknesses, sc in ch sp, [ch 2, sc in next ch sp] rep around, with sc, ch 2, sc in each corner ch-2 sp, join in beg sc, ch 1.

Rnd 2: [Sc in 1 sp, 2 dc, ch 2, 2 dc in next ch sp (shell)] rep around, with [3 dc, ch 2, 3 dc] in each of 3 corner ch-2 sps, [3 dc, ch 18 (hanging lp), sl st in first ch of ch-18, 3 dc] in 4th corner ch-2 sp, join in beg st, ch 1.

Rnd 3: Sc in next sc, [ch 2, sc, ch 2, sc in ch-2 sp of shell, ch 2, sc in next sc] rep around, working [ch 3, sc, ch 3, sc] in each ch-2 sp of 3 corner shells, [ch 3, sc in next sc] on 4th corner at hanging lp, ch 3, sc in sp between dc and ch, 24 sc over ch, sc in sp between ch and next dc, ch 3, sc in next sc, join in beg st, fasten off.

Weave in loose ends.

Hexagonal Pot Holder
Front

Rnd 1: With amethyst, ch 4, join to form a ring, ch 1, 12 sc in ring, join in beg sc, ch 1. (12)

Rnd 2: [Sc in sc, 2 dc, ch 2, 2 dc in next sc] rep around, join in beg sc, ch 1.

Rnd 3: [Sc in sc, ch 2, sc, ch 2, sc in ch-2 sp of shell, ch 2] rep around, join in beg sc.

Rnd 4: [Sc in sc, ch 2, sc, ch 3, sc in ch-2 sp of shell, ch 2] rep around, join in beg sc, fasten off.

Rnd 5: Draw up a lp of true blue in any ch-3 sp, ch 1, [sc, ch 2, sc in ch-3 sp, sc in next sc, 2 hdc in next ch-2 sp, dc in next sc, 2 hdc in next ch-2 sp, sc in next sc] rep around, join in beg sc.

Rnd 6: Ch 3 (counts as first dc), [dc, ch 2, dc in corner ch-2 sp, dc in each st across to next corner ch-2 sp] rep around, join in beg dc.

Rnd 7: Ch 3, dc, ch 2, 2 dc in ch-2 sp, [ch 1, sk 2 dc, 2 dc in next dc] 3 times, ch 1, sk 2 dc, *2 dc, ch 2, 2 dc in ch-2 sp, [ch 1, sk 2 dc, 2 dc in next dc] 3 times, ch 1, sk 2 dc, rep from * around, join in 3rd ch of beg ch-3.

Rnd 8: Ch 3, dc in each dc and each ch-1 sp around, with [2 dc, ch 2, 2 dc] in each ch-2 sp, join in 3rd ch of beg ch-3.

Rnd 9: Ch 3, dc in each dc around, with [dc, ch 2, dc] in each ch-2 sp, join in 3rd ch of beg ch-3.

Rnd 10: Ch 3, dc in same dc as ch-3, ch 1, sk 2 dc, 2 dc, ch 2, 2 dc in ch-2 sp, *[ch 1, sk 2 dc, 2 dc in next dc] 6 times, ch 1, sk 2 dc, 2 dc, ch 2, 2 dc in ch-2 sp, rep from * around, ending with rep between [] 5 times on last rep, ch 1, join in 3rd ch of beg ch-3.

Rnd 11: Sl st in next ch-1 sp, ch 3, dc in same ch sp, ch 1, 2 dc, ch 2, 2 dc in ch-2 sp, *[ch 1, 2 dc in next ch-1 sp] 7 times, ch 1, 2 dc, ch 2, 2 dc in ch-2 sp, rep from * around, ending with rep between [] 6 times on last rep, ch 1, join in 3rd ch of beg ch-3.

Rnd 12: Sl st into next ch-1 sp, ch 1, sc in ch-1 sp, *ch 2, sc, ch 2, sc in corner ch-2 sp, [ch 2, sc in next ch-1 sp] 8 times, rep from * around, ending with rep between [] 7 times on last rep, ch 2, join in beg st, fasten off.

Weave in loose ends.

Back

Rnds 1–6: Rep Rnds 1–6 of front, at end of Rnd 6, fasten off.

Rnd 7: With creme, draw up a lp in any dc, ch 3, dc in each dc around, with 2 dc, ch 2, 2 dc in ch-2 sp, join in 3rd ch of beg ch-3, fasten off.

Rnd 8: Attach true blue in any dc, ch 3, dc in each dc around, with [dc, ch 2, dc] in each ch-2 sp, join in 3rd ch of beg ch-3.

Rnd 9: Ch 3, dc in each dc around, with [2 dc, ch 2, 2 dc] in each ch-2 sp, join in 3rd ch of beg ch-3, fasten off.

Rnd 10: With creme, draw up a lp in 4th dc to left of any corner, ch 3, dc in each dc around, with [dc, ch 2, dc] in each ch-2 sp around, join in 3rd ch of beg ch-3.

Rnd 11: Rep Rnd 9, do not fasten off.

Rnd 12: Ch 1, [sc in dc, ch 2, sk 2 dc] rep around, with [sc, ch 2, sc] in each corner ch-2 sp, join in beg st, fasten off.

Weave in loose ends.

Border

Rnd 1: With WS tog, working through ch lps of both thicknesses, attach amethyst in ch-2 sp to left of corner sp, ch 1, 2 sc in same ch sp, ch 1, [2 sc in next ch sp, ch 1] rep around, with [sc, ch 2, sc] in each corner ch-2 sp, join in beg sc, sl st in next ch sp.

Rnd 2: Ch 1, sc in ch sp, ch 2, [sc in next ch sp, ch 2] rep around, with [sc, ch 2, sc] in each corner ch sp, join in beg sc, sl st in next ch sp.

Rnd 3: Ch 1, [sc in ch sp, 5 dc in next ch sp] rep around, at 1 corner ch-2 sp, make hanging lp of 3 dc in corner, ch 19, sc in 2nd ch from hook, sc in each rem ch across, turn ch to right and in back of last dc, sl st in end ch, sl st in side edge at top of last dc, work 2 dc in same corner ch sp, join in beg st, fasten off.

Weave in loose ends.

—Designed by Katherine Eng

Lacy Luncheon Set

Continued from Page 123

around, join in beg sc, fasten off.

Napkin Ring

Row 1: With white, ch 62, dc in 4th ch from hook, dc in each of next 3 chs, [ch 4, sk 4 chs, dc in each of next 4 chs] 7 times, ch 3, turn.

Row 2: Dc in each of next 3 dc, [ch 3, sc in next ch-4 sp, ch 3, dc in each of next 4 dc] 7 times, ch 3, turn.

Row 3: Dc in each of next 3 dc, [ch 4, dc in each of next 4 dc] 7 times, fasten off.

Edging

Row 1: Attach pale pink in Row 3 of napkin ring, ch 3, dc in each st across, fasten off.

Row 2: Attach white, ch 1, sc in same st, [ch 4, sk 2 dc, sc in next dc] rep across, ch 1, turn.

Row 3: Sl st in ch-4 sp, ch 1, [sc in ch-4 sp, ch 6, sc in 3rd ch from hook, ch 3, sc in same ch-4 sp] rep across, fasten off.

Rep Rows 1–3 in opposite side of foundation ch.

Sew ends of napkin ring tog. Starch pieces and allow to dry completely.

—Designed by Mary Viers

Home Sweet Home

The love and caring that make a house a home are evident in the warmth and comfort found inside. Add simple accents to your home that reflect the love within, or share a gift of caring with friends just starting a home of their own.

Doily Duet

Like early spring blossoms, a delicate red outline highlights the heart pattern in a decorative heart doily. And, seven pretty floral motifs joined together make for a striking accent doily.

Hearts in Blossom

Doily

Rnd 1: Ch 6, join to form a ring, ch 4 (counts as first tr), [4-tr cluster in ring, ch 5] 6 times, join in 4th ch of beg ch-4.

Rnd 2: Sl st to 3rd ch of ch-5, ch 4 (counts as first tr), 3 more tr in same st, [ch 5, 4 tr in center st of next ch-5] rep around, ending with ch 5, join in 4th ch of beg ch-4.

Rnd 3: Ch 4 (counts as first tr), [4-tr cluster over next 4 tr, ch 5, tr in next sp, ch 5] rep around, join in 4th ch of beg ch-4.

Rnd 4: *Ch 6, 3 tr in next tr, ch 6, sc in top of cluster, rep from * around, join in first ch of beg ch-6.

Rnd 5: Sl st to center of next sp, sc in same sp, ch 6, *2 tr in next tr, tr in next tr, 2 tr in next tr, [ch 6, sc in next sp] twice, ch 6, rep from * around, ending with [ch 6, sc in next sp] once, ch 3, tr in first sc to be in position for next rnd.

Rnd 6: Ch 6, sc in next sp, ch 6, *2 tr in next tr, tr in next tr, ch 1, sk 1 tr, tr in next tr, 2 tr in next tr, [ch 6, sc in next sp] 3 times, ch 6, rep from * around, ending with [ch 6, sc in next sp] once, ch 3, tr in first st.

Rnd 7: Ch 7 (counts as first tr and ch 3), tr in next sp, ch 3, dc in next sp, *2 tr in next tr, tr in next tr, ch 3, sk [tr, ch-1, tr], tr in next tr, 2 tr in next tr, ch 3, dc in next sp, [ch 3, tr in next sp] twice, ch 3, dc in next sp, ch 3, rep from * around, join in 4th ch of beg ch-7.

Rnd 8: Sl st to center of next sp, ch 4 (counts as first tr), [4 tr in center st of sp, ch 3, tr in next sp, ch 3, tr in next sp, ch 3, 2 tr in next tr, tr in next tr, ch 3, sk 1 tr, tr in next sp, ch 3, sk 1 tr, tr in next tr, 2 tr in next tr, ch 3, tr in next sp, ch 3, tr in next sp, ch 3, sk 1 tr] rep around, join in 4th ch of beg ch-4.

Rnd 9: Ch 4 (counts as first tr), *4-tr cl over next 4 tr, ch 6, sk 1 sp, 4 tr in center st of next sp, ch 6, sk 1 sp, 2 tr in next tr, tr in next tr, [ch 3, tr in next sp] twice, ch 3, sk 1 tr, tr in next tr, 2 tr in next tr, ch 6, sk 1 sp, 4 tr in center st of next sp, ch 6, rep from * around, join in 4th ch of beg ch-4.

Let's Begin!

Experience Level: Advanced

Size: 18" in diameter

Materials
☐ Crochet cotton size 10: 1 50-gram ball white and small amount red

☐ Size 6 steel crochet hook

Gauge: 8 tr and 2 tr rows = 1"

To save time, take time to check gauge.

Pattern Stitch
4-tr-cl: Retaining last lp of each tr on hook, tr in next 4 sts, yo, draw through all lps on hook.

Pattern Note: Join rnds with a sl st unless otherwise stated.

Rnd 10: Ch 7, *4-tr cluster in 4 tr, ch 7, 2 tr in next tr, tr in next tr, [ch 3, tr in next sp] 3 times, ch 3, sk 1 tr, tr in next tr, 2 tr in next tr, ch 7, 4-tr cluster in 4 tr, ch 7, sc in top of cluster, ch 7, rep from * around, join in first ch of beg ch-7.

Rnd 11: Ch 4 (counts as first tr), 4 tr in joining st, ch 3, sc in next sp, ch 7, sc in next sp, ch 7, *2 tr in next tr, tr in next tr, [ch 3, tr in next sp] 4 times, ch 3, sk 1 tr, tr in next tr, 2 tr in next tr, [ch 7, sc in next sp] twice, ch 3, 4 tr in sc, ch 3, sc in next sp, ch 7, sc in next sp, ch 7, rep from * around, join in 4th ch of beg ch-4.

Rnd 12: Ch 4 (counts as first tr), *4-tr cl over next 4 tr, [ch 7, sc in next ch-7 sp] twice, ch 7, 2 tr in next tr, tr in next tr, [ch 3, tr in next sp] 5 times, ch 3, sk 1 tr, tr in next tr, 2 tr in next tr, [ch 7, sc in next sp] twice, ch 7, rep from * around, join in 4th ch of beg ch-4.

Rnd 13: Sl st to center of next sp, [ch 7, sc in next sp] twice, ch 3, *2 tr in next tr, tr in next tr, [ch 3, tr in next sp] 6 times, ch 3, sk 1 tr, tr in next tr, 2 tr in next tr, ch 3, sc in next sp, [ch 7, sc in next sp] 5 times, ch 3, rep from * around, ending with ch 3, tr in first st of rnd.

Rnd 14: Ch 4, 3 tr in same st, ch 7, 2-tr cluster over next 2 sps, ch 7, *sk next sp, tr in 3rd tr, 3 tr in next sp, tr in next tr, [ch 3, tr in next tr] twice, 3 tr in next sp, tr in next tr, **[ch 3, tr in next tr] twice, 3 tr in next sp, tr in next tr, rep from ** once, ch 7, 2-tr cluster over next 2 sps, ch 7, 4 tr in center ch of next sp, ch 7, 2-tr cluster over next 2 sps, ch 7, rep from * around, join in 4th ch of beg ch-4.

Rnd 15: Ch 4 (counts as first tr), 4-tr cluster over 4 tr, ch 7, 2-tr cluster over next 2 sps, ch 7, *tr in first tr, ch 3, sk 3 tr, tr in next tr, [3 tr in next sp, tr in next tr] twice, ch 3, sk 3 tr, tr in next tr, [3 tr in next sp, tr in next tr] twice, ch 3, sk 3 tr, tr in next tr, ch 7, 2-tr cluster over next 2 sps, ch 7, 4-tr cluster over 4 tr, ch 7, 2-tr cluster over next 2 sps, ch 7, rep from * around, ending with ch 3, tr in top of first cluster.

Rnd 16: Ch 5, *sc in top of cluster, ch 5, sc in next sp, ch 5, sc in top of cluster, ch 5, sc in next sp, ch 5, sc in tr, ch 5, sc in next tr, [ch 5, sc in center of next tr group, ch 5, sc in last tr of same group], ch 5, sc in next tr, rep between [], ch 5, sc in next tr, ch 5, sc in next sp, ch 5, sc in top of cluster, ch 5, sc in next sp, ch 5, rep from *

around, ending with ch 2, dc in first st of rnd.

Rnd 17: [Ch 3, 4 tr in next sp, ch 3, sc in next sp] rep around, ending with sl st in first st of rnd.

Rnd 18: Sl st to center of sp, ch 5, *4-tr cluster over next 4 tr, ch 5, sc in next sp, ch 2, sc in next sp, ch 5, rep from * around, ending with sl st in first st of rnd, fasten off.

Rnd 19: Attach red with a sc in any ch-2 sp, *ch 3, sc in next sp, ch 5, sc in next sp, ch 3, sc in next ch-2 sp, rep from * around, join in beg sc, fasten off.

Heart Outline

Following close-up of doily below, attach red with a sc in bottom post inside heart, [ch 4, sc in first ch at edge on right side of heart] 5 times, ch 4, sc in corner of next ch, ch 4, sc over top post, ch 4, working down opposite side of heart, sc in corner corresponding to right side, [ch 4, sc in next ch] 5 times, ch 4, sl st in beg sc, fasten off.

Rep for each heart.

—Designed by Emma L. Willey

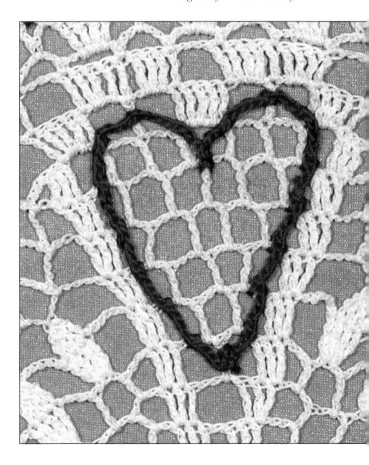

Floral Motif Doily

Let's Begin!

Experience Level: Advanced

Size: Approximately 12½" in diameter

Materials

☐ Crochet cotton size 10: 150 yds white

☐ Size 5 steel crochet hook

Gauge 4 dc = ½"; 3 dc rows = 1"

To save time, take time to check gauge.

Pattern Note: Join rnds with a sl st unless otherwise stated.

Pattern Stitches

Shell: [3 dc, ch 3, 3 dc] in indicated st.

4 dc tog: Work 4 dc into indicated st leaving last lp of each on hook, yo and draw through all 5 lps on hook.

Motif (Make 7)

Rnd 1: Ch 6, join to form a ring, ch 1, 12 sc in ring, join in beg sc. (12)

Rnd 2: Ch 1, sc in same st, [ch 7, sk 1 sc, sc in next sc] 5 times, ch 2, join with a tr in beg sc. (6 ch-7 sps)

Rnd 3: Ch 3, 4 dc in next sp, [ch 3, 5 dc in next sp] 5 times, ch 3, join in 3rd ch of beg ch-3.

Rnd 4: Ch 3, dc in each of next 4 dc, [ch 3, sc in next sp, ch 3, dc in each of next 5 dc] 5 times, ch 3, sc in next sp, ch 3, join in 3rd ch of beg ch-3.

Rnd 5: Ch 3, 4 dc tog, *[ch 5, sc in next sp] twice, ch 5, 5 dc tog (cluster), rep from * 4 times, [ch 5, sc in next sp] twice, ch 5, join in beg cluster.

Rnd 6: Sl st in each of next 2 chs, sc in next sp, *ch 5, sc in next sp, rep from * around, omitting last sc, join in beg sc.

Rnd 7: Sl st in each of next 2 chs, sc in next sp, *ch 5, sc in next sp, ch 3, [5 dc, ch 3, 5 dc] in next sp, ch 3, sc in next sp, rep from * 5 times, omitting last sc, join in beg sc, fasten off.

Complete 1 motif then attach subsequent motifs with a sl st in ch-5 sp between 5 dc of Rnd 7 as

you work each motif, [ch 2, sl st in 3rd ch of ch-5 sp, ch 2, sc in next sp, ch 2, 5 dc, ch 1, sl st in 2nd ch of ch-3 sp, ch 1] rep for patt.

Border

Rnd 1: Attach cotton with a sl st in 3rd dc after any joining, ch 1, sc in same sp *[shell in next ch-3 sp, sc in next ch-5 sp, shell in next ch-3 sp, sk 2 dc, sc in next dc], shell in next ch-3 sp, sk 2 dc, sc in next dc, rep from * once, rep between [] once, ch 2, sc next 2 ch-3 corner sps tog, ch 2, sk 2 dc, sc in next dc, rep from * around, join in beg sc.

Rnd 2: Ch 1, sc in same sp, *[ch 3, {2 sc, ch 3, 2 sc} in next ch-3 sp, ch 3, sc in next sc] 8 times, ch 3, sk 1 sc, sc in next sc, rep from * around, omitting last sc, join in beg sc, fasten off.

—Designed by Pamela McKee

Birdhouse Tissue Box

Add a touch of spring to your home's decor any time of year with this colorful tissue box cover.

Experience Level: Intermediate

Size: 8" tall at center point of roof

Materials

☐ Bernat® Berella "4"® 4-ply yarn: 3½ oz each pearl gray #8912 and scarlet #8933; ½ oz each white #8942, medium colonial blue #8861 and oak #8796; small amount black #8994; and scraps each baby pink #8943, baby yellow #8945, light lagoon #8820, pale colonial blue #8863 and light damson #8854

☐ Bernat® Nice 'n Soft® worsted weight yarn: 1 oz kelly green #4565 and scrap of bright yellow #4346

☐ Size D/3 crochet hook

☐ Size H/8 crochet hook or size needed to obtain gauge

☐ Yarn needle

☐ Fiberfill

☐ Boutique tissue box

☐ 2 (5½" x 6½") pieces cardboard

Gauge: 4 sc and 4 sc rows = 1" with larger hook

To save time, take time to check gauge.

Pattern Notes: Do not join rnds unless otherwise indicated; use a marker to mark rnds.

Use larger crochet hook unless indicated otherwise.

Birdhouse

Front

Row 1: With scarlet, ch 16, sc in 2nd ch from hook, sc in each rem ch across, ch 1, turn. (15)

Rows 2–4: Sc in each sc across, ch 1, turn.

Row 5: 2 sc in first sc, sc across to within last sc, 2 sc in last sc, ch 1, turn. (17)

Rows 6–9: Rep Row 2.

Row 10: Rep Row 5. (19)

Rows 11–14: Rep Row 2.

Row 15: Rep Row 5. (21)

Rows 16 & 17: Rep Row 2.

Row 18: Dec 1 sc over next 2 sc, sc in each sc across to within last 2 sc, dec 1 sc over next 2 sc, ch 1, turn. (19)

Note: *Mark beg and end of Row 18 for later use.*

Row 19: Rep Row 2.

Row 20: Rep Row 18. (17)

Row 21: Rep Row 18. (15)

Row 22: Rep Row 2.

Row 23: Rep Row 18. (13)

Row 24: Rep Row 2.

Row 25: Rep Row 18. (11)

Row 26: Rep Row 18. (9)

Row 27: Rep Row 2.

Row 28: Rep Row 18. (7)

Row 29: Rep Row 18. (5)

Row 30: Rep Row 18. (3)

Row 31: Dec 1 sc over next 2 sc, sc in next sc, ch 1, turn. (2)

Row 32: Dec 1 sc over next 2 sc, fasten off. Set aside.

Back
Rows 1–32: Rep Rows 1–32 of front.

Sides *(Make 2)*
Row 1: With scarlet, ch 16, sc in 2nd ch from hook, sc in each rem ch across, ch 1, turn. (15)

Rows 2–18: Sc in each sc across, ch 1, turn, at end of Row 18, fasten off, leaving a 24" length of yarn.

Joining Front & Sides
Alternating front and back with sides, matching sts, sew sides from bottom up 18 rows to markings to form square. Place over tissue box; set aside.

Roof *(Make 4)*
Row 1: With pearl gray, ch 24, sc in 2nd ch from hook, sc in each rem ch across, ch 1, turn. (23)

Rows 2–22: Sc in each sc across, ch 1, turn, at end of Row 22, fasten off, leaving a 36" length of yarn.

Joining roof
Holding 2 sections of roof tog, matching sts, sew around 3 sides. Insert 1 cardboard piece; sew 4th side closed.

Rep with rem 2 sections of roof.

Attaching roof
Sew 1 roof section to each side of house top, overlapping sides equally. Sew across center top of roof, leaving 2" sp at center for tissue opening.

Door
Rnd 1: With black, ch 2, 6 sc in 2nd ch from hook. (6)

Rnd 2: 2 sc in each sc around. (12)

Rnd 3: [Sc in next sc, 2 sc in next sc] rep around. (18)

Row 4: [Sc in each of next 2 sc, 2 sc in next sc] rep around, fasten off, leaving a length of yarn for sewing. (18)

Sew to front of birdhouse over Rows 5–14.

Perch
Rnd 1: With oak, ch 2, 6 sc in 2nd ch from hook. (6)

Rnd 2: [Sc in next sc, 2 sc in next sc] rep around. (9)

Rnds 3–12: Sc in each sc around, at end of Rnd 12, fasten off, leaving a length of yarn for sewing.

Stuff perch with fiberfill. Sew perch below birdhouse door.

Vines

Leaves *(Make 14)*
With kelly green, ch 7, sc in 2nd ch from hook, hdc in next ch, dc in each of next 2 chs, hdc in next ch, 2 sc in next ch, working on opposite side of foundation ch, sc in next ch, hdc in next ch, dc in next ch, hdc in next ch, sc in next ch, fasten off, leaving a 12" length for sewing.

Cut 2 (12") strands of kelly green. Sew 7 leaves in desired position along each strand. Tack 1 vine to each side of birdhouse from top of roof to bottom of house in desired position.

Flowers *(Make 2 each baby yellow, baby pink, light damson, pale colonial blue & pale lagoon)*
Rnd 1: With white, ch 2, 6 sc in 2nd ch from hook, join in beg sc, fasten off white, attach appropriate color yarn. (6)

Rnd 2: [Ch 6, sc in next sc] rep around, join in beg sc, fasten off, leaving 8" length of yarn for sewing.

Sew 1 flower of each color evenly sp across each vine.

Bird

Body
Rnd 1: With smaller crochet hook and medium colonial blue, ch 2, 6 sc in 2nd ch from hook. (6)

Rnd 2: 2 sc in each sc around. (12)

Rnd 3: Sc in each sc around.

Rnd 4: [Sc in next sc, 2 sc in next sc] rep around. (18)

Rnd 5: Rep Rnd 3.

Rnd 6: [Sc in next sc, dec 1 sc over next 2 sc] 3 times, sc in each of next 9 sc. (15)

Rnd 7: Rep Rnd 3.

Rnd 8: [Dec 1 sc over next 2 sc] 3 times. (12)

Rnd 9: Rep Rnd 3.

Rnd 10: Rep Rnd 4. (18)

Rnd 11: [Sc in each of next 2 sc, 2 sc in next sc] rep around. (24)

Rnd 12: Sc in each of next 21 sc, ch 7, sc in 2nd ch from hook, sc in each of next 5 chs, sc in each of next 3 sc. (30)

Rnd 13: Sc in each of next 21 sc, working on opposite side of ch-7 of Rnd 12, sc in each of next 5 chs, 2 sc in next ch, sc in each of next 9 sc. (37)

Rnd 14: Sc in each of next 26 sc, 2 sc in next sc, sc in next sc, 2 sc in next sc, sc in each of next 8 sc. (39)

Rnd 15: Sc in each of next 4 sc, [dec 1 sc over next 2 sc, sc in next sc] 3 times, sc in each of next 7 sc, dec 1 sc over next 2 sc, sc in each of next 13 sc, dec 1 sc over next 2 sc, sc in each of next 2 sc. (34)

Rnd 16: Sc in each of next 3 sc, [dec 1 sc over next 2 sc] 4 times, sc in each of next 6 sc, dec 1 sc over next 2 sc, sc in each of next 4 sc, dec 1 sc over next 2 sc, sc in next sc, dec 1 sc over next 2 sc, sc in each of next 3 sc, dec 1 sc over next 2 sc, sc in next sc. (26)

Rnd 17: Sc in each of next 18 sc, [dec 1 sc over next 2 sc] twice, sc in each of next 4 sc. (24)

Rnd 18: Sc in each of next 17 sc, [dec 1 sc over next 2 sc] twice, sc in each of next 3 sc. (22)

Rnd 19: [Dec 1 sc over next 2 sc] rep around. (11)
Stuff bird firmly. Continue to rep Rnd 19 until opening is closed, fasten off.

Tail

Row 1: With smaller crochet hook and medium colonial blue, ch 5, sc in 2nd ch from hook, sc in each rem ch across, ch 1, turn. (4)

Row 2: Sc in each sc across, ch 1, turn.

Row 3: 2 sc in first sc, sc in each sc across to within last sc, 2 sc in last sc, ch 1, turn. (6)

Rows 4 & 5: Rep Row 2.

Row 6: Rep Row 3. (8)

Row 7: Rep Row 2.

Row 8: Rep Row 3. (10)

Rows 9–11: Rep Row 2.

Row 12: Dec 1 sc over next 2 sc, sc in each sc across to within last 2 sc, dec 1 sc over next 2 sc, ch 1, turn. (8)

Row 13: Rep Row 2.

Row 14: Rep Row 12. (6)

Rows 15 & 16: Rep Row 2.

Row 17: Rep Row 12. (4)

Rows 18 & 19: Rep Row 2, at end of Row 19, fasten off, leaving a 24" length of yarn.
Fold Row 1 over to Row 19; sew around outer edge of tail. Sew Rows 1 and 19 (narrower end of tail) to back of bird body.

Wings (Make 2)

Rnd 1: With smaller crochet hook and medium colonial blue, ch 12, sc in 2nd ch from hook, sc in each of next 9 chs, 3 sc in next ch, working on opposite side of foundation ch, sc in each of next 9 chs, 2 sc in last ch. (24)

Rnd 2: Sc in each of next 10 sts, 2 sc in next st, sc in next st, 2 sc in next st, sc in each of next 11 sts. (26)

Rnd 3: Sc in each of next 2 sts, 2 hdc in next st, hdc in next st, 2 dc in next st, dc in next st, 2 dc in next st, hdc in each of next 3 sts, sc in each of next 2 sts, 2 sc in next st, ch 2, sl st in 2nd ch from hook, 2 sc in next st, sc in each of next 2 sts, hdc in each of next 2 sts, 2 hdc in next st, 2 dc in next st, dc in next st, 2 dc in next st, dc in next st, hdc in next st, sc in each of next 2 sts, fasten off, leaving a length of yarn for sewing.

Sew 1 wing to each side of body 1" from head, pointing toward tail.

Beak

Leaving a 2" length of yarn for tying, with smaller crochet hook and bright yellow, ch 3, fasten off, leaving a 2" length for tying.

Tie beak to front center of head.

Eyes (Make 2)

With yarn ndl and black, make 1 French knot on each side of head ½" from beak.

Underbelly Patch

Row 1: With smaller crochet hook and white, ch 4, sc in 2nd ch from hook, sc in each of next 2 chs, ch 1, turn. (3)

Row 2: 2 sc in first sc, sc across to within last sc, 2

Continued on Page 145

Old-Time Teddy Bear

*Tuck this lovable teddy bear into an empty chair or
corner to give your home a touch of sweet, old country charm!*

Head (*Make 2*)

Rnd 1: With light brown, ch 2, 6 sc in 2nd ch from hook. (6)

Rnd 2: 2 sc in each sc around. (12)

Rnd 3: [Sc in next sc, 2 sc in next sc] rep around. (18)

Rnds 4–10: Sc around, inc 6 sc evenly sp around. (60 sc at end of Rnd 10)

Rnd 11: Sc in each sc around, fasten off.

Ears (*Make 2*)

Row 1: With light brown, ch 2, 3 sc in 2nd ch from hook, turn. (3)

Row 2: Ch 1, 2 sc in each sc across, turn. (6)

Row 3: Ch 1, [2 sc in next sc, sc in next sc] 3 times, turn. (9)

Row 4: Ch 1, [2 sc in next sc, sc in each of next 2 sc] 3 times, turn. (12)

Row 5: Ch 1, [2 sc in next sc, sc in each of next 3 sc] 3 times, do not turn. (15)

Rnd 6: Ch 1, 3 sc in same sp (corner), sc evenly sp across straight edge (side edges of rows), 3 sc in corner, sc in each sc across Row 5 of curve, join with a sl st in first sc of corner, fasten off.

Sew head tog with ears between halves, leaving 3½" between ears at top of head and leaving 8 sts open each half at neck edge (16 sts total front and back). Stuff head firmly.

Body

Rnd 1: Attach light brown with a sl st at neck edge, ch 1, sc in same st, 19 sc evenly sp around neck edge. (20)

Rnd 2: 2 sc in each sc around. (40)

Rnds 3–9: Sc in each sc around.

Rnd 10: Sc around, inc 4 sc evenly sp around. (44)

Rnd 11: Rep Rnd 3.

Rnd 12: Rep Rnd 10. (48)

Rnds 13–17: Rep Rnd 3.

Rnds 18–24: Sc in each sc around, dec 6 sc evenly sp around.

Stuff with fiberfill at end of Rnd 21, adding stuffing as opening closes.

At end of Rnd 24, sl st in next st, fasten off, leaving a length of yarn.

Thread yarn ndl; weave through rem sts and pull

Let's Begin!

Experience Level: Intermediate

Size: 16" tall

Materials

- ☐ Worsted weight 4-ply yarn (3½ oz per skein): 2 skeins light brown and scraps of vermilion and black
- ☐ Size G/6 crochet hook or size needed to obtain gauge
- ☐ Fiberfill
- ☐ Yarn needle
- ☐ 1 yd 1½"-wide cream lace
- ☐ 1 yd ½"-wide cream satin ribbon
- ☐ Cream sewing thread and needle

Gauge: 4 sc and 4 sc rows = 1"

To save time, take time to check gauge.

Pattern Note: Do not join rounds unless otherwise stated; mark rnds with CC yarn marker.

tight to close opening. Weave loose end into work.

Muzzle

Rnds 1–4: Rep Rnds 1–4 of head. (24)

Rnds 5–7: Sc in each sc around. At end of Rnd 7, sl st in next sc, fasten off.

Sew muzzle to front of head, stuffing with fiberfill as you close.

Facial Features

With black and yarn ndl, make 3–4 small satin sts for each eye. Make 3–4 satin sts for nose. St mouth and line from nose to mouth.

Arms (Make 2)

Rnds 1–3: Rep Rnds 1–3 of head. (18)

Rnds 4–23: Sc in each sc around. (18)

Stuff firmly.

Rnds 24 & 25: Sc around, dec 6 sc evenly sp around, adding fiberfill as opening closes.

Close opening as for body. Sew arms firmly to body at shoulders.

Legs (Make 2)

Rnds 1–5: Rep Rnds 1–5 of head. (30)

Rnd 6: Working in back lps only, sc in each sc around.

Rnd 7: Sc in each sc around.

Rnd 8: Sc in each of next 11 sc, [dec 1 sc over next 2 sc] 4 times, sc in each of next 11 sc. (26)

Rnd 9: Sc in each of next 10 sc, [dec 1 sc over next 2 sc] 3 times, sc in each of next 10 sc. (23)

Rnd 10: Sc in each of next 9 sc, dec 1 sc over next 2 sc, sc in next sc, dec 1 sc over next 2 sc, sc in each of next 9 sc. (21)

Rnds 11–28: Sc in each sc around. Stuff.

Rnds 29 & 30: Sc around, dec 6 sc sts evenly sp around, adding fiberfill as opening closes.

Rnd 31: [Dec 1 sc over next 2 sc] rep around.

Close opening as for body. Sew legs firmly to sides of body in line with arms.

Heart

Row 1: With vermilion, ch 3, sc in 2nd ch from hook, sc in next ch, turn. (2)

Row 2: Ch 1, 2 sc in each sc across, ch 1, turn. (4)

Row 3: Ch 1, 2 sc in first sc, sc in next sc, turn.

Row 4: Ch 1, 2 sc in first sc, dec 1 sc over next 2 sc, turn. (3)

Row 5: Ch 1, dec 1 sc over next 2 sc, sc in next sc, fasten off, leaving a length of yarn. (2)

Sew heart to chest.

Gather 1 edge of lace with sewing thread and needle to fit around bear's neck. Center ribbon on gathered edge of lace; stitch.

Tie lace and ribbon in a bow around neck of bear; trim ends at an angle.

—Designed by Carolyn Christmas

Popcorn Edging

Use this edging to finish yarn projects, or work in crochet cotton with a corresponding steel hook.

[Ch 4, 4 dc in 3rd ch from hook, remove hook from lp, insert in top of beg ch-4, pick up dropped lp, yo and draw through both lps on hook (popcorn made)] rep for a continuous string of popcorns.

Sew edging to project.

Pretty Bath Set

Crochet this pretty ensemble to spruce up your bathroom. Instructions for a toilet tissue topper, bath sign and liquid soap cover are included.

Tissue Topper

Body

Rnd 1: With mint ch 2, 6 sc in 2nd ch from hook, join to first sc, ch 1, turn. (6)

Rnd 2: 2 sc in each sc around, join, ch 1, turn. (12)

Rnd 3: [Sc in next sc, 2 sc in next sc] rep around, join, ch 1, turn. (18)

Rnd 4: [Sc in each of next 2 sc, 2 sc in next sc] rep around, join, ch 1, turn. (24)

Rnd 5: [Sc in each of next 3 sc, 2 sc in next sc] rep around, join, ch 1, turn. (30)

Rnd 6: [Sc in each of next 4 sc, 2 sc in next sc] rep around, join, ch 1, turn. (36)

Rnd 7: [Sc in each of next 5 sc, 2 sc in next sc] rep around, join, ch 1, turn. (42)

Rnd 8: [Sc in each of next 6 sc, 2 sc in next sc] rep around, join, ch 1, turn. (48)

Rnd 9: [Sc in each of next 7 sc, 2 sc in next sc] rep around, join, ch 1, turn. (54)

Rnd 10: [Sc in each of next 8 sc, 2 sc in next sc] rep around, join, ch 1, turn. (60)

Rnd 11: Sc in each sc around, join, turn. (60)

Rnd 12: Working in front lps only, ch 3, sc in next sc, [dc in next sc, sc in next sc] rep around, join to 3rd ch of beg ch-3, turn.

Rnds 13–27: Ch 3, sc in next sc, [dc in next dc, sc in next sc] rep around, join, turn, fasten off at end of Rnd 27.

Trim

Rnd 1: With top (Rnd 1) of tissue topper facing, join white with a sc in any free lp left from Rnd 12, sc in each lp around, join to first sc, turn.

Rnd 2: Ch 3, working in front lps only around, 2 sc in same sc, sl st in next sc, [3 dc in next sc, sl st in next sc] rep around, join to top of beg ch, fasten off.

Soap Cover

Body

Row 1: Beg at bottom, with mint ch 5, sc in 2nd ch from hook and in each ch across, ch 1, turn. (4)

Rows 2–9: Sc in each sc across, ch 1, turn. (4)

Rnd 10: Working in ends of rows and in each sc, sc around outer edge of piece, making 3 sc in corners, join to first sc. (32)

Rnd 11: Ch 3, working in back lps only, sc in next sc, [dc in next sc, sc in next sc] rep around, join to 3rd ch of beg ch-3, turn.

Let's Begin!

Experience Level: Beginner

Size
Tissue Topper: Fits 5" tissue roll (for smaller roll, use size F hook)
Bath Sign: 7" x 8"
Soap Cover: Fits standard oval soft soap bottle

Materials
- ☐ Worsted weight yarn (3½-oz/100-gram skeins): 4½ oz mint and 1 oz white
- ☐ Size G/6 crochet hook
- ☐ Tapestry needle
- ☐ 40" ¼"-wide matching satin ribbon
- ☐ 3¾" wooden heart
- ☐ Paint markers: black and white
- ☐ Crafter's cement
- ☐ 1 sheet 7-count plastic canvas

Gauge: 4 sc and 4 sc rnds = 1"
To save time, take time to check gauge.

Pattern Note: Join all rnds with a sl st unless otherwise stated.

Rnds 12–26: Ch 3, sc in next sc, [dc in next dc, sc in next sc] rep around, join, turn.

Rnd 27: Ch 1, sc in same place as joining, ch 1, sk next sc, [sc in next dc, ch 1, sk next sc] rep around, join to first sc, turn.

Rnd 28: Ch 1, sc in same place as joining, sc in next ch sp, [sc in next sc, sc in next ch sp] rep around, join to first sc, fasten off.

Trim
Rnd 1: With bottom of soap cover facing, join white with a sc in any st of Rnd 28, sc in each sc around, join to first sc, *do not turn.*

Rnd 2: Rep Rnd 2 of tissue topper trim, fasten off.

Finishing
Cut 20" length of ¼"-wide satin ribbon. Thread ribbon through sps of Rnd 27; gather and tie into a bow in front. Trim ends.

Bath Sign

Front & Back (*Make 2*)
Row 1 (WS): With mint, ch 27, sc in 4th ch from hook, dc in next ch, [sc in next ch, dc in next ch] rep across, turn.

Rows 2–15: Ch 3, sc in next sc, [dc in next dc, sc in next sc] rep across, dc in 3rd ch of beg ch-3, turn.

Rnd 16: Working in ends of rows and in each st, sc around outer edge of side, making 3 sc in corners, join to first sc, fasten off.

Front Trim
Rnd 1: With RS facing, join white with a sl st in any st of Rnd 16 of front, ch 1, working in front lps only around, sc in each sc around, working 3 sc in corners, join to first sc, turn.

Rnd 2: Ch 3, dc in same place, sl st in next sc, [3 dc in next sc, sl st in next sc] rep around, join to 3rd ch of beg ch-3, fasten off.

Joining
Cut 2 pieces plastic canvas slightly smaller than crocheted front.

Holding front and back with WS tog, matching sts and working in both back lps only around, join mint in any lp left from Rnd 1 of trim, sl st in both lps around, joining sides tog and inserting plastic canvas before closing, fasten off.

Wooden Heart
Paint wooden heart with white marker; allow to dry.

With black marker write "BATH" using Fig. 1 as a guide; allow to dry.

Glue heart to front of sign.

Finishing
From remaining ribbon, cut 2 (10") pieces. Tie 1 piece into a bow and glue to top center of sign; trim ends.

Glue rem ends of ribbon to back for hanger.

—Designed by Jocelyn Sass

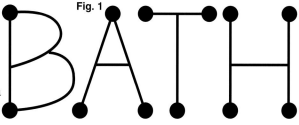

Fig. 1

Missy Mop Doll

*Spruce up your kitchen with our lovable **Missy Mop Doll!***

Let's Begin!

Experience Level: Beginner

Size: 14" tall

Materials

☐ 4-ply yarn: 1¾ oz winter white; small amount each light blue, light rose, moss green, yellow and beige; scrap of black

☐ Size G/6 crochet hook

☐ Small amount synthetic blond curly hair

☐ Fiberfill

☐ Hot-glue gun

☐ Yarn needle

Gauge: 4 sc = 1"; 4 sc rnds = 1"

To save time, take time to check gauge.

Pattern Note: Do not join rnds unless otherwise indicated, use a scrap of yarn to mark rnds.

Body & Dress

Cut 90 strands of winter white yarn each 24" long. Cut another 24" strand of winter white and tie strands tightly around the center of the 90 strands. Set aside.

Head

Rnd 1: With winter white yarn, ch 2, 6 sc in 2nd ch from hook. (6)

Rnd 2: Work 2 sc in each sc around. (12)

Rnd 3: Sc around, inc 6 sc evenly sp around. (18)

Rnd 4: Sc in each sc around.

Rnds 5 & 6: Rep Rnd 3. (30)

Rnds 7–11: Rep Rnd 4.

Rnd 12: Sc around, dec 6 sc evenly sp around. (24)

Rnd 13: Rep Rnd 4.

Stuff head with fiberfill.

Rnd 14: Rep Rnd 12. (18)

Rnd 15: [Dec 1 sc over next 2 sc] 9 times, sl st in next st, leaving a length of yarn, fasten off. (9)

Arms

Note: *Arms are crocheted in 1 long tube.*

Rnd 1: With winter white yarn, ch 2, 6 sc in 2nd ch from hook. (6)

Rnd 2: Sc in each sc around.

Rnd 3: Sc around, inc 2 sc evenly sp. (8)

Rnds 4 & 5: Rep Rnd 2.

Rnd 6: Rep Rnd 3. (10)

Stuff arm lightly with fiberfill and continue to stuff as work progresses.

Rnds 7–32: Rep Rnd 2.

Rnd 33: Sc around, dec 2 sc evenly sp. (8)

Rnds 34 & 35: Rep Rnd 2.

Rnd 36: Rep Rnd 33. (6)

Rnd 37: [Sk next st, sl st in next st] 3 times, leaving a length of yarn, fasten off.

Place arms under center of body and dress strands of yarn. Pull strands down over arms. Cut a 22" length of each light blue and light rose. Holding the 2 strands tog, tie around strands at what would be the underarms to form bodice. Tie strands in a bow at center front. Trim strands even with bottom of dress.

Pull arms forward, with the rem length of yarn at end of arms, tack hands tog.

Sew head in place to top of body.

Features

With a length of black yarn and yarn needle, embroider eyes in satin stitch over Rnds 7–9 of head. With a length of light rose and yarn needle, embroider a V-shaped mouth over Rnds 11 and 12 of head.

Make clusters from curly hair about 4" long. With hot-glue gun, glue at Rnd 4 of head at sides, curving downward to Rnds 11 and 12 at back of head. Do not put hair on top of head; hat will cover bald spot. For bangs, cut 2" lengths of hair. Rub lengths lightly into a ball in palm of your hand. Glue at top of head. Trim ends as needed.

Hat

Rnd 1: With light blue yarn, ch 2, 6 sc in 2nd ch from hook. (6)

Rnd 2: Work 2 sc in each sc around. (12)

Rnd 3: Rep Rnd 2. (24)

Rnd 4: [Sc in next sc, 2 sc in next sc] rep around. (36)

Rnds 5–8: Sc in each sc around.

Rnd 9: Sl st in next st, [ch 2, sk next st, sc in next st] rep around, ending with ch 2, sk next st, sl st in next st.

Rnd 10: Sl st into ch-2 sp, ch 3, 3 dc in same ch-2 sp, work 4 dc in each rem ch-2 sp around, sl st to join in 3rd ch of beg ch-3, leaving a length of yarn, fasten off.

Cut a length of light rose. Weave through ch-2 sps of Rnd 9. Tie ends in a bow. Trim ends as desired.

Place hat on doll with light rose bow at center back. With rem length of light blue, sew hat to head.

Basket

Rnd 1: With beige yarn, ch 2, 6 sc in 2nd ch from hook. (6)

Rnd 2: Work 2 sc in each sc around. (12)

Rnd 3: [Work 2 sc in each of next 3 sc, sc in next 3 sc] twice. (18)

Rnd 4: *[Sc in next sc, 2 sc in next sc] 3 times, sc in next 3 sc, rep from * once. (24)

Rnds 5 & 6: Hdc in each st around.

Rnd 7: Sl st in next st, ch 13, sl st in 2nd ch from hook, sl st in each rem ch across, fasten off.

Flowers *(Make 2 each light blue & light rose)*
[Ch 6, sl st in first ch] 6 times, fasten off.

Run a strand of yarn through the center of flower and pull up tightly. Tack to secure.

With a length of yellow yarn and yarn needle, make a French knot in the center of each flower.

Leaves *(Make 2)*
With moss green, ch 5, sl st in 2nd ch from hook, sl st in next ch, sc in next ch, hdc, ch 2 and sl st in last ch, fasten off.

Sew flowers and leaves around edge of the basket. Arrange handle of basket up through arms. Sew end of handle to opposite side of top of basket.

Hanging Loop

With light blue yarn, ch 18, fasten off. Thread chain through sts at center back Rnd 1 of hat. Sew ends of chain tog.

—Designed by Sheila Leslie

Birdhouse Tissue Box

Continued from Page 139

Continued from Page 139

sc in last sc, ch 1, turn. (5)

Row 3: Rep Row 2. (7)

Rows 4–10: Sc in each sc across, ch 1, turn.

Row 11: Dec 1 sc over next 2 sc, sc across to within last 2 sc, dec 1 sc over next 2 sc, ch 1, turn. (5)

Rows 12 & 13: Rep Row 4.

Row 14: Rep Row 11. (3)

Rows 15–19: Rep Row 4, at end of Row 19, fasten off, leaving a length of yarn.

Sew underbelly patch down front of body from neck to tail.

Finishing

Sew bottom of bird body to perch.

Pull tissue through opening at top.

—Designed by Lori Jean Karluk

Afghan Jamboree

What more could a crocheter ask for than two beautiful afghans?
Each of these treasures will be a pleasure to crochet and to snuggle up in!

Diamond Delight

Diamond Squares *(Make 48)*

Rnd 1: With violet, ch 3, join to form a ring, ch 3 (counts as first dc), 2 dc in ring, ch 1, 3 dc in ring, change to Springfield, [3 dc, ch 1] twice in ring, join in 3rd ch of beg ch-3, turn.

Rnd 2: Continuing with Springfield, sl st into sp just made, ch 3, 2 dc in same sp, ch 1, [3 dc, ch 1, 3 dc] in next ch-1 sp, ch 1, [3 dc (change to violet), ch 1, 3 dc] in same sp, ch 1, [3 dc, ch 1, 3 dc] in next ch-1 sp, ch 1, 3 dc in beg ch-1 sp, ch 1, join in 3rd ch of beg ch-3, turn.

Rnd 3: Continuing with violet, sl st into ch-1 sp just made, ch 3, 2 dc in same sp, ch 1, 3 dc in next ch-1 sp, ch 1, [3 dc, ch 1, 3 dc] in next ch-1 sp, ch

Let's Begin!

Experience Level: Advanced beginner

Size
Afghan: 46" x 61"
Each square: 6¼"

Materials
☐ Lion Brand Jiffy 2-ply acrylic yarn: 6 (3-oz) skeins violet #191 and 6 (2.5-oz) skeins Springfield #337
☐ Size K/10½ crochet hook
☐ Yarn needle

Gauge: 3 sc, 1 dc row and 2 sc rows = 1"

To save time, take time to check gauge.

Pattern Notes: Design is worked in squares then sewn together to form patt.

To change colors, work last dc until 2 lps rem, pull through a lp of new color.

Do not carry colors; simply drop where indicated and pick up again when required.

Join rnds with a sl st unless stated otherwise.

1, 3 dc in next ch-1 sp, ch 1, 3 dc in next ch-1 sp, change to Springfield, ch 1, 3 dc in same sp, ch 1, 3 dc in next ch-1 sp, ch 1, [3 dc, ch 1, 3 dc] in next ch-1 sp, ch 1, 3 dc in next ch-1 sp, ch 1, 3 dc in next ch-1 sp, ch 1, join in 3rd ch of beg ch-3, turn.

Rnd 4: Continuing with Springfield, sl st into ch-1 sp just made, ch 3, 2 dc in same sp, [ch 1, 3 dc in next ch-1 sp] twice, ch 1, [3 dc, ch 1, 3 dc] in next ch-1 sp, [ch 1, 3 dc in next ch-1 sp] twice, ch 1, 3 dc in next sp, change to violet, ch 1, 3 dc in same sp, [ch 1, 3 dc in next sp] twice, ch 1, [3 dc, ch 1, 3 dc] in next sp, [ch 1, 3 dc in next ch-1 sp] twice, ch 1, 3 dc in next ch-1 sp, ch 1, join in

3rd ch of beg ch-3, fasten off, leaving approximately 12" for sewing.

Assembly
Thread yarn into yarn ndl. With RS tog, whipstitch through back lps only. Sew squares tog vertically to join 6 squares across. Sew strips tog in same manner.

Border
Rnd 1: With RS facing and violet, [sc, ch 2, sc] in any corner sp of afghan, *sc in each dc and ch-1 sp across square, hdc in corner ch-3 sp, hdc in joining of squares, hdc in next corner ch-1 sp of next square, rep from * around, working corner as before, join in beg sc.

Rnds 2 & 3: Ch 1, sc in each st around, with [sc, ch 2, sc] in each corner, join in beg sc, fasten off at end of Rnd 3, turn.

Rnd 4: Attach Springfield in any corner, *[sc, ch 3, sc] in corner sp, [ch 1, sk 1 sc, sc] in next sc, rep from * around, join in beg sc, turn.

Rnd 5: Dc in each sc and each ch-1 sp around, working [2 dc, ch 2, 2 dc] in each corner, join in beg dc.

Rnd 6: [Hdc, ch 1, hdc] in each corner, [ch 1, hdc in next dc, sk 1 dc] rep around, join in beg hdc, fasten off.

Rnd 7: With violet, [sc, ch 3, sc] in each corner, sc in each hdc and ch-1 sp around, join in beg sc.

Rnd 8: *Sc in each of next 3 sc, ch 3, sl st in 3rd ch from hook for picot, rep from * around, working picot in each corner, join in beg sc, fasten off.

Block lightly on WS if desired.

—*Designed by Colleen Sullivan*

Open Swirls

Afghan
Row 1 (WS): With Aran, ch 233, dc in 4th ch from hook, dc in each rem ch across, ch 3, turn. (231 sts counting turning ch)

Row 2: Sk first st, dc in each rem st across **, ch 3, turn.

Row 3: Rep Row 2, ending at **, ch 1, turn.

Row 4: Join light blue velvet with sc in first st, sc in each of next 9 sts, [{open swirl in next st, sc in each of next 5 sts, open swirl in next st}, sc in each of next 27 sts] 6 times, rep between {}, sc in each

Let's Begin!

Experience Level: Advanced

Size: 48" x 73" without fringe

Materials
☐ Brunswick® Windrush® worsted weight yarn (3.5 oz/100 grams per skein): 8 skeins Aran #90400, 2 skeins each light wicker green #90461 and maize #9031, and 1 skein each light blue velvet #90813, colonial blue #90181, pale terra cotta #90195, terra cotta #90191, medium wicker green #90462 and canary #90083

☐ Size H/8 crochet hook or size needed to obtain gauge

Gauge: 10 dc sts = 3"

Pattern Stitches
Front post treble crochet (fptr): Yo twice, insert hook from front to back and to front again around vertical post of next st, draw up lp, [yo, draw through 2 lps] 3 times.

Front post double treble crochet (fpdtr): Yo 3 times, insert hook from front to back and to front again around vertical post of next st, draw up lp, [yo, draw through 2 lps] 4 times.

Open swirl: Work fpdc, fptr and fpdtr around post of same st from top to bottom; sc in top 2 lps of same st.

of last 10 sts, fasten off, turn.

Row 5 and all odd-numbered rows following open swirl rows: Join Aran with a sl st in first st, ch 3, dc in each sc across including sc of swirl, fasten off, turn.

Row 6: Join colonial blue with sc in first st, sc in each of next 12 sts, [open swirl in next st, sc in each of next 33 sts] 6 times, open swirl in next st, sc in each of last 13 sts, fasten off, turn.

Row 8: Rep Row 4.

Row 10: Join pale terra cotta with sc in first st, sc in each of next 26 sts, [rep between [] of Row 4] 6 times, fasten off, turn.

Row 12: Join terra cotta with sc in first st, sc in each of next 29 sts, [rep between [] of Row 6] 5 times, open swirl in next st, sc in each of last 30 sts.

Row 14: Rep Row 10.

Row 16: With light wicker green, rep Row 4.

Row 18: With medium wicker green, rep Row 6.

Row 20: Rep Row 16.

Row 22: With maize, rep Row 10.

Row 24: With canary, rep Row 12.

Row 26: Rep Row 22.

Row 27: Rep Row 5.

[Rep Rows 4–27] 4 times, [rep Rows 4–8] once.

Next Row: Rep Row 5, do not fasten off, ch 3, turn.

Next 2 Rows: Rep Row 2, ending last row at **, fasten off.

Fringe

Omitting all Aran rows, knot 6 (18") yarn lengths of matching color at each end of each row except Aran rows; trim fringe.

—Designed by Mary Lamb Becker for Designs for America

Piglets-for-Sale Doorstop

*Crochet this pair of adorable piglets to keep a door
from blowing shut! You'll delight any guests too!*

Let's Begin!

Experience Level: Beginner

Size: 10" wide x 13½" tall

Materials

- [ ] Coats & Clark Red Heart Classic 4-ply yarn: 3½ oz tan #334, 2½ oz pale rose #755 and small amount black #12
- [ ] Size G/6 crochet hook
- [ ] 2-pound bag unpopped popcorn or rice
- [ ] Fiberfill
- [ ] 1 oz One and Only Creations Fancy Fiber
- [ ] Tacky glue
- [ ] 2" x 3" blackboard
- [ ] White acrylic paint
- [ ] Paintbrush
- [ ] Pink straw satin raffia ribbon
- [ ] 2 (6") lengths ⅜"-diameter wooden dowels
- [ ] Masking tape
- [ ] 1 sheet 7-count plastic canvas
- [ ] 2 (3"-diameter) plastic canvas circles
- [ ] Yarn needle

Gauge: 4 sc and 4 sc rnds = 1"

To save time, take time to check gauge

Pattern Notes: Weave in loose ends as work progresses.

Do not join rnds unless otherwise indicated. Use a scrap of CC yarn to mark rnds.

Do not stuff ears with fiberfill.

Feed Sack

Rnd 1: Beg at bottom, with tan, ch 32, 2 sc in 2nd ch from hook and in each of next 29 chs, 4 sc in last ch, working on opposite side of foundation ch, sc in each of next 29 chs, ending with 2 sc in same sc as beg 2 sc. (66)

Rnd 2: 2 sc in each of next 2 sc, sc in each of next 29 sc, 2 sc in each of next 4 sc, sc in each of next 29 sc, 2 sc in each of next 2 sc. (74)

Rnds 3 & 4: Sc in each sc around.

At the end of Rnd 4, draw up a lp and remove

crochet hook.

Using crocheted section as a pattern, cut 2 pieces plastic canvas slightly smaller. Set aside.

Rnd 5: Sc in each sc around, join with a sl st in beg sc.

Rnd 6: Ch 3 (counts as first dc), sc in next sc, [dc in next sc, sc in next sc] rep around, join with a sl st in 3rd ch of beg ch-3, turn.

Rnds 7–31: Ch 3, sc in next sc, [dc in next dc, sc in next sc] rep around, join with a sl st in 3rd ch of beg ch-3, turn, fasten off at end of Rnd 31.

Insert plastic canvas sections into base of feed sack.

To reinforce bag of popcorn or rice, wrap with masking tape. Place wrapped bag crosswise inside crocheted feed sack. Stuff remainder of feed sack with fiberfill. Set aside.

Head *(Make 2)*

Rnd 1: With pale rose, ch 2, 6 sc in 2nd ch from hook. (6)

Rnd 2: 2 sc in each sc around. (12)

Rnd 3: [Sc in next sc, 2 sc in next sc] rep around. (18)

Rnd 4: [Sc in each of next 2 sc, 2 sc in next sc] rep around. (24)

Rnd 5: [Sc in each of next 3 sc, 2 sc in next sc] rep around. (30)

Rnd 6: [Sc in each of next 4 sc, 2 sc in next sc] rep around. (36)

Rnds 7–19: Sc in each sc around.

Rnd 20: [Sc in each of next 4 sc, dec 1 sc over next 2 sc] rep around. (30)

Rnd 21: [Sc in each of next 3 sc, dec 1 sc over next 2 sc] rep around. (24)

Rnd 22: [Sc in each of next 2 sc, dec 1 sc over next 2 sc] rep around. (18)

Stuff head with fiberfill and continue stuffing with fiberfill as work progresses.

Rnd 23: [Sc in next sc, dec 1 sc over next 2 sc] rep around. (12)

Rnd 24: [Dec 1 sc over next 2 sc] rep around, sl st in next st, fasten off.

Ears *(Make 4)*

Rnd 1: With pale rose, ch 2, 6 sc in 2nd ch from hook. (6)

Rnd 2: Sc in each sc around.

Rnd 3: [Sc in next sc, 2 sc in next sc] rep around. (9)

Rnds 4 & 5: Rep Rnd 2.

Rnd 6: [Sc in each of next 2 sc, 2 sc in next sc] rep around. (12)

Rnds 7 & 8: Rep Rnd 2.

Rnd 9: [Sc in each of next 3 sc, 2 sc in next sc] rep around. (15)

Rnd 10: [Sc in each of next 4 sc, 2 sc in next sc] rep around. (18)

Rnd 11: [Sc in each of next 2 sc, 2 sc in next sc] rep around. (24)

Rnd 12: Sc in each sc around, sl st in next sc, fasten off, leaving a length of yarn.

Do not sew bottom of Rnd 12 of ear tog.

Ears are sewn to each side of head over Rnds 5–12. With yarn ndl and rem length of yarn, holding Rnd 12 open in an oval shape, sew around entire outer edge to head. Fold Rnds 1–6 downward at a slight angle (see photo for assistance) and tack in place.

Snout (*Make 2*)
Rnds 1–4: Rep Rnds 1–4 of head. (24)

At the end of Rnd 4, sl st in next sc.

Rnd 5: Ch 1, working in back lps for this rnd only, sc in each st around, sl st to join in beg sc. (24)

Rnd 6: Ch 1, sc in each sc around, sl st to join in beg sc, leaving a length of yarn, fasten off.

Cut 4 bars off each plastic canvas circle to fit inside of first 4 rnds of snout. Insert plastic canvas. Sew snout to front of head over Rnds 13–20, stuffing with fiberfill as work progresses.

Eyes
With yarn ndl and black, embroider satin-stitch eyes over Rnds 11 and 12 with 1" sp between eyes.

Nostrils
With yarn ndl and black, embroider 1 straight stitch for each nostril over center of snout.

Finishing
Push crochet hook into bottom opening of head to form an opening in the fiberfill. Place a small amount of glue on end of dowel. Insert glued end of dowel into bottom of head opening. Allow to dry completely.

Rep same process with 2nd dowel.

Place glue over rem length of dowel and push into feed sack, positioning heads as desired.

Cut 4 pieces of Fancy Fiber each 6" in length. Pull strands apart and crumple into a ball. Glue to top of feed sack around pigs. Continue until surface is covered. Trim if desired.

Cut pink straw satin raffia ribbon into 4 (55") lengths. Using thumb, open creases of straw satin. Holding all 4 lengths tog, tie and knot around center of bag and tie in a bow at center front. Glue in place.

Paint "Piglets for Sale" on blackboard.

Cut an 8" length of raffia; open out and tie into a bow. Glue bow to side of 1 pig's head.

—*Designed by Jocelyn Sass*

Crocheting With Rag Strips

The large gauge of rag strip projects makes them go so quickly they are seldom left abandoned.

The procedure for crocheting garments from rag strips is basically the same as for rugs. Here are some helpful hints:

• To make your rag strips, select firmly woven or knitted light- to medium-weight fabrics. Fabric strips tend to twist as you work with them, so try to find fabrics that are the same color on both sides.

• Be sure the fiber content of your fabrics is compatible with your project. Cotton and cotton blends have more body, while rayons tend to be more clinging. Polyesters are extremely stiff when crocheted. Make a trial swatch, using hooks sizes J to Q, depending upon your fabrics.

• For a size 12 women's long-sleeved sweater you will need approximately 600 yards of fabric strips. The usual strip width is ¾", so you will need approximately 11 yards of 45"-wide fabric.

• For lighter weight sweaters, cut strips narrower and use a smaller hook, but be sure you have chosen fabrics that don't ravel easily.

• Strips may be cut all at once before you begin crocheting, or as work progresses.

• Strips may be sewn together as work progresses, or before crocheting begins. Reduce frequent seaming by cutting strips on the bias, stopping just short of the selvedge, and beginning again at the selvedge edge a strip-width from the previous cut.

Little Pretties

Share your love of crochet with those who mean the most to you by giving a thoughtful hand-crocheted gift. Scented sachets, pretty doilies, lacy decorations and many more keepsake patterns await you!

Patchwork Heart

*Fill this pretty sachet with your favorite potpourri. Then,
either tuck it into your lingerie drawer or give as a sweet-scented gift.*

Heart *(Make 2)*

Patch No. 1

With dark lavender, ch 23, beg Row 1 in 2nd ch from hook.

Row 1 (RS): Sc in each st across, ch 1, turn. (22)

Row 2 (WS): Dec 1 sc over next 2 sts, sc in each rem st across, ch 1, turn. (21)

Row 3 (RS): Sc in each st across to within last 2 sts, dec 1 sc over next 2 sts, ch 1, turn. (20)

Rows 4–7: Rep Rows 2 and 3. (10)

Row 8: Rep Row 2. (10)

Row 9: Sc in each st across, ch 1, turn.

Row 10: Dec 1 sc over next 2 sts, sc in each rem st

across, ch 1, turn. (9)

Rows 11 & 12: Rep Rows 9 and 10. (8)

Row 13: Rep Row 3. (7)

Row 14: Rep Row 9.

Row 15: Rep Row 3. (9)

Rows 16 & 17: Rep Rows 9 and 3. (8)

Row 18: Rep Row 2. (7)

Row 19: Rep Row 3. (6)

Row 20: Rep Row 2. (5)

Row 21: Rep Row 3. (4)

Patch No. 2

Rows 1–16: With WS facing, attach delft in

Let's Begin!

Experience Level: Advanced beginner

Size: Approximately 4" across

Materials

- ☐ J. & P. Coats Knit-Cro-Sheen: small amounts white #001, dark lavender #37, French pink #515, delft #180 and lilac #522
- ☐ Size 7 steel crochet hook
- ☐ 18" ⅛"-wide pink satin ribbon
- ☐ 18" ⅛"-wide lavender satin ribbon
- ☐ Fiberfill
- ☐ Small amount potpourri
- ☐ Yarn needle

Gauge: 4 sc = ½"; 4 sc rows = ½"
To save time, take time to check gauge.

opposite side of foundation ch (this will be at the center of the heart), ch 1, rep Rows 1–21 of patch No. 1.

Patch No. 3

Row 1: With RS facing (patch No. 1 at left bottom and patch No. 2 at right bottom), attach French pink in Row 1 of dark lavender, ch 1, sc in each row across, inc 1 sc across, ch 1, turn. (21)

Row 2: Sc in each st across, ch 1, turn.

Row 3: Rep Row 2.

Row 4: Dec 1 sc over next 2 sts, sc in each rem st across, ch 1, turn. (20)

Rows 5–7: Rep Row 2.

Rows 8–12: Rep Row 4. (15)

Row 13: Dec 1 sc over next 2 sts, sc in each st across to within last 2 sts, dec 1 sc over next 2 sts, do not sl st to corresponding row, ch 1, turn. (13)

Row 14: Dec 1 sc over next 2 sts, sc in each st across to within last 2 sts, dec 1 sc over next 2 sts, ch 1, turn. (11)

Row 15: Rep Row 13. (9)

Row 16: Dec 1 sc over next 2 sts, sc in next st, hdc in each of next 2 sts, sc in each of next 2 sts, dec 1 sc over next 2 sts, fasten off. (7)

Weave in loose ends.

Patch No. 4

Row 1: With RS facing (patch No. 3 just completed to the left), attach lilac in Row 16 of patch No. 2, ch 1, sc across, inc 1 sc, sl st to corresponding Row 1 of previous patch, sl st up 1 row, ch 1, turn. (21)

Rows 2–16: Rep Rows 2–16 of patch No. 3.

Border

Beg at left-hand seam in end of first lavender sc row below seam, draw up lp of white, ch 1.

Rnd 1: Sc evenly around (in end of each row or in sc) working sc, ch 2, sc in end ch at point of heart, work 2 sc in end sc (right and left) of lilac and French pink patches at top of heart, sl st to join, ch 1.

Rnd 2: Sc in first sc, ch 1, sk 1 sc, [sc in next sc, ch 1, sk 1 sc] rep around, with sc, ch 2, sc in ch-2 sp at point of heart, sl st to join.

Rnd 3: Ch 1, [2 sc, ch 2, 2 sc in ch-1 sp] rep in each ch-1 sp around, in ch-2 sp at point of heart, work 2 sc, ch 3, 2 sc, sl st to join, fasten off.

Weave in loose end.

Flower for Front Heart

Rnd 1: With French pink, ch 4, join to form a ring, ch 1, 6 sc in ring, sl st to join, fasten off.

Rnd 2: With white, draw up a lp in any sc, [ch 4, retaining last lp of each st on hook, work 2 tr in same st as ch-4, yo, draw through all lps on hook, ch 4, sl st in same sc, sl st in next sc] 6 times, fasten off.

Weave in loose ends to back of flower. Sew flower to center of front heart.

Ribbon

Holding pink and lavender ribbon together, draw ribbon through center of back heart, tie ends in a bow.

Assembly

Rnd 1: Attach white in any st on outer edge of heart. With WS tog, working through both thicknesses, ch 1, sc halfway around.

Stuff heart with fiberfill. Make a pocket in fiberfill, insert a small amount of potpourri and then insert more fiberfill. Continue to sc around, stuffing with extra fiberfill as needed before closing.

Rnd 2: Ch 2, sc in each sc around, fasten off.

—Designed by Katherine Eng

Pineapple Star Doily

This delicate crochet cotton doily is just the right size for placing under a favorite framed photograph, or vase of fresh flowers.

Doily

Rnd 1: Ch 5, join to form a ring, ch 1, 20 sc into ring, join to beg sc.

Rnd 2: Ch 4, sk 1 sc, [dc in next sc, ch 1, sk 1 sc] 9 times, ch 1, join in 3rd ch of beg ch-4.

Rnd 3: Sl st to first ch-1 sp, ch 3, dc in same sp, [{ch 2, 2 dc} in next sp] 9 times, ch 2, join in 3rd ch of beg ch-3, turn.

Rnd 4: Sl st to first ch-2 sp, [ch 3, 2 dc, ch 1, 3 dc (beg shell)] in same sp, [{3 dc, ch 1, 3 dc (shell)} in next ch-2 sp] 9 times, join in 3rd ch of beg ch-3.

Rnd 5: Sl st to first ch-1 sp, beg shell in same sp, ch 3, [shell over shell, ch 3] 9 times, join in 3rd ch of beg ch-3.

Rnd 6: Sl st to first ch-1 sp, beg shell in same sp,

Let's Begin!

Experience Level: Advanced beginner

Size: 12" in diameter

Materials
☐ Crochet cotton size 10 (150 yds per ball) : 1 ball ecru
☐ Size E/4 crochet hook

Gauge: 3 rnds of shells = 1⅛"; width of 1 shell = ⅞"

To save time, take time to check gauge.

Pattern Note: Join rnds with a sl st unless otherwise stated.

ch 2, 9 tr in next shell, ch 2, [shell over shell, ch 2, 9 tr in next shell, ch 2] 5 times, join in 3rd ch of beg ch-3.

Rnd 7: Sl st to first ch-1 sp, beg shell in same sp, [ch 3, sc between tr] 8 times, ch 3, [shell over shell, {ch 3, sc between tr} 8 times, ch 3] 3 times, join in 3rd ch of beg ch-3.

Rnd 8: Sl st to first ch-1 sp, [beg shell, ch 1, 3 dc] in same sp, [ch 3, sc in next ch-3 sp] 7 times, ch 3, [{shell over shell, ch 1, 3 dc} in same sp, {ch 3, sc in ch-3 sp} 7 times, ch 3] 3 times, join in 3rd ch of beg ch-3.

Row 9 (First point): Sl st to ch-1 sp, turn, beg shell in same sp, [ch 3, sc in ch-3 sp] 6 times, ch 3, shell over first ch-1 sp, turn.

Rows 10–14: Ch 3, shell over shell, [ch 3, sc] in each ch-3 sp, ch 3, shell over shell, turn.

Row 15: Ch 3, [shell over shell] twice, fasten off.

Attach thread to 2nd ch-1 sp to left of point just made. Rep Rows 9–15 for 2nd, 3rd, 4th and 5th points.

—Designed by Starlinne Garrett

Keepsake Barrettes

Crochet these lovely barrettes to coordinate with your favorite outfits.

Popcorn Barrette

Body

Row 1: With mid rose, ch 30, sc in 2nd ch from hook, sc in each rem ch across, ch 1, turn. (29)

Row 2: Pc in 3rd st from hook, [ch 1, sk 1 st, pc in next st] rep across, ch 1, turn. (14 pc)

Row 3: Sc in top of each pc and sc in each ch-1 sp across, fasten off.

Finishing

Glue finished piece across length of barrette. Press firmly into place and allow to dry.

Herringbone Barrette

Body

Row 1: With white, ch 30, sc in 2nd ch from

Let's Begin!

Experience Level: Intermediate

Size: 3" x ½"

Materials

☐ J. & P. Coats Knit-Cro-Sheen: 10 yds each white #001, mid rose #46A and delft #180

☐ Size 3 steel crochet hook

☐ Hot-glue gun

☐ 3 (3") barrettes

Gauge: Work evenly and consistently

Pattern Stitch

Popcorn (pc): Retaining last lp of each st on hook, work 3 dc in same st, yo, draw through all 4 lps on hook.

hook, sc in each rem ch across, turn. (29)

Row 2: Ch 2 (first dc), sk 2 sts, 1 tr in next st, working behind the tr, dc in sk sts, *sk 2 sts, tr in next st, working behind the tr, dc in the 2 sk sts, rep from * across, ending with dc in last st, turn. (9 diagonal tr)

Row 3: Ch 2, tr in 4th st, working in front of tr, dc in 2nd and 3rd sts, *sk 2 sts, tr in next st, working in front of tr, dc in each of next 2 sk sts, rep from * across, ch 1, turn.

Row 4: Sc in each st across, fasten off.

Finishing

Glue finished piece across length of barrette. Press firmly into place and allow to dry.

Cross-Stitch Barrette

Body

Row 1: With delft, ch 30, sc in 2nd ch from hook, sc in each rem ch across, ch 1, turn. (29)

Row 2: Working in back lps for this row only, sc in each st across, ch 1, turn.

Row 3: Sc in each sc across, turn.

Note: *The cross-stitches in Row 4 are worked in the rem free lps of Row 1.*

Row 4: Ch 1, sc in first st, [sk 1 st, tr in next st, sc in next st, tr in sk st, sc in next st] rep across, ch 1, turn. (7 cross-sts)

Row 5: Sc in each st across, fasten off.

Finishing

Glue finished piece across length of barrette. Press firmly into place and allow to dry.

—Designed by Jane Routte

Floral Greeting Card

When you care enough to send the very best, send a loved one your very own crocheted greeting card. It's a snap to make, and the effort you take is sure to be appreciated.

Let's Begin!

Experience Level: Advanced beginner

Size: 4½" x 6"

Materials
- ☐ Embroidery floss in colors of choice
- ☐ Size 7 steel crochet hook
- ☐ 12" ⅛"-wide satin ribbon
- ☐ Glue
- ☐ 6" x 9" piece heavy paper

Gauge: Work evenly and consistently throughout

Pattern Notes: Work all parts with 2 strands of embroidery floss, except work large flower centers with 1 strand.

Cut embroidery floss into 42" lengths.

Pattern Stitch

2-tr cluster (2-tr cl): Retaining the last lp of each tr on hook, work 2 tr in same st, yo and pull through all 3 lps on hook.

Large Flower *(Make 4)*

With 2 strands of embroidery floss, ch 5, 2-tr cl in 4th ch from hook, ch 3, sl st in same place, [ch 3, 2-tr cl in same place as first petal, ch 3, sl st in same place] 4 times, fasten off. (5 petals)

Flower Center *(Make 4)*

With 1 strand of embroidery floss, ch 5, sl st in 5th ch from hook, [ch 4, sl st in same place as first petal] 3 times, fasten off.

Attach flower center to centers of large flowers.

Cluster Flowers *(Make 2)*

Ch 5, *sl st in 5th ch from hook, [ch 4, sl st in same place as first petal] 4 times *, ch 8, rep from * to * once, ch 8, rep from * to * once, fasten off. (3 flowers per cluster)

3-Leaf Cluster *(Make 3)*

Ch 7, *2-tr cl in 4th ch from hook, ch 2, sc in top

of last cl worked, ch 3, sl st in base of leaf *, ch 4, rep from * to * once, sl st in base of first leaf, ch 4, rep from * to * once, sl st in next 3 chs on stem, fasten off.

Vine *(Make 4)*

Ch 7, sl st in 4th ch from hook, [ch 5, sl st in 4th ch from hook] 3 times, working down side, *sl st in next ch on stem between last 2 leaves, sl st in base of next leaf, ch 4, sl st in 4th ch from hook, rep from * twice, sl st in next 3 chs on stem, fasten off.

Finishing

Make single leaves and small flowers to fill in as necessary.

Continued on Page 163

Heirloom Sachets

Delight the bride-to-be with a scented, pastel-colored set of delicate lingerie sachets. She'll treasure them for years after her wedding day!

Peach Sachet

Let's Begin!

Experience Level: Intermediate

Size: 2½" x 3½"

Materials

- ☐ Bernat® Handicrafter® Traditions crochet cotton: 100 yds pale peach #510
- ☐ Size 7 steel crochet hook or size needed to obtain gauge
- ☐ 14" ¼"-wide peach satin ribbon
- ☐ ½" peach silk rose
- ☐ Small amount potpourri
- ☐ Glue

Gauge: First 4 rnds = ⅜"; 4 sc = ⅜"

To save time, take time to check gauge.

Pattern Note: Join rnds with a sl st unless otherwise stated.

Body

Rnd 1: Ch 27, sc in 2nd ch from hook, sc in each rem ch across, ending with 3 sc in last ch, working on opposite side of foundation ch, sc in each ch across, ending with 2 sc in last ch, join, ch 1.

Rnd 2: Sc in each sc around, join, ch 1.

Rnd 3: Sc in first sc, *sk 1 sc, 3 dc in next sc, sk 1 sc in next sc, rep from * around, ending with sk 1 sc, 3 dc in next sc, join in beg sc. (14 shells)

Rnd 4: Ch 3 (counts as first dc), 2 dc in same sc as ch-3, sc in center dc of 3-dc group, [3 dc in sc, sc in center dc of 3-dc group] rep around, join.

Rnds 5–15: [Work a sc in center dc of each 3-dc group and work 3 dc in each sc] rep around, join,

ch 1 to beg with sc and ch 3 to beg with dc.

Rnd 16: [Work 1 sc in each dc and 1 hdc in each sc] rep around, join.

Rnd 17: Ch 1, sc in each st around, join.

Rnd 18: Ch 4 (counts as first dc, ch 1), sk 1 sc, [dc in next sc, ch 1, sk 1 sc] rep around, join in 3rd ch of beg ch-4.

Rnd 19: Sc in ch-1 sp, shell of [2 dc, ch 2, 2 dc] in next ch-1 sp, [sc in next ch-1 sp, shell of {2 dc, ch 2, 2 dc} in next ch-1 sp] rep around, join in beg sc.

Rnd 20: Ch 3 (counts as first dc), shell of [2 dc, ch

2, 2 dc] in ch-2 sp, [dc in next sc, shell of {2 dc, ch 2, 2 dc} in next ch-2 sp of shell] rep around, join.

Rnd 21: Ch 1, sc in same st as ch-1, ch 2, sc, ch 3, sc in next ch-2 sp, ch 2, [sc in single dc between shells, ch 2, sc, ch 3, sc in ch-2 sp, ch 2] rep around, join.

Rnd 22: Ch 1, sc in first sc, ch 2, sc, ch 3, sc in ch-3 sp, ch 2, [sc in next sc, ch 2, sc, ch 3, sc in next ch-3 sp, ch 2] rep around, join, fasten off.

Weave in loose ends.

Finishing

Weave ribbon over and under dc sts of Rnd 16.

Fill pocket with potpourri. Tie ribbon tightly, then tie ends in a bow. Wrap stem of rose around knot of bow. Secure rose with a dab of glue. Trim ribbon ends as desired.

Cream Sachet

Let's Begin!

Experience Level: Intermediate

Size: 2¾" wide x 3¾" long

Materials
☐ Bernat® Handicrafter® crochet cotton: 100 yds cream #502

☐ Size 7 steel crochet hook or size needed to obtain gauge

☐ 14" ¼"-wide peach satin ribbon

☐ Small amount potpourri

☐ ½" peach silk rose

☐ Glue

Gauge: First 4 rnds = ⅜"; 4 sc = ⅜"

To save time, take time to check gauge.

Pattern Note: Join rnds with a sl st unless otherwise stated.

Body

Rnd 1: Ch 29, sc in 2nd ch from hook, sc in each rem ch across, ending with 3 sc in last ch, working on opposite side of foundation ch, sc in each ch across, ending with 2 sc in last ch, join, ch 1. (60)

Rnds 2 & 3: Sc in each st around, join, ch 1.

Rnd 4: Working in back lps only, sc in each st around, join, ch 1.

Rnds 5 & 6: Rep Rnd 2.

Rnd 7: Rep Rnd 4.

Rnd 8: Sc in each st around, working a dec 1 sc over next 2 sc at each side, join, ch 1. (50)

Rnd 9: Sc in first sc, dc in next sc, [sc in next sc, dc in next sc] rep around, join in beg sc, ch 3 (first dc on Rnd 10).

Rnds 10–16: [Sc in each dc, dc in each sc] rep around, join, ch 1 to beg a rnd with a sc, ch 3 to beg a rnd with dc.

Rnd 17: Sc in each st around, working a dec 1 sc over next 2 sc at each side, join, ch 1. (48)

Rnd 18: Sc in each sc around, join, ch 1.

Rnds 19–23: Rep Rnds 9–13.

Rnds 24 & 25: Rep Rnds 17 and 18. (46)

Rnd 26: Ch 4 (counts as first dc, ch 1), sk 1 sc, dc in next sc, [ch 1, sk 1 sc, dc in next sc] rep around, join in 3rd ch of beg ch-4, ch 1.

Rnd 27: Sc in ch-1 sp, [ch 2, sc in next ch-1 sp] rep around, ending with ch 2, join in beg sc, sl st in next ch-2 sp, ch 1.

Rnds 28 & 29: Rep Rnd 26, working ch 3 (instead of 2).

At the end of Rnd 29, join, do not ch 1.

Rnd 30: In each ch-3 sp work, [sl st, ch 3, 2 dc] rep around, ending with sl st in beg sl st, fasten off.

Bottom Trim

Rnd 1: Beg in rem front lp of Rnd 3, attach cotton, ch 1, sc in same st as ch-1, ch 2, sk 1 st, [sc in next st, ch 2, sk 2 sts] rep around, join.

Rnd 2: Sl st into ch-2 sp, ch 1, sc in same ch sp as ch-1, ch 3, [sc in next ch-2 sp, ch 3] rep around, join.

Rnd 3: In each ch-3 sp work [sl st, ch 3, 2 dc] rep around, ending with sl st to join, fasten off.

Rep bottom trim in rem free lps of Rnd 6.

Weave in loose ends.

Finishing

Weave ribbon through dc sts of Rnd 26. Fill pocket with potpourri. Tie ribbon tightly in a knot. Tie ends in a bow. Secure rose around knot of bow. Glue to secure in place. Trim ribbon ends evenly as desired.

Peach & Cream Sachet

Let's Begin!

Experience Level: Intermediate

Size: 5" square

Materials
☐ Bernat® Handicrafter® Traditions crochet cotton: small amount pale peach #510

☐ Bernat® Handicrafter® crochet cotton: 100 yds cream #502

☐ Size 7 steel crochet hook or size needed to obtain gauge

☐ 2 lengths 14" ¼"-wide peach satin ribbon

☐ Small amount potpourri

☐ 2 (½") coordinating silk roses

☐ Glue

Gauge: First 2 rnds = ¾"

To save time, take time to check gauge.

Pattern Stitch
Popcorn: Work 5 dc in same st, draw up a lp, drop lp from hook, insert hook from front to back in first dc of 5-dc group, pick up dropped lp, pull through st on hook.

Pattern Note: Join rnds with a sl st unless otherwise stated.

Body *(Make 2)*
Rnd 1: With cream cotton, ch 5, join to form a ring, ch 1, work 8 sc in ring, join, ch 3 (counts as first dc in following rnd.)

Rnd 2: 2 dc in first sc, *ch 1, popcorn in next sc, ch 1, 3 dc in next sc, rep from * around, ending with popcorn, ch 1, join in 3rd ch of beg ch-3, ch 1.

Rnd 3: Sc in top of each of next 2 dc, *work corner: sc in next ch-1 sp, ch 3, sc in next ch-1 sp, sc in each of next 3 dc, rep from * around, ending with corner pattern, join to beg sc, ch 4 (counts as first dc, ch 1 of Rnd 4).

Rnd 4: Popcorn in next dc, ch 1, dc in each of next 2 sc, *work corner: ch 1, popcorn, ch 3, popcorn in ch-3 sp, ch 1, dc in each of next 2 sc, ch 1, popcorn in next sc, ch 1, dc in each of next 2 sc, rep from * around, ending with corner pattern,

dc in last sc, join in 3rd ch of beg ch-4, ch 1.

Rnd 5: Sc in each dc and ch-1 sp around, working 2 hdc, ch 2, 2 hdc in each corner ch-3 sp, join, ch 1.

Rnd 6: Sc in each sc around, working sc, ch 2, sc in each corner ch-2 sp, join, sl st in next sc, ch 1.

Rnd 7: Sc in first sc, *sk 2 sc, 5 dc in next sc, sk 1 sc, sc in next sc, sk 2 sc, 7 dc in corner ch-2 sp, sk 1 sc, sc in next sc, sk 2 sc, 5 dc in next sc, sk 1 sc, sc in next sc, rep from * around, ending last pattern repeat with sk 1 sc, join in beg sc, ch 3 (counts as first dc of next row).

Rnd 8: 4 dc in same sc as ch-3, [sc in center dc of 5-dc group, 5 dc in next sc] rep around, working at each corner, sc in 2nd dc of 7-dc group, 7 dc in 4th dc, sc in 6th dc, join last sc to top of beg ch, fasten off.

Rnd 9: Draw up a lp of peach in any sc on edge, ch 3, *hdc in next dc, sc in each of next 3 dc, hdc in next dc, dc in next sc, rep from * around, working corners with hdc in first 3 dc, hdc, ch 2, hdc in next dc, hdc in each of last 3 dc, dc in next sc, end last pattern rep with hdc in next dc, join, ch 1.

Rnd 10: Sc in each st around, working sc, ch 2, sc in each corner ch-2 sp, join, fasten off.

Border
Note: Work ruffle around 1 sachet square only. With cream cotton, draw up a lp in 2nd sc to the left of any corner ch-2 sp, ch 1.

Rnd 1: Sc in first sc, *ch 2, sk 1 sc, sc in next sc, rep from * around, working corners, ch 2, sk 1 sc, sc, ch 2, sc in corner ch-2 sp, at end of rnd, join last ch-2 to beg sc, sl st in next ch-3 sp, ch 1.

Rnd 2: Sc in first ch-2 sp, *ch 3, sc in next ch-2 sp, rep from * around, working each corner with ch 3, sc, ch 3, sc in corner ch-2 sp, at end of rnd, join last ch-3 to beg sc, sl st in next ch-3 sp, ch 1.

Rnd 3: Rep Rnd 2, working in ch-3 sps, join, sl st in next ch-3 sp.

Rnd 4: Ch 3, 4 dc in same ch sp, [sc in next ch-3 sp, 5 dc in next ch-3 sp] rep around, join last sc to beg ch-3, sl st to center dc of 5-dc group, ch 1.

Rnd 5: Sc, ch 3, sc in center dc of 5-dc group, *ch 3, sc in next sc, ch 3, sc, ch 3, sc in center dc of next 5-dc group, rep from * around, working corners, sc, ch 3, sc, ch 5, sc, ch 3, sc in center dc of corner dc groups, at the end of the rnd, ch 3, sc

Continued on Page 173

Pretty Tissue Holder

Tuck a packet of tissues inside this lovely tissue packet holder specially sized for your purse!

Body

Row 1: With steel crochet hook size 8 and ecru, ch 33, sc in 2nd ch from hook, sc in each rem ch across, ch 1, turn. (32)

Row 2: Sc in first sc, dc in next sc, [sc in next sc, dc in next sc] rep across, ch 1, turn.

Row 3: [Sc in next dc, dc in next sc] rep across, ch 1, turn.

Rows 4–9: Rep Row 3.

Row 10: [Sc in next dc, dc in next sc] 3 times, ch 19, sk 19 sts, dc in next sc, [sc in next dc, dc in next sc] 3 times, ch 1, turn.

Row 11: Sc in dc, [dc in next sc, sc in next dc] 3 times, [dc in next ch, sc in next ch] 9 times, dc in next ch, [sc in next dc, dc in next sc] 3 times, ch 1, turn.

Rows 12–19: Rep Row 3.

At the end of Row 19, fasten off, turn.

Row 20: With ecru, ch 6, [sc in next dc, dc in next sc] 16 times, ch 7, turn.

Row 21: Sc in 2nd ch from hook, [dc in next ch, sc in next ch] 2 times, dc in next ch, [sc in next dc, dc in next sc] 16 times, [sc in next ch, dc in next ch] 3 times, ch 1, turn. (44)

Rows 22–32: Rep Row 3.

Row 33: Sl st in next 6 sts, sl st, ch 1 and sc in next dc, dc in next sc, [sc in next dc, dc in next sc] 15 times, leaving rem 6 sts unworked, ch 1, turn. (32)

Rows 34–42: Rep Row 3.

Row 43: Sc in next dc, [dc in next sc, sc in next dc] 14 times, draw up a lp in next sc, sk next dc, draw up a lp in next sc, yo, draw through 2 lps on hook, yo, draw through 2 lps on hook, ch 1, turn. (30)

Let's Begin!

Experience Level: Beginner

Size: 2¾" x 4¾"

Materials
- ☐ Coats Opera crochet cotton size 5: 1 (50=gram) ball ecru #503
- ☐ Coats Opera crochet cotton size 20: 20 yds each coral #517, misty spruce #518, orchid #519 and dusty rose #523
- ☐ Sizes 8 and 11 steel crochet hooks
- ☐ 15-tissue pocket pack
- ☐ 2 size 4/0 snap fasteners
- ☐ Clear 6mm bead
- ☐ 9 silver 3mm beads
- ☐ Ecru sewing thread and needle
- ☐ Tapestry needle

Gauge: 7 sts = 1" with size 8 steel crochet hook; 3 patt rows = ½"

To save time, take time to check gauge.

Pattern Note: Weave in loose ends as work progresses.

Row 44: Sc in next dc, [dc in next sc, sc in next dc] rep across to within last 3 sts, draw up a lp in next sc, sk next dc, draw up a lp in next sc, yo, draw through 2 lps on hook, yo, draw through 2 lps on hook, ch 1, turn. (28)

Rows 45–51: Rep Row 44. (14)

Row 52: Sc in next dc, [dc in next sc, sc in next dc] 3 times, ch 8, sl st in top of last sc (button loop), [dc in next sc, sc in next dc] 3 times, ending with sc in last st, fasten off.

With tapestry needle and length of ecru, sew side edge of Rows 1–19 to side edge of Rows 20–32. Rep on opposite edge.

With sewing needle and thread, sew snap fasteners to Row 1 and Row 33 evenly sp across.

Trim

With RS facing and with steel crochet hook size 8, attach ecru, with a sl st in side edge of Row 33, working evenly sp down side edge to within button loop work [5 dc, sl st] 7 times evenly sp across edge, work 16 sc over ch-8 button loop, sl st in next st, [5 dc, sl st] 7 times evenly sp across opposite edge ending in side edge of Row 33, fasten off.

Insert tissue pack and snap the fasteners.

Button

Rnd 1: With steel crochet hook size 8 and ecru, ch 2, 6 sc in 2nd ch from hook, join in beg sc. (6)

Rnd 2: Ch 1, 2 sc in same sc as beg ch-1, sc in next sc, [2 sc in next sc, 1 sc in next sc] rep around, join in beg sc. (9)

Rnd 3: Ch 1, sc in each sc around, join in beg sc, leaving a length of cotton, fasten off.

With tapestry needle, thread rem length of cotton and weave through sc sts of Rnd 3, place 6mm bead in center of crocheted piece, pull woven length gently to close opening, knot to secure, do not fasten off.

Fold flap closed to find placement of button. Sew button to tissue cover.

Flowers (Make 9)
Note: Make 3 flowers each of coral, orchid and dusty rose crochet cotton.

Rnd 1: With steel crochet hook size 11 and crochet cotton, ch 5, join to form a ring, ch 1, sc in ring, [ch 2, 2 dc in ring, ch 2, sc in ring] 5 times, fasten off.

Leaves (Make 5)
Row 1: With steel crochet hook size 11 and misty spruce crochet cotton, ch 8, sl st in 2nd ch from hook, sl st in next ch, sc in next ch, dc in each of next 3 chs, sc in last ch, fasten off.

Sew leaves and flowers to front flap of tissue holder as desired. Sew a 3mm bead to the center of each flower.

—*Designed by Agnes Russell*

Floral Greeting Card

Continued from Page 158

To form greeting card, fold heavy paper in half.

With a small amount of glue applied to center back of each piece, glue leaves and flowers to card.

Tie ribbon in a bow and glue center of bow and ribbon ends to card.

—*Designed by Rosanne Kropp*

Bowery Baskets

You'll find dozens of perfect uses and places for these sweet lacy baskets! You can fill them with potpourri and dried rose petals for your bathroom or bedroom.

Clockwise from top left: Latticework Basket, Garden Wall, Morning Web and Trellised Vines.

Morning Web Basket

Additional Materials
- [ ] 200 yds white crochet cotton
- [ ] 8-oz whipped topping container
- [ ] 18" ¼"-wide light blue satin ribbon
- [ ] 2 light blue lilies

Basket Base
Rnd 1: Ch 5, join to form a ring, ch 3 (counts as first

Let's Begin!

Experience Level: Intermediate

Sizes
Morning Web: 6" in diameter x 3" deep
Trellised Vines: 6" in diameter x 4" deep
Latticework: 4½" in diameter x 2" deep
Garden Wall: 7½" in diameter x 3" deep

Materials
☐ Crochet cotton size 10: as listed with basket

☐ Size 7 steel crochet hook

☐ Fabric stiffener

☐ White floral wire

☐ Hot-glue gun

Gauge: Morning Web, Trellised Vines and Garden Wall: 4 sts and 2 dc rnds = ½"

Latticework: 4 sc = ½"

To save time, take time to check gauge.

Pattern Note: Join rnds with a sl st unless otherwise stated.

dc), 15 dc in ring, join in 3rd ch of beg ch-3. (16)

Rnd 2: Ch 3, dc in same st, work 2 dc in each rem dc around, join in 3rd ch of beg ch-3. (32)

Rnd 3: Ch 1, sc in same st, [ch 3, sk 1 dc, sc in next dc] rep around, ending with ch 1, join with dc in beg sc (ch 1, dc sets you up in the middle of lp for next rnd). (16 ch lps around)

Rnd 4: Ch 1, sc in same lp, [ch 8, sc in same lp, ch 2, sc in next lp] rep around, ending with ch 2, join in beg sc. (16 ch-8 lps around)

Rnd 5: Sl st to the 4th ch of next ch-8 lp, ch 1, sc in same lp, [ch 5, sc in center of next ch-8 lp] rep around, ending with ch 3, join with dc in beg sc. (16 ch-5 lps around)

Rnd 6: Ch 1, sc, ch 3, sc in same lp, [ch 5, {sc, ch 3, sc} in next ch-5 lp] rep around, ending with ch 3, join with dc in starting sc.

Rnds 7 & 8: Rep Rnd 6.

Rnd 9: Ch 1, sc, ch 3, sc in same lp, [ch 6, {sc, ch 3, sc} in next ch-5 lp] rep around, ending ch 3, join with tr in beg sc.

Rnd 10: Ch 1, sc, ch 3, sc in same lp, [ch 6, {sc,

ch 3, sc} in next ch-6 lp] rep around, ending with ch 3, join with tr in beg sc.

Rnd 11: Ch 1, sc, ch 3, sc in same lp, [ch 7, {sc, ch 3, sc} in next ch-6 lp] rep around, ending with ch 4, join with tr in beg sc.

Rnds 12–19: Ch 1, sc, ch 3, sc in same lp, [ch 7, {sc, ch 3, sc} in next ch-7 lp] rep around, ending with ch 4, join with tr in beg sc.

Rnd 20: Ch 4, [3 tr, {ch 3, sc} at base of ch-3 (picot), 4 tr] in same ch-7 lp, ch 3, [4 tr, picot, 4 tr in next lp, ch 3] rep around, join in 4th ch of beg ch-4, fasten off.

Handle
Row 1: Ch 90, sc in 10th ch from hook, [ch 2, sk 1 ch, sc in next ch, ch 8, sc in same ch as last sc] rep across, turn.

Row 2: Sl st to center of ch-8 lp, ch 1, sc in same lp, [ch 2, sc in center of next ch-8 lp] rep across, turn.

Row 3: Ch 1, sc in first sc, [ch 3, sc in top of next sc at center of ch-8 lp] rep across, fasten off.

Finishing
Saturate basket and handle with stiffener. Place basket over container. Lay handle on flat surface. Allow pieces to dry completely. Weave ribbon through center ch sps of handle. For extra handle support, weave 2 lengths of white floral wire through handle under ribbon. Hot-glue handle to inside edge of basket. Glue a lily to each side over handle.

Trellised Vines Basket

Additional Materials
☐ 150 yds white crochet cotton

☐ 6"-diameter x 4"-deep container

☐ 2 yds ¼"-wide rose satin ribbon

☐ 2 (25mm) rose satin roses

Basket
Rnd 1: With white crochet cotton, ch 6, join to form a ring, ch 3, 15 dc in ring, join in 3rd ch of beg ch-3. (16)

Rnd 2: Ch 3, dc in same st, work 2 dc in each rem dc around, join in 3rd ch of beg ch-3. (32)

Rnd 3: Ch 1, sc in same dc, ch 5, sk 1 dc, [sc in next dc, ch 5, sk 1 dc] rep around, join in beg sc. (16 lps)

Rnd 4: Sl st to next lp, ch 3, dc, ch 2, 2 dc in same lp, [2 dc, ch 2, 2 dc in next lp] rep around, join in 3rd ch of beg ch-3.

Rnd 5: Sl st to next ch-2 sp, ch 3, dc, ch 3, 2 dc in same ch-2 sp, [2 dc, ch 3, 2 dc in next ch-2 sp of next shell] rep around, join in 3rd ch of beg ch-3.

Rnd 6: Sl st to next ch-3 sp of shell, ch 3, [2 dc, ch 3, 3 dc] in same ch-3 sp of shell, [work shell of 3 dc, ch 3, 3 dc in next ch-3 sp] rep around, join in 3rd ch of beg ch-3.

Rnd 7: Sl st to next ch-3 sp of shell, ch 3, 2 dc, ch 3, 3 dc in same ch-3 sp of shell, ch 2, [shell of 3 dc, ch 3, 3 dc in next ch-3 sp of shell, ch 2] rep around, join in 3rd ch of beg ch-3.

Rnd 8: Rep Rnd 7.

Rnd 9: Sl st to next ch-3 sp of shell, ch 3, 2 dc, ch 3, 3 dc in same ch-3 sp of shell, ch 3, [shell of 3 dc, ch 3, 3 dc in next ch-3 sp of shell, ch 3] rep around, join in 3rd ch of beg ch-3.

Rnd 10: Sl st to next ch-3 sp of shell, ch 3, 2 dc, ch 3, 3 dc in same ch-3 sp of shell, ch 2, sc in next ch lp between shells, ch 2, [shell of 3 dc, ch 3, 3 dc in next ch-3 sp of shell, ch 2, sc in next ch lp between shells, ch 2] rep around, join in 3rd ch of beg ch-3.

Rnd 11: Sl st to next ch-3 sp of shell, ch 3, 2 dc, ch 3, 3 dc in same ch-3 sp of shell, ch 4, [shell of 3 dc, ch 3, 3 dc in next ch-3 sp of shell, ch 4] rep around, join in 3rd ch of beg ch-3.

Rnds 12–15: Rep Rnds 10 and 11.

Rnd 16: Sl st in ch-3 sp of shell, ch 3, 2 dc, ch 3, sc at base of ch-3 (picot), 3 dc all in the same ch-3 sp of shell, [3 dc, picot, 3 dc] in next ch-4 lp between shells, [{3 dc, picot, 3 dc} in next ch-3 sp of shell, {3 dc, picot, 3 dc} in next ch-4 lp between shells] rep around, join in 3rd ch of beg ch-3, fasten off.

Handle

Row 1: Ch 8, dc in 3rd ch from hook, ch 4, sk 4 chs, 2 dc in last ch, turn.

Row 2: Ch 3, dc in next dc, ch 2, sc in ch-4 lp, ch 2, dc in each of next 2 dc, turn.

Row 3: Ch 3, dc in next dc, ch 4, dc in each of next 2 dc, turn.

Rep Rows 2 and 3 until handle measures 11", fasten off.

Finishing

Saturate basket and handle with fabric stiffener. Shape basket over container; allow to dry completely.

Place handle on flat surface and allow to dry completely. Cut a 10" length of ribbon and weave through sps of handle. Glue handle to inside edges of basket.

Cut remaining ribbon into 4 equal pieces. Tie 2 lengths of ribbon into a double bow; glue to side of handle. Rep on other side of handle. Glue a satin rose to center of each bow.

Latticework Basket

Additional Materials

☐ 100 yds white crochet cotton

☐ 1 yd ⅛"-wide peach satin ribbon

☐ Butter tub: 4½" top diameter x 2" deep

Basket

Rnd 1: Ch 5, join to form a ring, ch 3, 15 dc in ring, join in 3rd ch of beg ch-3. (16)

Rnd 2: Ch 3, dc in same dc as ch-3, 2 dc in each rem dc around, join in 3rd ch of beg ch-3. (32)

Rnd 3: Ch 6 (counts as 1 dc, ch 3), sk 1 dc, [dc in next dc, ch 3, sk 1 dc] rep around, join in 3rd ch of beg ch-6.

Rnd 4: Ch 1, 3 sc in each ch-3 lp around, join in beg sc.

Rnd 5: Sl st in 2nd st, ch 1, sc in same st, ch 5, [sc in center sc of next lp, ch 5] rep around, join in beg sc.

Rnd 6: Ch 1, 5 sc in each lp around, join in beg sc.

Rnd 7: Sl st to center st of next lp, ch 1, sc in same st, ch 7, [sc in center st of next lp, ch 7] rep around, join in beg sc.

Rnd 8: Ch 1, 7 sc in each lp around, join in beg sc.

Rnd 9: Rep Rnd 7.

Rnd 10: Rep Rnd 8.

Rnd 11: Sl st in center st of next lp, ch 1, sc in same st, ch 9, [sc in center st of next lp, ch 9] rep around, join in beg sc.

Rnd 12: Ch 1, 9 sc in each lp around, join in beg sc.

Rnds 13–18: Rep Rnds 11 and 12. At the end of Rnd 18, fasten off.

Handle

Rnd 1: Ch 75, dc in 3rd ch from hook, [ch 2, sk 1 ch, dc in next ch] rep across.

Rnd 2: 3 sc across end just completed, 2 sc in each sp between dc sts up side edge, 3 sc across end, working on opposite side, 2 sc in each sp between dcs, join in beg sc, fasten off.

Finishing

Saturate basket and handle with stiffener. Shape basket over container; place handle on flat surface. Allow to dry completely.

Weave ribbon through handle. For extra handle support, weave 2 lengths of white floral wire through handle under ribbon. Glue handle in place. Glue a small bow to each side of handle on outer edge of basket.

Garden Wall Basket

Additional Materials

☐ 200 yds white crochet cotton

☐ 7½" x 3" empty container

☐ 1½ yds ¼"-wide burgundy satin ribbon

☐ 6 (25mm) burgundy satin roses

Pattern Stitch

Cluster st: Holding back last lp of each dc, work 3 dc in indicated sp, yo, pull through all lps on hook.

Basket

Rnd 1: Ch 5, join to form a ring, ch 3, 14 dc in ring, join in 3rd ch of beg ch-3. (15)

Rnd 2: Ch 3, dc in same st as ch-3, 2 dc in each rem dc around, join in 3rd ch of beg ch-3. (30)

Rnd 3: Ch 3, dc in same st as ch-3, [dc in each of next 2 dc, 2 dc in next dc] rep around, join in 3rd ch of beg ch-3.

Rnd 4: Ch 3, dc in same st as ch-3, [dc in each of next 2 dc, 2 dc in next dc] rep around, join in 3rd ch of beg ch-3.

Rnd 5: Ch 3, dc in same st as ch-3, [dc in each of next 3 dc, 2 dc in next dc] rep around, join in 3rd ch of beg ch-3.

Rnd 6: Ch 3, dc in same st as ch-3, [dc in each of next 4 dc, 2 dc in next dc] rep around, join in 3rd ch of beg ch-3.

Rnd 7: Ch 3, dc in same st as ch-3, [dc in each of next 5 dc, 2 dc in next dc] rep around, join in 3rd ch of beg ch-3.

Rnd 8: Ch 3, dc in same st as ch-3, [dc in each of next 6 dc, 2 dc in next dc] rep around, join in 3rd ch of beg ch-3.

Rnds 9–11: Ch 3, dc in each dc around, join in 3rd ch of beg ch-3.

Rnd 12: Ch 1, sc in same st, ch 4, sk 1 dc, [sc in next dc, ch 4, sk 1 dc] rep around, ending with ch 2, join with dc in beg sc. (This will set you up in the middle of lp for next rnd.)

Rnd 13: Ch 3 (counts as first dc), work 2 more dc in same ch lp holding back last lp of each dc, yo, pull through all lps on hook, ch 2, [cluster st in next ch-4 lp, ch 2], rep around, join in 3rd ch of beg ch-3.

Rnds 14–19: Sl st to next ch-2 sp, ch 3, holding back the last lp of each dc, work 2 more dc in same lp, yo, pull through all lps on hook, ch 2, [cluster st in next ch-2 sp, ch 2] rep around, join in 3rd ch of beg ch-3.

Rnd 20: Sl st to next ch-2 sp, ch 5 (counts as dc, ch 2), [dc in next ch-2 sp, ch 2] rep around, join in 3rd ch of beg ch-5, fasten off.

Handle

Ch 110, dc in 4th ch from hook, [ch 1, sk 1 ch, dc in next ch] rep across, ch 4, sl st in opposite side of foundation ch at base of last dc, ch 3, [cluster st in next ch sp, ch 2] rep across edge, ch 4, sc at top of first dc at beg of handle, ch 3, [cluster st in next ch sp, ch 2] rep across, fasten off.

Finishing

Saturate basket and handle with stiffener. Shape basket over container; place handle on flat surface. Allow to dry completely.

Weave ribbon through dc sps in center of handle. For extra handle support, weave 2 lengths of white floral wire through handle under ribbon. Weave ribbon through Rnd 20 of basket.

Glue handle to inside edge of basket over Rnds 16–20. Glue 3 roses to outside edge of each side of basket where handle is attached.

—Designed by Mary Viers

Lacy Hat Decoration

Hang this pretty hat on a wall to display your handiwork and give your home a decorative touch too!

Hat

Rnd 1: With white, ch 5, join to form a ring, ch 3, 14 dc in ring, join. (15)

Rnd 2: Ch 3, dc in same dc, 2 dc in each rem dc around, join. (30)

Rnd 3: Ch 3, 2 dc in next dc, [dc in next dc, 2 dc

Let's Begin!

Experience Level: Advanced beginner

Size: 14" in diameter

Materials
☐ Crochet cotton size 10: (325 yds/ball):
1 ball white; small amounts yellow, green,
pink, purple

☐ Size 2 steel crochet hook

☐ 3 yds ⅛"-wide pink satin ribbon

☐ 3 yds ⅛"-wide lavender satin ribbon

☐ White glue

☐ Plastic wrap

☐ 6" plastic foam ball, cut in half

Gauge: 4 dc = ½"; 3 dc rnds = 1"

To save time, take time to check gauge.

Pattern Note: Join rnds with a sl st in 3rd
ch of beg ch-3 unless otherwise stated.

Pattern Stitch
Cluster st: Holding back last lp of each tr, 5
tr over ch-3 lp, yo and draw through all lps
on hook.

in next dc] rep around, join. (45)

Rnd 4: Ch 3, dc in next dc, 2 dc in next dc, [dc in
each of next 2 dc, 2 dc in next dc] rep around,
join. (60)

Rnd 5: Ch 3, dc in each of next 2 dc, 2 dc in next
dc, [dc in each of next 3 dc, 2 dc in next dc] rep
around, join. (75)

Rnd 6: Ch 3, dc in each of next 3 dc, 2 dc in next
dc, [dc in each of next 4 dc, 2 dc in next dc] rep
around, join. (90)

Rnd 7: Ch 3, dc in each of next 4 dc, 2 dc in next
dc, [dc in each of next 5 dc, 2 dc in next dc] rep
around, join. (105)

Rnd 8: Ch 3, dc in each of next 5 dc, 2 dc in next
dc, [dc in each of next 6 dc, 2 dc in next dc] rep
around, join. (120)

Rnds 9–11: Ch 3, dc in each dc around, join.

Rnd 12: Ch 6, sk 2 dc, dc in next dc, ch 3, sk 2
dc, [dc in next dc, ch 3, sk 2 dc] rep around, join
in 3rd ch of beg ch-6.

Rnd 13: Ch 7, cluster st in ch-3 lp, ch 3, tr in
next dc of previous rnd, ch 3, cluster st in next
ch-3 lp, ch 3, [tr in next dc, ch 3, cluster st in
next ch-3 lp, ch 3] rep around, join in 4th ch of
beg ch-7.

Rnds 14–18: Ch 7, cluster st in next ch-3 sp, ch 3,
[tr in next tr, ch 3, cluster st in next ch-3 sp, ch 3]
rep around, join in 4th ch of beg ch-7.

Rnd 19: Ch 1, sc in same st, [ch 8, sl st in 3rd ch
from hook (picot), ch 4, sc in next tr] rep around,
join in beg sc, fasten off.

Flowers *(Make 1 pink & 1 purple)*
Row 1: Ch 45, tr in 4th ch from hook, tr in each
rem ch across, ch 4, turn.

Row 2: Tr in each tr across, turn.

Rnd 3: [Ch 6, sl st in next tr] rep around, join in
first ch of beg ch-6, fasten off.

Stamen
With yellow, ch 45, fasten off.

Fold into 2–3 lps and glue in center of flower for
stamen, using photo as a guide.

Leaves
Rnd 1: With green, ch 10, dc in 3rd ch from hook,
dc in each rem ch across, dc in each ch on opposite
side of foundation ch, join.

Rnd 2: Ch 4, [dc in next dc, ch 1] rep around, join
in 4th ch of beg ch-4, fasten off.

Finishing
Starch hat using white glue. Cover half of plastic
foam ball with plastic wrap; shape hat over ball on
flat surface. Let dry completely.

Weave ribbon through Rnd 12. Tie in a double
bow at back, leaving 8" ends; trim. Tie rem ribbon
in a single bow, leaving 7" ends; glue in place over
first bow, using photo as a guide.

Weave a length of matching cotton through
foundation ch of each flower; draw tog tightly and
tie. Fasten off.

Stitch edge of flower tog. Work loose ends into
piece. Starch flowers into shape; allow to dry.

Glue flowers and leaves to hat, using photo as a
guide.

—Designed by Mary Viers

Valentine Plant Poke

Insert this sweet poke into a pretty flowering plant as a thoughtful gift for a special friend.

Let's Begin!

Experience Level: Advanced beginner
Size: 3" wide x 2½" long
Materials
☐ Crochet cotton size 10: 18 yds French rose, small amount white
☐ Size 5 steel crochet hook
☐ Yarn needle
☐ 8" ¼"-wide white satin ribbon
☐ Fiberfill
☐ Bamboo skewer
☐ Glue

Gauge: Work evenly and consistently
Pattern Note: Join rnds with a sl st unless otherwise indicated.

Hearts *(Make 2)*

Rnd 1: With French rose, ch 20, 6 dc in 4th ch from hook, dc in each of next 5 chs, dc next 5 chs tog as follows: [Yo, insert hook in next st, yo and pull through, yo and draw through 2 lps on hook] 5 times, yo and draw through all 6 lps on hook, dc in each of next 5 chs, 7 dc in last ch, working on opposite side of foundation ch, dc in each of next 7 chs, 5 dc in next ch, dc in each of next 7 chs, sl st to join in 3rd ch of beg ch-3. (44)

Rnd 2: Ch 3, dc in same st, 2 dc in each of next 6 dc, dc in each of next 3 dc, dc next 5 dc tog, dc in each of next 3 dc, 2 dc in each of next 7 dc, dc in each of next 9 dc, 5 dc in next dc, dc in each of next 9 dc, join in 3rd ch of beg ch-3. (58)

Rnd 3: Ch 3, dc in same st, [dc in next dc, 2 dc in next dc] 6 times, dc in each of next 2 dc, dc next 5 dc tog, dc in each of next 2 dc, [2 dc in next dc, dc in next dc] 6 times, 2 dc in next dc, dc in each of next 11 dc, 5 dc in next dc, dc in each of next 11 dc, join in 3rd ch of beg ch-3, fasten off. (72)

Joining

Rnd 1: With bottom 5-dc point facing, attach white in first dc of 5-dc group of point, ch 1, sc in same st, sc in next dc, 3 sc in next dc, dc in each of next 2 dc, holding WS of 2nd heart to back of first heart, matching sts and working through both thicknesses, sc in each of next 32 dc, [insert hook in next dc, yo, draw up a lp] 3 times, yo and draw through all 4 lps on hook, sc in each of next 32 sts, join in beg sc.

Rnd 2: Sl st to next st, ch 1, sc in same st, ch 3, [sk next st, sc in next st, ch 3] rep around, join in beg sc, leaving a rem length of 6", fasten off.

Finishing

Stuff heart with fiberfill through opening at bottom point.

Apply glue to 1" of end of bamboo skewer. Insert skewer into opening. With rem length of cotton, sew opening closed.

Tie ribbon in a bow. Glue to center front of heart.

—Designed by Sharon Volkman

Picture-Perfect Frame

Display treasured family photographs in this delicately crocheted frame.

Front

Rnd 1: Ch 92, join to form a ring, ch 3, dc in each ch around, join in 3rd ch of beg ch-3. (92)

Rnd 2: Ch 3, dc, ch 2, 2 dc in same st as ch-3, ch 3, sk 3 dc, [2 dc, ch 2, 2 dc in next dc, ch 3, sk 3 dc] rep around, join in 3rd ch of beg ch 3. (23 shells)

Rnd 3: Sl st into ch-2 sp of shell, ch 3, dc, ch 2, 2 dc in same ch sp, ch 3, sc in ch-3 lp, ch 3, [2 dc, ch 2, 2 dc in next ch-2 sp of shell, ch 3, sc in next ch-3 lp, ch 3] rep around, join in 3rd ch of beg ch-3.

Rnd 4: Sl st into ch-2 sp of shell, ch 3, 1 dc, ch 2, 2 dc in same ch sp, ch 4, [shell of 2 dc, ch 2, 2 dc in next shell sp, ch 4] rep around, join in 3rd ch of beg ch-3.

Rnd 5: Sl st into ch-2 sp of shell, ch 4, 5 tr in same ch sp of shell, ch 3, sc in ch-4 sp, ch 3, [6 tr in next ch sp of shell, ch 3, sc in next ch-4 sp, ch 3] rep around, join in 4th ch of beg ch-4.

Rnd 6: Ch 4, [ch 1, tr in sp between tr sts, ch 1, tr in next tr] 5 times, [ch 3, sc in next ch-3 lp] twice, ch 3, *tr in next tr, [ch 1, tr in sp between tr sts, ch 1, tr in next tr] 5 times, [ch 3, sc in next ch-3 lp] twice, ch 3, rep from * around, join in 4th ch of beg ch-4.

Rnd 7: Ch 6, sl st in 3rd ch from hook for picot, [dc in next tr, ch 3, sl st in top of dc for picot] 10 times, ch 3, [sc in next ch-3 lp, ch 3] 3 times, *[dc in next tr, ch 3, sl st in top of dc for picot] 11 times, ch 3, [sc in next ch-3 lp, ch 3] 3 times, rep from * around, join in base of beg ch-6, fasten off.

Let's Begin!

Experience Level: Advanced beginner

Size:
Frame: Approximately 9" x 8½" oval
Opening: Approximately 4¼" x 3¼"

Materials
- ☐ Crochet cotton size 10 (150 yards per ball): 1 ball white
- ☐ Size 7 steel crochet hook
- ☐ 16" x 24" piece burgundy taffeta
- ☐ Cardboard
- ☐ Quilt batting
- ☐ Pinning board
- ☐ Fabric stiffener
- ☐ Sewing needle and thread
- ☐ 40" ⅜"-wide burgundy satin ribbon
- ☐ Glue

Gauge: 4 sts = ½"

To save time, take time to check gauge.

Pattern Note: Join rnds with a sl st unless otherwise stated.

Continued on Page 173

Potpourri Hat

Stitch this sweetly scented sachet delightfully shaped like a hat.

Base

Rnd 1: With peach cotton, ch 5, join to form a ring, ch 3, work 11 dc in ring, join in 3rd ch of beg ch-3. (12)

Rnd 2: Ch 3 (counts as first dc), dc in same st as beg ch-3, work 2 dc in each dc around, join in 3rd ch of beg ch-3. (24)

Rnd 3: Ch 3 (counts as first dc), 2 dc in next dc, [dc in next dc, 2 dc in next dc] rep around, join in 3rd ch of beg ch-3. (36)

Brim

Rnd 4: Working in back lps for this rnd only, ch 1, [sc in next 3 dc, ch 2] 11 times, sc in next 3 dc, hdc in beg sc (this hdc represents the last ch 2 and positions hook to start the next rnd). (12 sps between groups of sc sts)

Rnd 5: Ch 3 (first dc), dc over hdc, [ch 1, 2 dc, ch 2 and 2 dc in next ch-2 sp] 11 times, ch 1, 2 dc over same hdc as beg 2 sts, hdc in top of beg ch-3. (12 shells)

Rnd 6: Ch 3 (counts as first dc), 2 dc over hdc, [ch 1, 3 dc, ch 2 and 3 dc in next ch-2 sp of shell] 11 times, ch 1, 3 dc over same hdc as beg 3 sts, ch 2, join in 3rd ch of beg ch-3. (12 shells)

Rnd 7: Ch 1, sc in same st as beg ch-1, ch 1, [sc in next st, ch 1] rep around entire outer edge, join in beg sc, fasten off.

Crown

Rnd 8: Attach peach cotton in rem front lp of Rnd 3, ch 1, sc in same st as beg ch-1, sc in each of next 35 sts, join in beg sc. (36)

Rnd 9: Ch 1, sc in same sc as beg ch-1, [ch 2, sk 1 sc, sc in next sc] 17 times, hdc in beg sc. (18 ch sps between sc sts)

Rnds 10–14: Ch 1, sc over hdc, [ch 2, sc over ch-2 sp] 17 times, hdc in beg sc. (18 ch sps)

Rnd 15: Ch 1, sc over hdc, [sc in next ch-2 sp] 17 times, join in beg sc. (18)

Fill crown of hat with potpourri.

Let's Begin!

Experience Level: Beginner

Size: 4" in diameter

Materials

☐ Crochet cotton size 10: 65 yds peach

☐ Steel crochet hook size 7

☐ 10 inches ¼"-wide peach ribbon

☐ ½" peach ribbon rose

☐ Potpourri

☐ Glue

☐ Yarn needle

Gauge: Work evenly and consistently throughout

Pattern Notes: Weave in loose ends as work progresses.

Join rnds with a sl st unless otherwise stated.

Rnd 16: Ch 1, sc in same sc as beg ch-1, sk 1 sc, [sc in next sc, sk 1 sc] 8 times, join in beg sc. (9)

Rnd 17: Ch 1, sc in same sc as beg ch-1, sk 1 sc, [sc in next sc, sk 1 sc] 4 times, join in beg sc. (5)

Rnd 18: Ch 1, sc in same sc as beg ch-1, sk 1 sc, sc in next sc, sk 1 sc, sc in next sc, join in beg sc, fasten off. (3)

Finishing

Wrap ribbon around base of crown. Overlapping ends, glue in place to secure. Glue ribbon rose to overlapped section of ribbon.

—Designed by Mildred Blankenship

Mini Flower Earrings

Complement a favorite outfit with these quick-to-stitch earrings to match!

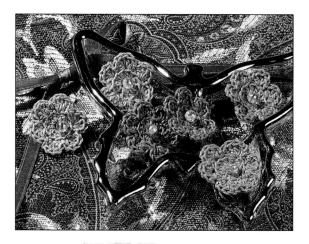

Let's Begin!

Experience Level: Beginner

Size: 1" in diameter

Materials
- ☐ Bernat® Handicrafter® Traditions crochet cotton size 10: 6 yds each pale pink #514, delft blue #526 and violet #521
- ☐ Size 9 steel crochet hook
- ☐ 3 pair post pearl or bead earrings

Gauge: 8 sts = 1"

To save time, take time to check gauge.

Pattern Note: To make smaller earrings, follow patt working hdc in place of dc.

Earring *(Make 2 each pink, blue & violet)*

Rnd 1: Ch 4, join to form a ring, ch 3, 11 dc in ring, join in 3rd ch of beg ch-3.

Rnd 2: Ch 3, working in back lps only, 4 dc in same st, [sl st in next st, 5 dc in next st], rep around, join in first ch of beg ch-3, fasten off.

Slip post earring through center of flower.

—Designed by Nyola Boley

Heirloom Sachets

Continued from Page 161

in next sc, ch 3, join, fasten off.

Weave in loose ends.

Finishing

With RS facing out, place pieces tog. With peach cotton and using a running st, sew tog 3 sides through sts of last sc rnd of peach. Stuff with potpourri. Sew last edge closed.

At 2 corners, tie peach ribbon around 1 corner sc of first cream border rnd. Tie bows over rose stems. Clip ribbon ends and stems to desired length. Secure roses with glue.

—Designed by Katherine Eng

Picture-Perfect Frame

Continued from Page 171

Finishing

Saturate crocheted piece with stiffener. Stretch and pin to pinning board in oval shape, adjusting ruffles for fullness. Allow to dry completely.

When dry, trace around outer edge on cardboard. Using cardboard as patt, cut 2 pieces batting. Cut 2 pieces taffeta, allowing ½" for seams. Layer 1 piece taffeta face down, 1 piece batting, cardboard, rem batting and taffeta face up. Turn edges of taffeta under; sew closed with sewing ndl and thread.

Weave ribbon through sps between shells of Rnd 2, beg at top. Tie ends in a bow.

Run a bead of glue around bottom half of frame. Center over taffeta backing; press. When dry, slip picture into frame from top.

Hanging Loop

With crochet cotton, ch 20, join to form a ring, fasten off. Sew lp to back top of frame back.

—Designed by Amanda Nygaard

173

General Instructions

Please review the following information before working the projects in this book. Important details about the abbreviations and symbols used and finishing instructions are included.

Hooks

Crochet hooks are sized for different weights of yarn and thread. For thread crochet, you will usually use a *steel* crochet hook. Steel crochet hook sizes range from size 00 to 14. The higher the number of hook, the smaller your stitches will be. For example, a size 1 steel crochet hook will give you much larger stitches than a size 9 steel crochet hook. Keep in mind that the sizes given with the pattern instructions were obtained by working with the size thread or yarn and hook given in the materials list. If you work with a smaller hook, depending on your gauge, your project size will be smaller; if you work with a larger hook, your finished project's size will be larger.

Gauge

Gauge is determined by the tightness or looseness of your stitches, and affects the finished size of your project. If you are concerned about the finished size of the project matching the size given, take time to crochet a small section of the pattern and then check your gauge. For example, if the gauge called for is 10 dc = 1 inch, and your gauge is 12 dc to the inch, you should switch to a larger hook. On the other hand, if your gauge is only 8 dc to the inch, you should switch to a smaller hook.

If the gauge given in the pattern is for an entire motif, work one motif and then check your gauge.

Understanding Symbols

As you work through a pattern, you'll quickly notice several symbols in the instructions. These symbols are used to clarify the pattern for you: Brackets [], curlicue brackets {}, asterisks *.

Brackets [] are used to set off a group of instructions worked a number of times. For example, "[ch 3, sc in ch-3 sp] 7 times" means to repeat the instructions inside the [] seven times. Brackets [] also set off a group of stitches to be worked in one stitch, space or loop. For example, the brackets [] in this set of instructions, "Sk 3 sc, [3 dc, ch 1, 3 dc] in next st" indicate that after skipping 3 sc, you will work 3 dc, ch 1 and 3 more dc all in the next stitch.

Occasionally, a set of instructions inside a set of brackets needs to be repeated too. In this case, the text within the brackets to be repeated will be set off with curlicue brackets {}. For example, "[Ch 9, yo twice, insert hook in 7th ch from hook and pull up a loop, sk next dc, yo, insert hook in next dc and pull up a loop, {yo and draw through 2 lps on hook} 5 times, ch 3] 8 times." In this case, in each of the eight repeats of the instructions included in brackets, you will work the section included in curlicue brackets five times.

Asterisks * are also used when a group of instructions is repeated. They may either be used alone or with brackets. For example, "*Sc in each of the next 5 sc, 2 sc in next sc, rep from * around, join with a sl st in beg sc" simply means you will repeat the instructions from the first * around the entire round.

"*Sk 3 sc, [3 dc, ch 1, 3 dc] in next st, rep from * around" is an example of asterisks working with brackets. In this set of instructions, you will repeat the instructions from the asterisk around, working the instructions inside the brackets together.

Front Loop (a) Back Loop (b)

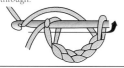

Chain (ch)

Yo, draw lp through hook.

Slip Stitch Joining

Insert hook in beg ch, yo, draw lp through.

Stitch Abbreviations

The following stitch abbreviations are used throughout this book.

beg . . . . .begin(ning)
bl(s) . . . . .block(s)
bpdc . . . . .back post dc
ch(s) . . . . .chain(s)
cl(s) . . . . .cluster(s)
CC . . . . .contrasting color
dc . . . . .double crochet
dec . . . . .decrease
dtr . . . . .double treble crochet
fpdc . . . . .front post dc
hdc . . . . .half-double crochet
inc . . . . .increase
lp(s) . . . . .loop(s)
MC . . . . .main color
p . . . . .picot
rem . . . . .remain(ing)
rep . . . . .repeat
rnd(s) . . . . .round(s)
RS . . . . .right side facing you
sc . . . . .single crochet
sk . . . . .skip
sl st . . . . .slip stitch
sp(s) . . . . .space(s)
st(s) . . . . .stitch(es)
tog . . . . .together
tr . . . . .treble crochet
trtr . . . . .triple treble crochet
WS . . . . . . .wrong side facing you
yo . . . . .yarn over

Front Post/Back Post Dc

Fpdc (a): Yo, insert hook from front to back and to front again around the vertical post (upright part) of next st, yo and draw yarn through, yo and complete dc.

Bpdc (b): Yo, reaching over top of piece and working on opposite side (right side) of work, insert hook from right to left around vertical post of next st, yo and draw yarn through, yo and complete dc.

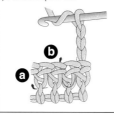

Single Crochet (sc)

Insert hook in st (a), yo, draw lp through (b), yo, draw through both lps on hook (c).

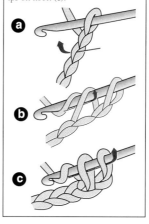

Half-Double Crochet (hdc)

Yo, insert hook in st (a), draw lp through (b), yo, draw through all 3 lps on hook (c).

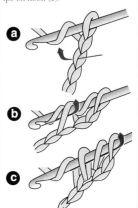

Double Crochet (dc)

Yo, insert hook in st (a), yo, draw through 1 lp (b), [yo, draw through 2 lps] twice (c, d).

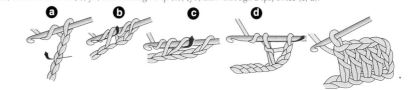

Treble Crochet (tr)

Yo hook twice, insert hook in st (a), yo, draw lp through (b), [yo, draw through 2 lps on hook] 3 times (c, d, e).

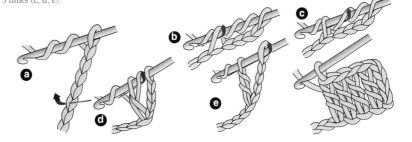

Yarn Conversion

Ounces to Grams		Grams to Ounces	
1	.28.4	25	7⁄8
2	.56.7	40	1⅓
3	.85.0	50	1¾
4	.113.4	100	3½

Double Crochet Color Change (dc color change)

Work dc until 2 lps rem, drop first color, yo with new color, draw through last 2 lps of st.

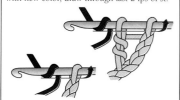

Chain Color Change (ch color change)

Yo with new color, draw through last lp on hook.

Special Stitches

Reverse Single Crochet (reverse sc)

Working from left to right, insert hook in next st to the right (a), yo, draw through st, complete as for sc (b).

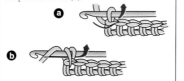

Decreasing

Single Crochet Decrease

Dec 1 sc over next 2 sc as follows: Draw up a lp in each of next 2 sts, yo, draw through all 3 lps on hook.

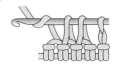

Half-Double Crochet Decrease

Dec 1 hdc over next 2 hdc as follows: [Yo, insert hook in next st, yo, draw lp through] twice, yo, draw through all 5 lps on hook.

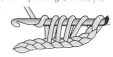

Index